BIBLICAL BOOKS TRANSLATED FROM THE ARAMAIC

By Frank Zimmermann

KTAV PUBLISHING HOUSE, INC.

NEW YORK

Library of Congress Cataloging in Publication Data

Zimmermann, Frank.
  Biblical books translated from the Aramaic.

  Bibliography: p.
  Includes indexes.
    1. Bible. O.T. Hagiographa. Aramaic—Versions.   2.
Bible. O.T. Hagiographa—Language, style. I. Title.
BS1308.A4A78   221   74-34107
ISBN 0-87068-252-0

To Rebecca, dear wife
—of the merry eye in the loving look—
this book is affectionately dedicated
by the author.

TABLE OF CONTENTS

PREFACE

The present study provides the student investigating the Hebrew biblical text with an additional tool. As a regular procedure, the investigator collates manuscripts, looks into the Ancient Versions, into the Septuaguint, the Peshitta, the Vulgate, and the Targums, as well as the fragments of Aquila, Symmachus and Theodotion to insure and to test the transmitted text. He will comb the vocabularies of the Semitic languages for new meanings of difficult words, and for enlightenment on difficult passages. He may employ conjectural emendation to remove a difficulty. This study offers him an additional procedure to solve some problems that he is confronted with, viz., that underlying his Hebrew text in certain books there may be an original Aramaic document.

Several books in the Hebrew Bible show a strong Aramaic coloring. This is assuredly true for Daniel, written both in Hebrew and Aramaic, as well as for Ezra, which is a part really of one work, Nehemiah and Chronicles. The late book of Esther, too, transmitted in no less than six versions of the story (see Chapter Five) was likewise translated. The evidence shows that the same holds true for the folk-tale of Jonah, and the book of Ecclesiates. The latter book received detailed treatment in the writer's "Inner World of Qohelet".

The Aramaic, in which these books were composed, was of a particular character, that of Eastern Aramaic. Taken into the Hebrew text, these Aramaic words the Hebrew translator considered to be of the same meaning as their Hebrew cognates. He incorporated them unchanged into his own copy. The Aramaic words, however, have their own special meaning, indigenous to Aramaic only. They manifest themselves as coming from a vocabulary of what might be called proto-Syriac, actually a linguistic complex of what is now transmitted as Babylonian (Talmudic) Aramaic, Syriac, and Mandaic, not of the Palestinian Talmud or Midrash.

Since we are dealing with the older forms of the language ca. 300-200 B.C.E., I have not, in retroverting to the putative Aramaic documents, hewed to the line of Eastern Aramaic exclusively. The reader will find *de* and *di* flexibly used, nominal forms with Aleph and He, —m and —n suffixes, and the like. The reader should have mainly in mind however the Eastern Aramaic provenance.

Needless to say, these writings were composed in the Diaspora, to the north of Palestine where Aramaic was the common language, as Josephus, who prepared his "Wars of the Jews" in that language for his people in Mesopotamia, expressly states in his Preface. It is simply dogma to assert that all biblical books have to be written in Palestine. The other great centers of Jewish population, whether in Antioch on-the-Orontes, or in the twin capital, Seleucia on-the-Tigris, or in Babylonia, could very well be the fertilizing literary force for the writing of such books. As they gained in significance, or as M. L. Margolis would say in "classicity", they were translated. Esther and Jonah, beautifully translated, were given their Hebraic cast in Palestine.

The analysis and accumulation of examples will carry conviction, I hope, for the soundness of the thesis advanced here. Standard lexical indexes, in Hebrew-Aramaic, and in Aramaic-Hebrew, are as yet an unfulfilled desideratum for scholars.

It is my pleasant duty to thank the editors of the Journal of Biblical Literature, and those of the Jewish Quarterly Review for permission to use some material printed previously; also to thank Joel Burstein and Bernard Scharfstein for valuable assistance in preparing the manuscript for printing, as well as to my wife to whom this volume is dedicated.

Summer, 1974.

1

Introduction

Aramaic was one of the great, widespread languages of Asia Minor. In all its manifold dialects, it became diffused throughout the Near East and Middle East from earliest antiquity. Today much more circumscribed, it is still alive. It has had its ebb and flow, but the evidence of inscriptions shows that it had penetrated most of the known world of ancient times. The earliest inscriptions belong to a period between the tenth and eighth centuries B.C.E. especially that of Sam'al, that of the so-called Panamuwa inscription, and that of the Bar-Rakib inscription and still others from Damascus, Hama, and Arpad. There are inscriptions from Nerab (near Aleppo) from the seventh century, and bronze lion weights with Aramaic upon them from Nineveh. Still others are extant from Cilicia fifth to fourth century, Tema in Arabia in the fifth, the well-known Elephantine papyri, the inscription from Saqqara in the fifth with its marked Hebraisms, then at the beginning of the common era the Nabatean inscriptions from North Arabia, particularly those from El-Hejra, as well as the well-known ones from the Palmyrene area with the important tariff text. It is evident then that Aramaic reached from Mesopotamia to the Northwest of Asia Minor, to the Southeast (Petra), to the bottom of the Arabian Peninsula, extending moreover to North Africa, going south as far as Elephantine, and then, even north into Europe, with the unexpected inscription in the important harbor of Puteoli, Italy[1].

[1] M. Lidzbarski, *Handbuch der nordsemitischen Epigraphik*, Weimar, 1898, and the subsequent volumes of his *Ephemeris*; G. A. Cooke, *A Text-Book of North Semitic Inscriptions*, Oxford, 1903; H. Donner and W. Röllig, *Kanaanäische und Aramäische Inschriften*, 3 Bände, Wiesbaden, 1962; Moscati, S. ed. *An Introduction to the Comparative Grammar of the Semitic Languages*, Wiesbaden, 1964, and bibliography, 173f.

The Hebrews in the earlier period, as well as the Jews of later centuries, had a marked attachment for Aramaic. The reasons are not far to seek. There were unconscious "chords of memory" that bound them to their Aramaean kinsmen. If we follow the biblical tradition, their ancestor Abraham came from Aram-Naharayim, Aram of the Two Rivers (Mesopotamia)[2]. Then again in Deut. 26.5, part of the cultic ritual consists of a statement in the proem, "A wandering *Aramaean* was my ancestor". Josh. 24.2 repeats and confirms this origin of the ancient Hebrews, "Thus says Yahweh, the God of Israel, 'Your ancestors dwelt across the River from time immemorial' ". Isaac, the son of Abraham, in conversation with his parents, undoubtedly spoke Aramaic as his mother tongue; at any rate, he certainly had to speak Aramaic with his wife Rebecca, the sister of Laban, the Aramaean. When furthermore Jacob remained with Laban twenty years, he assuredly spoke Aramaic to Rachel and Leah, his wives. They were Aramaean women. When Jacob and Laban parted, the latter designated the stones that were erected as a covenant between them as *yegar sahadutha*[3] "The Cairn of Witness". There can hardly be any question that the children of Jacob born in these Aramaean surroundings spoke Aramaic with their mothers in their daily language.

It was Hebrew however that possessed the soul of the Hebrew people, and Aramaic became secondary. Nonetheless, Aramaic must have been known and spoken, certainly among the educated classes. The Assyrian staff commander was asked to speak in Aramaic by the envoys sent by Hezekiah (2 Kings 18.26). The prefect, the secretary, the chancellor, who composed the commission, did not want the Hebrew populace at the barricades to understand the insolent demands of the Assyrian. Aramaic patently was the *lingua franca* in the Middle East.

With the collapse of the Hebrew state, Aramaic increasingly took the field. It is well recognized that it was not Ezra, Nehemiah,

[2] That is, more specifically, from Ur Kasdim, Gen. 11.31; but in Gen. 24.10, the city of Naḥor, Abraham's brother, was Aram-Naharayim.

[3] Gen. 31.47.

or the returning colonists from Babylon who brought back Aramaic with them. Rather, Aramaic was already there *in situ* (cf. W. Wright, *A Comparative Grammar of the Semitic Languages*, p. 16). The exilic Ezekiel exhibits more Aramaisms than any other prophet [4]. So pervasive did Aramaic become, and so widespread its influence, that it found its way among the biblical books, Dan. 2–7, as well as the books of Ezra-Nehemia composed and edited in the two languages of Hebrew and Aramaic. It had gained official sanction as *Reichsaramäisch*[5] through the authority of the Persian government. It insinuated itself as an equal partner in the bilinguality of the people. By virtue of Daniel and Ezra, it became a holy language. Nehemiah 13 attests that the Jewish governor sought to suppress alien tongues from the midst of the young colony. It is to be remarked however that Nehemiah sought to eradicate "Ashdodite", and presumably the Ammonite and Moabite languages, but no mention is made of suppressing Aramaic. It went on to be used in prayer, and in translations of the Bible (Targums), almost as a matter of course.

Some counter forces undoubtedly were at work that provided some restraint nevertheless. Perhaps it was felt that certain forms of literature could not be composed in Aramaic. Later tradition asserted that God spoke to Adam and Eve in Hebrew, as the terms *'ish* and *'issah* imply[6]. Stories and narratives might be permitted *aramaice* but not prophecy, or any eschatological discourse, which purported to come from God himself. It was hardly possible that God should speak in Aramaic. So Daniel 8–12, as a piece of prophetic eschatological literature, was translated from Aramaic to Hebrew.[7]

Within the twentieth century, scholars have become increasingly

---

[4] Comp. G. A. Cooke, *Book of Ezekiel*, in the ICC series. There are, however, more Aramaisms in Ezekiel than are recognized by Cooke. On the other hand, his steady use of E. Kautzsch, *Die Aramäismen in A. T. Halle,* 1902 should have been more discriminating. Comp. H. H. Powell, *The Supposed Hebraisms in the Grammar of the Biblical Aramaic*, 1906.

[5] Cf. F. Rosenthal, *A Grammar of Biblical Aramaic*, Wiesbaden, 1961.

[6] Comp. Gen. Rabbah, sec. 18 and 31.

[7] Dan. 4.26 is an angelic voice.

aware that there are translated documents in the Hebrew Bible. In 1906, C.H.H. Wright in his work on Daniel became convinced that many difficulties could be resolved in the Danielic text if the presumption were made that the book were a translation.[8] Beyond this mere assertion however he went no further. Dalman asserted that chapter seven of Daniel was originally written in Hebrew; but to make an appropriate framework for the stories of the book, and the distinct prophecies that followed, someone undertook to translate into Aramaic the eschatological chapter seven as a transition.[9] C.C. Torrey pointed out, in addition, that chapters 1–2.4a were likewise an Aramaic composition originally.[10] Marti, too, essayed to prove Daniel a translation although Montgomery judged the results meagre.[11]

In 1938 the present writer undertook to make a further study of the possibilities, and came to the conclusion that there could hardly be any question that Dan. 8–12 (with the exception of the prayer in c. 9) was translated.[12] In subsequent articles more evidence was supplied.[13] In his "Studies in Daniel", 1948, H.L. Ginsberg furnished further convincing and instructive examples. Other biblical books in addition were holding the attention of scholars elsewhere. In 1922, F. C. Burkitt in an article entitled "Is Ecclesiastes a Translation?" examined a number of passages in Qohelet with the hypothesis that Qohelet might have some passages whose underlying document was Aramaic.[14] The present writer had been pursuing the same line of inquiry and the analysis seemed to point to an inevitable verdict. See the "Aramaic Provenance of

---

[8] C.H.H. Wright, *Daniel and His Critics*, London, 1906, 17, 200.

[9] G. Dalman, *Worte Jesu*, translated by D. M. Kay as *Words of Jesus*, 1909, 13. Montgomery, op. cit. p. 91 adds, "And so exactly Torrey". The latter however asserts that c. 7 was originally written in Aramaic. Comp. his "Notes on the Aramaic Part of Daniel" in the Transactions of the Connecticut Academy of Arts and Sciences (15), 1909, 249.

[10] Torrey, op. cit., 249 n.

[11] Montgomery, op. cit. pp. 91–2.

[12] "The Aramaic Origin of Dan. 8–12" in JBL, vol. LVII, 3, 1938, p. 255f; LVIII, 1939, p. 349.

[13] JQR, vol. LI, 3, 1961 "Hebrew Translation in Daniel", 198–208.

[14] Journal of Theological Studies, 23, 1922, p. 23ff.

Qohelet" in the JQR, 36, 1945, p. 17f (and now, Zimmermann, *Inner World of Qohelet.* p. 98f.). This idea of translation in Qohelet was further advanced by a study published by C.C. Torrey in which he wholeheartedly espoused the cause of translation from Aramaic.[15] H.L. Ginsberg, with the notable chapter "Koheleth Wrote in Aramaic", followed through with his *Studies in Koheleth,* 1950.

J. Muilenberg published a fragment of Qohelet recovered from Qumran with the strong implication that Qohelet could not be consequently a translation.[16] This argument falters, because even if the fragment be dated extremely early at 100 B.C.E., this in no way gainsays the circumstance that a translation may have been made a hundred or a hundred and fifty years before. The Hebrew of Qohelet, if the development and evolution of the Hebrew language be part of philological equipment at all, cannot belong to the Hebrew of 250–200 B.C.E., when idiomatic beautiful Psalms were still being written, portions to the book of Proverbs were still being added, and to some extreme critics even sections to the Prophets. No,—the alternate hypothesis, translation, would most naturally and most simply account for the disproportionate percentage of the Aramaic words in relation to the Hebrew text, the lack of Waw conversives, the compound particles, the abuse of particles and prepositions, the misunderstanding of forms, the misapprehension of Aramaic roots as if they were Hebrew, and most significantly the mistranslations, the discovery of which replaces with sense where nonsense appeared before. As always, internal evidence is the determining factor.

There seems strong evidence of translation in other biblical books. Torrey essayed to show that Esther is a translation with his usual acuminous presentation.[17] The present volume contains additional information in support of translation in Esther. In addition, Chronicles, Ezra-Nehemiah, as well as the book of

---

[15] JQR, vol. 39, p. 151f.

[16] "A Qoheleth Scroll from Qumran", Bulletin of the School of Oriental Research, 135, (1954) pp. 20–8.

[17] "The Older Book of Esther", HTR, 37, (1944) pp. 1–40.

Jonah, are evidenced as examples of the wide activity in translation among the scribes and Jewish teachers. Among other books Tur Sinai in successive commentaries on Job has attempted to show that that book was translated from Aramaic.[18] In other fields, as in the Apocrypha and Pseudepigrapha, evidence for original Aramaic is constantly on the increase. We now know that quite a number of books, for centuries presumed to have been written originally in Greek, are now considered to have been written wholly in Aramaic or partially in Aramaic and partially in Hebrew (Enoch, IV Ezra), and in addition such books as Tobit, Bel and the Dragon, the Three Guardsmen, Wisdom, Testament of Job).[19] Many scholars consider that the Gospels (certainly the Synoptics, John partially) go back to Urtexts in Aramaic.[20]

The idea that certain books of the Bible are translations has received a mixed reception. Some are pained by the circumstance that we do not have the *ipsissima verba* of the author; others counter on dogmatic and theological grounds, still others object on the ground that the Hebrew genius has been impugned by the fact of translation. Undoubtedly this may all be distressing to sincere, piously-minded persons, but should be no more so than when critics have to emend a text, assign a Psalm to the Babylonian exile or the Maccabean period, or deny authorship of the Pentateuch to Moses. Authority cannot depend exclusively on the written word. The scientific procedure is to offer evidence, and evidence is the decisive factor.

[18] *Sefer Iyyob*, 2 vols. 1941; *Book of Job* (1957). Ibn Ezra at Job 2.12 held that Job was translated. Foster's "Is the Book of Job a Translation from an Arabic Original?" AJSL, 49, (1932/33) pp. 21–45 does not have any acceptable evidence.

[19] See the summaries in the writer's *Inner World of Qohelet*.

[20] Comp. C. C. Torrey, *Our Translated Gospels;* Matthew Black, *An Aramaic Approach to the Gospels.*

2

The Book of Daniel in the Light of a Translation Hypothesis

The reader of the Book of Daniel is struck by the phenomenon that two languages alternate with each other in the book. Why do sections 1–2.4a, and 8–12 appear in Hebrew while 2.4b–7 are written in Aramaic? A number of theories have been advanced to explain this bilingual peculiarity.

One view is that the author composed in two languages. In 2.4b he transits easily into Aramaic, quite in accordance with the occasion, as he imagined the "Chaldeans" to be Aramaic-speaking. With chapter 8, he resumed the Hebrew as it was more fitting to have the divine revelation in the sacred tongue of Hebrew. Unusual as this procedure may be, it would be no more peculiar, as critics argue, than the interspersed sections that manifest themselves in Ezra. It will be seen that the resolution of this question is the same for Daniel in that the Hebrew in Ezra-Nehemiah is a translation from Aramaic[1]. The chief objection to the above mentioned theory in Daniel, however, is that the apocalyptic visions begin with chapter 7, written in Aramaic. Why does the Hebrew start with chapter 8?

Another explanation offered by scholars is that the Book of Daniel existed in two versions, Hebrew and Aramaic. Part of the Hebrew was lost. A scribe replaced the missing portion of the Hebrew with an Aramaic version. Antiochus Epiphanes' edict to destroy the Law is cited as evidence for this view. "But that hypothesis", as Montgomery well says, "stumbles on the fact that the Aramaic begins neatly at the appropriate point"[2].

An hypothesis given prominence by Jahn maintains that the

---

[1] See the discussion in the chapter on Ezra-Nehemiah.
[2] J. A. Montgomery, *Book of Daniel*, p. 92; for further discussion and liter-

book was written in Hebrew. In addition, the Greek is supposed to contain the original Hebrew as against the bilingual version of the extant Daniel. Jahn however overrated the Greek too highly. This theory found no credence nor acceptance among scholars[3].

On the other hand, just the opposite view has been advanced. The book, it is maintained, was originally composed in Aramaic, and then translated into Hebrew. During the Maccabean struggle, a segment of the Hebrew was lost and an Aramaic portion was substituted. This is the view advocated by Buhl, Marti, and Charles in their commentaries[4]. The two latter scholars have tried to prove on linguistic grounds that the Hebrew was translated from the Aramaic. Marti's evidence is so slim that it cannot be called proof ("meagre"-Montgomery). Charles' argument that there were three translators in Daniel was subjected to penetrating criticism by Joseph Reider[5]. Reider demonstrates conclusively that the supposed Aramaic constructions and characteristics have their Hebrew parallels throughout. There is scarcely a single shred of evidence to show for an Aramaic original, or that the extant Hebrew is a translation.

Another type of hypothesis dealing with the composition of the book took the field. Dalman suggested[6] that Daniel is composed of two books, chapters 1–6 and 7–12. The editor of Daniel translated chapter 1 into Hebrew, and then translated chapter 7 from the Hebrew into Aramaic, so as to unite the book into one framework. Chapters 7 and 8 then would be variations on the same theme, the rise and fall of Antiochus Epiphanes, chapter 7 in Aramaic and chapter 8 in Hebrew. So too C. C. Torrey,[7] and Montgomery

ature, A. Bentzen, *Daniel*,[2] S. 9.

[3] Montgomery, *op. cit.,* 36f.

[4] A. A. Bevan, *A Short Commentary on the Book of Daniel*, 1892; K. Marti, *Das Buch Daniel*, 1902; R. H. Charles, *A Critical and Exegetical Commentary on the Book of Daniel*, 1929.

[5] "The Present State of Old Testament Criticism", HUCA, VII, 305f.

[6] *The Words of Jesus*, Eng. Trans., 1909, 13f.

[7] So Montgomery assumed; however, Torrey really says that the Daniel II author wrote c. 7 originally in Aramaic, in contrast to Dalman's hypothesis. Comp. Torrey's "Notes on the Aramaic Part of Daniel" in the "Transactions of the Connecticut Academy of Arts and Sciences", XV, 1909, p. 250.

concurred. The theory indeed is ingenious, but the same criticism must be levelled against it as may be countered against all the others. None of the hypotheses rests on significant criteria. The question of the two languages in Daniel is obviously a linguistic one which cannot be settled by an a priori judgement or arbitrary conclusion.

The present writer took up the question in a more detailed fashion in two articles in the Journal of Biblical Literature 1938–39[8], though but a preliminary survey and all the evidence could not be presented. H.L. Ginsberg followed through with his impressive *Studies in Daniel* (1948) with a number of important illuminatory observations which I have taken the liberty to incorporate in the present study. Ginsberg can rarely be matched for perception and insight in the Hebrew text, and his analysis is always keen and valuable. Through difference of temperament and approach, I cannot follow him completely, however, in his slashing attacks on the Hebrew text, the atomization of sentences, bisection of half verses, and wholesale emendation of words and phrases. I shy away from emending Aramaic texts I have never seen. His book however is an important landmark in Danielic studies, especially section 5, where I have borrowed and quoted in his name.

The evidence that Danielic Hebrew is a translation is borne out by a number of multifaceted examples, particularly signalized in the differentia between Aramaic and Hebrew.

A. *Many idioms and constructions in the text of the Hebrew betray their Aramaic origin.*

Thus 8.1 אני דניאל = 7.15 אנה דניאל; 8.9 ותגדל יתר = obviously the Aramaic ורבת יתיר/ורבת יתיר ושגיאת יתיר; cf. the Peshitta ורבת יתיראית; 8.13 אחד קדוש plainly חד קדיש with the numeral preceding; 8.25 באפס יד = 2.34 לא בידין; 8.5.8 צפיר העזים corresponds to צפירי עזין Ezr. 6.17 instead of the usual שעיר עזים; 11.21.24. בשלוה = מן שליא "suddenly" as in Aramaic, not the inappropriate "in peace"; 9.24,25,26 שבעים = Heb. שבועות but the Aramaic masculine ending of שבועין suggested for the translator the masculine ending in the Hebrew. Actual Aramaic words in the Hebrew text exhibit

[8] "The Aramaic Original of Daniel 8–12", JBL, 57, 1938, pp. 255f.; "Some Verses in Daniel in the Light of a Translation Hypothesis" ibid. 1939, 349ff.

further an Aramaic provenience as in 11.30 ונכאה (Montgomery, 456); 11.45 אפדנו an Aramaized Persian word, perhaps from Accadian *appu dannu*, Brockelmann 40, but see also the *Additamenta ad librum Aruch Completum Alexandri Kohut*, 53b; perhaps 11.44 בחמא. There are Aramaic constructions as 8.11 וממנו הרים התמיד where מן plus the suffix is syntactically placed first as for example in the frequent מני שים טעם Ezr. 7.13; Dan. 3.29; 4.3. See further the comments on the construction below, (p. 42), . . . אתרים אתרמי is a word play as well (Ginsberg differently). In 1.10 אשר למה is a mechanical reproduction of an underlying Aramaic די למא which however has the fundamental signification of "perhaps" (Torrey). The peculiar עד עת 11.2, which ends the verse lamely and abruptly, translated oddly as "but until the time", merely reproduces what Eastern Aramaic employs as עד זבן "for a while". Comp. Payne Smith, 400; similarly Dan. 11.33 where ימים is conventionally rendered "many (?) days", the translation should run "for some time". Cf. יומתא "for some time", Payne Smith, 190 .

B. *There are many nouns whereto the definite article is added superfluously; on the other hand, the definite article is peculiarly omitted in many cases where it is expected.*

As a rule, a noun mentioned for the first time is indefinite; thereafter, repetition of the noun carries with it the definite article. Thus the books of Samuel and Job open with איש אחד. Thereafter איש is prefixed with the definite article ה. The exceptions to this rule are confined to such nouns where there can be no doubt as to identification, e.g. השמים, הארץ. It is striking that within the five Hebrew chapters of Daniel (not 9.4–19), as well as the introductory 1.2.4a, an unusual number of examples occur wherein the definite article is prefixed to the noun, although it is mentioned for the first time. Thus for instance in 8.5 "And I continued to observe and behold! a צפיר העזים came from the West"; 9.24 הפשע; 9.25 ובת הנשים 11.17 ; ולקץ העתים שנים 11.13; ויבא אל החיל 11.7; העתים; 11.22 וזרעות השטף 11.31; המקדש המעוז 12.13; הימין and similarly 1.12 הזרעים "pulse", with the article unnecessary, cf. the following ומים. On the other hand, the definite article is missing when expected: 8.14 ונצדק קדש "Then shall *the* sanctuary be victorious (Jewish Version), but קדש was mentioned in the preceding verse; 8.22 "Four kingdoms shall rise out of *the* nation", Jewish Version, מגוי; 9.21: Gabriel came to Daniel "about the time of *the* evening offering" JV, כעת מנחת ערב; 9.25 "Know therefore and discern from the going forth of *the* word, JV, מן מצא דבר. The word דבר however was mentioned in v.23; 9.26 "And after 62 weeks an anointed will be cut down," יכרת משיח but comp. v. 25 משיח נגיד; 11.2 "And now I will declare unto thee *the* truth", JV, אמת but comp. 10.21; 11.21 "Upon whom there had not been conferred the majesty of the kingdom. . . .and shall obtain the kingdom by blandishments", JV, מלכות however without the article (*bis*). 11.14: "Also the children of the violent among thy people shall lift themselves up to establish *the* vision" JV, but חזון; 11.23 "And after the league made with him, he shall work deceitfully", JV, ומן התחברות אליו; 12.10 "And none of the wicked shall understand", JV, רשעים but רשעים was mentioned previously in the same verse. In 9.26 both משיח mentioned in the previous verse, and מלחמה "the war", JV, should have had the article.

How is one to explain these divergencies from grammatical rule? The thought must be dismissed that they are due to corruptions of the text. On the other hand, the peculiar use of the definite article, as well as its omission, might conceivably be a feature of the writer's style. Perhaps indeed he was careless with regard to the definite article. Aside from the fact that this phenomenon would be almost unique in the classical literature, the text nonetheless shows that the writer was conscious of the force of the definite article. Thus in 8.3 he mentions the Buck first as איל and in v. 6 as האיל, v. 7. האיל (*bis*). In 10.1 a דבר was revealed to Daniel. . . . . .and *the* word was true (see p. 17). In 11.33 משכילי עם occurs, but in v. 35 מן המשכילים.

The present writer believes that the only hypothesis that takes account of and explains throughout the superfluous use of the definite article, or its lack in so many instances, is the theory advanced above that the Hebrew rests upon an Aramaic original. In Aramaic, it is well known that the definite form is expressed by affixing ———*a* to the noun, e.g. מלך, מלכא. Already in biblical Aramaic, it can be observed that the sharp differentiation between the stat. absol. and the stat. determ. began to be blurred. Comp. Bauer-Leander, *Grammatik des biblisch-aramäischen,* 1927, par. 88h for some exx. In fact as early as the Elephantine papyri the distinction between the absolute and determinate cases started to be effaced. Cf. Zimmermann, JQR, vol. 36, (1945), p. 23 and note. This breakdown between the cases reached such lengths in Syriac that it becomes difficult at times to determine the status and formation of a noun. In fact, a large number of substantives in Syriac appear only in the emphatic state[9]. The same process went on in the later Jewish Aramaic[10].

A translator therefore would have to be quite sensible to the nuances in Aramaic as to whether קודשא should be rendered by קדש or הקדש. Thus if we look at any of the narratival chapters in Daniel, as c. 5, we observe that a translator has to keep his wits about him lest he fall into pitfalls that encompass him on every side. If he wished to be exact, he would carefully render חמרא in v. 1 by יין, but in v. 2 by היין despite the fact that חמרא is used in both instances. He would have to keep his head clear to translate the nouns in v. 4 לאלהי זהבא וכספא נחשא פרזלא אעא ואבנא without the article. In v. 5 היכלא די מלכא would be of course היכל המלך although the Hebrew translator erroneously translated this type of construction at 8.13 החזון התמיד, 11.31 השקוץ משומם; ibid. המקדש המעוז (see p. 32). It is not necessary to labor the point. Only a skilled translator in so many instances of stat. emph. could distinguish those cases when the article was or was not required. In Dan. 8–12 where the number of nouns runs into the hundreds, it is not surprising that a number of slips should be made. The Aramaic hypothesis explains therefore both the peculiar addition *and* the omission of the definite article.

Thus the singular passage in 10.4 presents an anomaly to the reader: "And in the fourth and twentieth day of the first month as I was by the side of the great river which is the Tigris. . . . "

There is only one great river in the Hebrew Bible, *the* River *par excellence*, the Euphrates, Gen. 15.18; Deut. 1.7; Josh. 1.4. The Tigris never receives this designation. So anomalous is our

---

[9] T. Nöldeke, *A Compendious Syriac Grammar*, Eng. Trans. p. 151f.

[10] M. L. Margolis, *A Manual of the Aramaic Language of the Babylonian Talmud*, Eng. ed., 1910, p. 62.

reading that the Peshitta by accident or otherwise has "the great river, Perat". For this reason, some commentators would eliminate הוא חדקל as a gloss. In line with what has been advanced, however, the matter is quite simple. The translator should have rendered נהרא רבא as *a* great river, i.e. Ḥidekel. He should have translated נהר גדול. He confused the absolute and emphatic cases by copying what, to him, the Aramaic suggested. Hence—

C. *An unconscious prompting in the translating process is the suggestibility of the Aramaic text. The translator will frequently copy out the Aramaic locution in front of him, especially if the Aramaic and Hebrew words are identical, without realizing however that Hebrew and Aramaic each go their own way.*

In 9.26 for example: "And after the threescore and two weeks, shall an anointed one be cut off, ואין לו and he shall have nothing . . . (?)" The Hebrew is most peculiar, and is emended to ואיננו (Ehrlich, BH). There is however no need to emend; *lectio difficilior praestat*. The translator had difficulty with the under-lying Aramaic ולא אתי לה, specifically in translating the copulative אתי, Hebrew cognate יש; so he left it out helplessly. He did the same thing again (p. 35). The Aramaic expression means, "And he shall be no more, he will die", exactly what we require. Comp. Payne Smith, *Dictionary*, p. 15.

Similarly in 11.6, the translator copied his Aramaic again making for a mysterious sense in a number of phrases:". . . .And the daughter of the king of the south shall come to the king of the north to make an agreement; but she shall not retain the strength of her arm; nor shall he stand, nor his arm; but she shall be given up, and they that brought her, and he that begot her (?), and he that obtained her (?), in times (?)." ותנתן היא ומביאיה והילדה ומחזקה בעתים.

Probably "to make an agreement", Heb. לעשות מישרים is an off-translation of the Aramaic root תרץ "be upright, correct, *amend*" Brockelmann, 838: למעבד תריצותא "to adjust differences, make amends".

"He that begot her" if that be the sense, is strange, since the form in the Hebrew implies יולד anomalously, and ultimately rests on a confusion in the Aramaic on the part of the translator between ילודא yālōda (a faʻola form) "a parent, one who brings forth" and yalūda "an infant, babe," (Payne Smith, 192) where others have reckoned the latter to be the original meaning through the different road of emendation.

"He that obtained her", מחזקה is impossible. We should assume a mistranslation of *gabrah* "her husband" (Ginsberg).

"In times", in this category of unconsciously reproducing the Aramaic, reflects here the Aramaic עתא[11] meaning "troubles, stress" / חמס Prov. 4.17 Peshitta, which the translator did not understand, and simply copied *hebraice* as עתים "times" making for no sense. We should now translate:

"And the daughter of the king of the south will come to the king of the north to make amends. . . .and she and her entourage, and her babe and her husband will be caught up in difficulties".

11.11 starts with the clause ויתמרמר מלך הנגב "And the king of the south shall become embittered (or enraged)", not a notable observation in the circumstances. The context really demands something else. What is required is that the king of the south shall *rebel* against the king of the north. This is the true picture of affairs as the struggle between the two kings ebbs and flows with the fortunes of war. Because the Aramaic had והתמרמר "rebelled", comp. its employment for וימרו בי Ez. 20.8, *memarmerana*/ Num. 17.25 בני מרי, Ez. 2.8, 6.1 (מרי), lexically again for מרי Deut.31.27; 1 Sam.15.23 i.e. rebellion, the Hebrew translator followed through the cue of his Aramaic text with ויתמרמר. The latter however has the entirely different connotation of "embittered", rt. *mrr*.

In 8.7 the probable meaning of ויתמרמר is "he attacked, he charged him" which the translator undoubtedly associated with *mrh* "contend", Aramaic *mari* (Paʻel) "contend".

A similar picture is conveyed to us at 11.40: ובעת קץ יתנגח עמו, usually translated, "At the time of the end, the king of

---

[11] עתא < עאתא (so in rabbinic texts, Jastrow, *Dictionary*, s.v.) < *עעתא (very much like * עע "wood" becomes אע to avoid two Ayins coming in sequence) in turn coming from or parallel to עקתא "trouble, distress". Comp. F. Zimmermann, "עיר ,קיר and Related Forms" in *The Seventy Fifth–Anniversary Volume of the Jewish Quarterly Review*, 1967, p. 583f.

the south shall push at him", so JV. Of course, נגח is used only for the goring ox. The Aramaic had יתגח (קרבא). The word here יתגח with or without קרבא means "wage war", Levy, *Chaldäisches Wörterbuch*, s.v. גוח/גיח, and this is the requisite sense here. Probably the Aramaic text ran: ובעדן סופא יתגח עמה מלכא די דרומא which the translator rendered with יתגח as a close possibility.

At 10.5, the strange בכתם אופז "with the fine gold of Uphaz", usually emended to Ophir, as no place as Uphaz is known, and awkwardly explained by Montgomery as ו = או and therefore like כתם [ו]פז, Song 5.11, can simply be explained as a miscopying, or misreading of the Aramaic text running together כתמאאופזא (Jastrow 1160).

Finally, in this category of the suggestibility of the Aramaic text to the translator, may be mentioned the passage in 8.9: And there came forth from one of them a horn, a small one, Hebrew מצעירה. This word has caused all sorts of difficulties to commentators, and their conclusions seem to be to read *maẓ'ira* or *miẓ'ira* (F. Delitzsch, *Lese u. Schreibfehler im A.T.*, 98b). Still, the word looks strange. It is obvious however that we have an almost transliterated word here. The Aramaic yields what should have been the correct sense מן זעירא "from the small one". The translator equated צעיר = זעיר for the Hebrew, and so precisely in 7.8. For the continuity, comp. the following ורבת יתיר / ושגיאת ותגדל יתר / / describing how the small horn grew.

Closely associated with these translations from the underlying Aramaic are certain Aramaic locutions that are marked features of the language. Thus in 1.17 והילדים האלה ארבעתם is clearly identical with 3.23, וגבריא אלך תלתהון with the numeral postpositive. In 9.21 commentators have remarked upon the play האיש גבריאל which in Aramaic is brought out more graphically גברא גבריאל. Then in 8.11 הרים .... השלך in Aramaic forms a wordplay אתרמי .... אתרים. The phrase בעא בעותא (Dan. 6.14) simply meaning "pray" was not recognized by the translator as an idiomatic expression i.e. a verb with the cognate accusative. He rendered the phrase word for word by לבקש תפלה at 9.3, a construction not found anywhere in the Hebrew Bible. The meaning is illogical;

one cannot ask for prayer. The interpretation given "to apply oneself to prayer" is reading something into the text which is not there. It is evident that the translator, rendering word for word, was misled and translated the Aramaic verb by "seek, ask for". Perhaps he should have translated (ותחנונים) להתפלל תפלה 1 Kings 8.28.29.30.

There are a number of syntactical features of the Aramaic which the translator misapprehended, two in particular. The Aramaic will employ the Lamed as a sign of the dative reference like the Hebrew, and in addition use the Lamed as a sign of the accusative, Hebrew ʾet. Then again Aramaic has a number of nominal and verbal forms identical with one another externally, different naturally in declension and paradigm, but lending themselves to confusion to an unwary translator. Hence—

D.   *There are misconstructions of the prepositional Lamed for the accusatival Lamed and vice versa.*

A clear-cut instance of the prepositional Lamed misconstrued as the *nota accusativi* is found at 11.2. The passage reads: "And now I will declare unto thee the truth. Behold, there shall stand up three kings in Persia; and the fourth shall be far richer than they all; and when he is waxed strong through his riches יעיר הכל את מלכות יון he shall stir up all, the kingdom of Greece." The latter part of this verse is translated conventionally; it will be discussed *in extenso* below. If our passage refers to Darius III (Montgomery); Artaxerxes, (Bevan et al.), then the Hebrew is obscure. One thing that the Persian king did not do was to arouse the Greeks to war. On the contrary, he waged war against them. The question properly posed by critics is that in the text there is no *against*. The suggestion of Torrey cited with approval by Montgomery is that we should read שר הכל יעמיד את מלכות יון where the designation מלכות יון is not the Grecian states as such but the Seleucid empire in Asia. It must be confessed however that the emendation (שר הכל) is unsupported (and seemingly unexampled) and the historical identification here (the kingdom of Greece = the Seleucid empire in Asia?) would be problematical.

The present writer believes that the original Aramaic ran: יעיר כלא למלכותא די יון. The translator, it is clear, misunderstood the Lamed in this instance. He should have retained the Lamed, or rendered it by אל. Instead he assumed that it was the sign of the accusative. The translation of the verse should have been given as: He shall arouse all *against* the kingdom of the Greeks.

Similarly in 10.1 a misunderstanding of this small particle threw the whole verse out of kilter. The passage runs: In the third year of Cyrus, king of Persia, a word was revealed unto Daniel whose name was Belteshazzar; and the word was true, even a great warfare (?) (but see below); he gave heed to the word, and had understanding of the vision ואמת הדבר וצבא גדול ובין את הדבר ובינה לו במראה and so the Jewish Version. In the first place, "great warfare" is impossible and without sense. The passage most likely read in Aramaic מהימנא מלתא ויציבא שגיא "The word was true, and very *sure*" where the translator misapprehended ויציבא Dan. 7.16.19 as וצבא. Comp. almost exactly the passage in Dan. 2.45 ויציב חלמא ומהימן פשרה. Daniel constantly wishes to convince his readers that what he saw was true, and so in the latter passage and at 10.21; 12.7. Secondly, בין cannot be a verb on two counts: the form is anomalous except as an imperative; then the construction בינה לו i.e. noun plus pronoun is the required attractive syntax in the parallelism. The Aramaic text read probably וסכל למלתא where: 1) The translator mistook סכל as a verb and should have taken it as a noun (Jastrow, 990 seq.); 2) The Lamed should have been understood prepositionally and not as the sign of the accusative. We should translate therefore: The word made sense, and there was meaning to the vision.

Conversely there seems to be an instance where the accusatival Lamed was mistaken for a preposition. The passage reads in the Hebrew (11.7): ועמד מנצר שדשיה כנו ויבא אל החיל ויבא במעוז מלך הצפון ועשה בהם והחזיק. The phrase ויבא אל החיל is meaningless. The words obviously must contain some reference to a campaign. Comp. the similar descriptions immediately following in v. 10 ושב מלך הצפון והעמיד המון רב v.13 ובניו יתגרו ואספו המון חיילים רבים. In Aramaic the original may have been misread וְיֵעַל לְחֵילָא "he shall come to the army" instead of וְיָעֵל לְחֵילָא "he shall bring an army". Although חילא the noun is in the determinate state, it may be indefinitely translated. Clearly the Lamed was misapprehended as a preposition instead of the Lamed as *nota accusativi*. The passage now has excellent coherence and continuity, "He shall bring an army and come into the stronghold of the king of the north etc.". For the phrase עשה בהם see p. 37.

The translator's knowledge and odd grammar is evidenced in a curious fashion elsewhere. Daniel is called איש חמודות 10.11,19, and is designated as "beloved" in 9.23 חמודות אתה. It is true that Gen. 27.15 and Dan. 10.3 may be offered as an analogy, but on examination, it will be seen that חמודות is always used of things, never of persons (Bevan, *Daniel*, 153). It appears from biblical usage that one may say in Hebrew בחור חמד or ארץ חמדה but not איש חמדה (see presently). The Hebrew plural here is puzzling moreover as a feminine. Where did this form come from? It is interesting that whereas Hebrew, on the whole, will forbid a combination בחור חמדה the Aramaic will permit its formation. Thus for בחורי חמד of Ez. 23.6.12.23 the Targum has עלמי חמדתא (the Peshitta גלודי רגתא); for שדי חמד Is. 32.12 the Targum has חקלי חמדתא; in Amos 5.11 כרמי חמד the Targum has כרמי חמדתא. חמידתא (Levy). It is likely that in our Daniel passage the original Aramaic had גבר חמידתא. The translator however was at a loss quite obviously in couching his rendering. His חמודות is an error in three directions. He should have made it masculine. He misread חמידתא as a plural, the consonants being identical. He considered חמידתא as a pe'il form, and so rendered it in Hebrew with a participial passive formation. Likewise in 9.23 (א)די חמידתה should have been rendered by כי נחמד/חמוד אתה, not חמודות אתה.

In two instances, because his knowledge of Aramaic was not comprehensive, he was misled in translating the word בית/בינת. In 8.16 Daniel says that he had heard the voice of a man between (!) the (river) Ulai. It is clear that this is a most extraordinary expression. Commentators suppose that the voice came up from the river which indeed would be natural, though the Hebrew in no way expresses such an idea. In Aramaic the word "between" is בינת, contracted to בית and even later to בי. בית however bears the signification of "place, area", French *chez*, e.g. Onqelos Gen.1.10 מקוה המים / בית כנישת מיא. It becomes attached to the names of places בי לפט, בי חוזאי, בי גובר, בי בריצתא and most interesting of all, though there are variants to the passages cf. A. Kohut, *Aruch Completum*, s.v. בי, we have בי פרת "at the Euphrates", בי יאורי "at the rivers". By contrast, our translator understood בית as "between". He should have understood the word as "*at* the River Ulai", which would have made good sense, and would have been the correct translation.

He misunderstood ביתֿ/בינת in another connection. In 8.5.21 the Buck is described as having a great horn between his eyes, בין עיניו. To have a horn *between* the eyes is a bit bizarre, and something of a caricature, when it is expected that the horn should be on his forehead. "Forehead" in Aramaic is בית עינוהי e.g. Ex. 28.38 מצח/בית עינוהי in Onqelos. I am aware of Ex. 13.16 (= Deut. 6.8) and parallels always employed in connection with the *ṭoṭafot* rite, mistranslated to this day by "between the eyes" harking back to the Authorized Version. Nevertheless I must insist that בין עיניו is a mistranslation, for if the author of Daniel had been writing Hebrew originally he would have used מצח, the biblical proportion of this word being 13 to 6, actually 13 to 2, as בין העינים is found in Ex. (= Deut. parallel as above) and twice in Dan. which is translation Hebrew as I am proceeding to argue for. The translator, rendering word for word, considered בית to mean "between" and so misrendered, likewise at 8.21.

E. *The temporal sequence is at times disruptive and illogical. Retroversion to the underlying Aramaic discloses the true chronological sequence.*

The beginning of 8.22 has a most peculiar sequence: והנשברת ותעמדנה ארבע תחתיה ארבע מלכיות מגוי יעמדנה. . . . . The translation of the Jewish Version fingerposts the difficulty at the outset: "And as for that which was broken, in the place whereof four stood up . . ." But והנשברת is a participle. We should expect ואשר נשברה in the perfect. The word והנשברת is usually explained as a casus pendens: writers generally cite Gesenius-Kautzsch, par. 116w, giving 1 Sam. 2.13 כל איש זבח זבח ובא הנער הכהן as a parallel. The reference does not apply. None of the examples found there are congruous to our case, a casus pendens followed by an imperfect with a Waw Conversive. A little farther down the page there, והנשברת is regarded as an exception: "On the other hand, והנשברת

Dan. 8.22 is a mere catchword (?) (equivalent to that which was broken to call to mind the contents of v.8)". But why did the catchword take the form of the present participle?

For narrative purposes, particularly for the description of events in the past, the perfect tense of the Aramaic is employed; but it is highly characteristic of Aramaic to employ the participle in the narration of past events, with the participle obtruding even in the middle of a sentence. Comp. M.L. Margolis, *Aramaic Language of the Babylonian Talmud*, p. 80 and as an example ואתו ותפסין לרבא . . . "And the officers came and arrested Rabba". For this verse which describes the events of v.8, the Aramaic probably ran ודי מתברה וסלקן ארבע. Off guard however in the midst of translating, or possibly because ודי מתברה began the sentence, the translator unconsciously took the participle in the present. He should have rendered the participle by ואשר נשברה "And that which was broken". Note also, in connection with this verse, the indeterminate עמא/גוי and יעמדנה the Aramaic formation instead of ותעמדנה.

At 10.9 the verse reads: ואשמע את קול דבריו וכשמעי את קול דבריו ואני הייתי נרדם על פני ופני ארצה. "But I heard the sound of his words; and when I heard the sound of his words, after I had fallen in a deep sleep on my face, with my face toward the ground". The construction ואני הייתי נרדם is puzzling. The clause is taken by Bevan as circumstantial, inserted parenthetically. But one cannot regard the clause as inserted in that fashion. The verse does not seem to have a conclusion. If the clause וכשמעי את קול דבריו were absent from the text, then ואני הייתי נרדם could be regarded as a parenthesis. But as the text stands, it is directly dependent on וכשמעי וגו' "And as I heard etc." The normal construction appears exactly in 8.18 ובדברו עמי נרדמתי על פני "As he spoke with me, I fell on my face".

The translator erred twice. In the first place, as Ginsberg pointed out, he mistranslated the Aramaic דמך, a standard equivalent for שכב and alternately רדם in the Targums, so that he should have translated "I lay upon my face, my face to the ground", not "I slept". Then again the translator rendered word for word, הוא + the participle which in Aramaic however expresses the simple past

"I lay", and not "I *was* lying". The Waw is to be translated as "there-upon, then", a case of the so-called redundant "and" in Aramaic, and Semitic generally. See C.C. Torrey, *Our Translated Gospels*, c.3.

As mentioned, the translator reproduced יעמדנה as a third feminine plural imperfect at 8.22. On the other hand he mistook the form at 8.8: וצפיר העזים הגדיל עד מאד וכעצמו נשברה הקרן הגדולה ותעלנה חזות ארבע תחתיה לארבע רוחות השמים. The difficulty lies in the plural verb ותעלנה. If it be explained as a *constructio ad sensum*, חזות nevertheless disturbs the whole set-up of the sentence. In fact, if חזות were not there, the whole verse would run smoothly. Accordingly some critics believe that חזות was carelessly inserted from v.5; still others propose to read אחרות, Greek *hetera*. But then how is it that it appears before ארבע?

In Aramaic that particular part of the verse ran וסלקה חזיא (see below). The translator, with an anticipatory eye towards ארבע, took סלקה as the third feminine plural perfect *seliqa* instead of the feminine participle סלקה *salqa*. The latter would be the correct vocalization. Observe how the retroversion secures agreement with the subject חזות and discloses the idiomatic Aramaic deployment of the narrative participle. The translator in short should have rendered ותעלנה/ותעל.

The חזות in v.5 is likewise peculiar. To translate the Hebrew והצפיר קרן חזות בין עיניו "And the Buck had a conspicuous horn on his forehead" may give the sense of the phrase, but it scarcely conveys the bizzarerie of the Hebrew. What would impel an author to describe the horn in such terms when he could have easily used קרן גבוהה (v. 21) or קרן גדולה to express conspicuousness? The Aramaic original probably ran: וצפירא קרן חזיא בית עינוה "And the Buck (casus pendens), a horn was seen on his forehead," (*ut supra*). The translator was misled into believing that קרן without the determinate ending was construct to חזיא which he apprehended as some sort of noun (so indeed חזיא another form of חזוא found in rabbinic texts, Syriac *ḥezāyā*). He should have vocalized the word as *ḥāzyā*, the passive feminine participle, and then rendered והצפיר קרן נראתה במצחו.

F. *Difficult or seemingly corrupt passages in the Hebrew are cleared up when retroverted into the underlying Aramaic.*

8.13 is a very puzzling verse, but its general drift is clear. How long will this state of affairs continue, wherein the Constant Sacrifice will be suspended, and the Holy Place desecrated? The answer given in v.14 is, "And he said unto me, 'Until mornings and evenings, two thousand three hundred, and ונצדק קדש, the Holy Place will be. . . .''. What is the verb to be supplied? "Justified" is not the word that suits. Moreover, the Nif'al of צדק is used nowhere else. The remark of Bevan, p. 136: "The justification of the sanctuary is the vindication of its cause, for as long as it is *polluted* (emphasis mine) it lies under condemnation", would ascribe to נצדק the idea of vindication. Whether the verb will bear this meaning or not, this very observation contains the clue to the correct solution. The Aramaic in back of the Hebrew seems to have ויזכא קודשא. Cf. זכי in the Targums for צדק at Job 33.12 Deut. 25.1; and lexically for נקי Jer. 25.29 and זך Job 33.9 good synonyms for טהר. Either the translator misunderstood זכי in the sense of "justified", whereas he should have translated the phrase in the sense of "cleanse", or he confused the roots of זכי and דכי "purify, cleanse". Actually, while זכי and דכי are apparently different, in reality they are one and the same (so Brockelmann, 153, 196, *purgavit* for both roots), and note how interchangeably they are deployed for Hebrew זכי in Job 9.30; 15.14, and occasionally employed in Jewish Aramaic one for the other, Jastrow, 307, 399. The translation here should have carried the meaning of "The sanctuary shall be cleansed". The purification of the sanctuary would be precisely the concern of our author (11.31) According to the accounts of 1 Macc. 46.47 and of Jos. Ant. Jud. XII, 5.4 a herd of swine were brought into the Holy Place and slaughtered there. An abstract vindication in the eyes of the pious was of less importance than the cleansing away of the defiling objects. Comp. the statement of Judas Maccabaeus in 1 Macc. 4.36: "Behold our enemies are discomfited; let us go up and *cleanse* and dedicate the sanctuary".

9.27 is a crux of long standing, and modern commentators admit their inability to deal with the verse. "The latter half of v. 26 and the whole of v. 27 are involved in such extraordinary difficulties that hardly any two interpreters take the same view. Any attempt

to construe or emend the passages must be regarded as purely
conjectural" (Bevan, 110). The passage runs: והגביר ברית לרבים
שבוע אחד וחצי השבוע ישבית זבח ומנחה ועל כנף שקוצים משמם ועד כלה
ונחרצה תתך על שמם. "And he shall make a firm covenant with many
for one week; and for half of the week he shall cause the sacrifice
and the offering to cease; and upon the wing of detestable things
shall be that which causeth appalment; and until the extermination
wholly determined be poured upon that which causeth appalment"
(JV). The first difficulty revolves around והגביר ברית לרבים. The
locution first of all is anomalous, found nowhere else in the Bible.
Secondly, Antiochus IV did not strengthen the Covenant. On the
contrary, he did his best to stamp out the Jewish religion. To relieve
the difficulty, numerous emendations have been proposed. Montgomery quotes no less than seven, though all the Versions, the
Peshitta, Aquila, Symmachus, Theodotion, the Vulgate, support the masoretic text.

The Aramaic hypothesis offers a suggestion for the solution
of this difficult phrase. What Antiochus really did was to *profane*
the Covenant, not strengthen it (the Hebrew חלל ברית). The
Aramaic probably ran ויחיל קימא, the Haf'el imperfect of חלל
"profane". The translator however pointed differently וְיְחַיֵּל the
Pa'el imperfect of חול and therefore his והגביר. חול is used in the
Targums גבר, תקף, אמץ; comp. Brederek, *Konkordanz zum Targum
Onqelos*, s.v. גבר. The translator may have been led astray by the
plene spelling of חלל > ויחיל so written almost universally in the
editions of the Targums, and he thought it to be the consonantal
Yod instead of the vocalic sign.

The latter part of the verse the commentators regard as equally
hopeless ועל כנף שקוצים משמם. Bevan follows Kuenen in proposing
על כנף/על כנו, an emendation which he regards as "well nigh
certain". But something is missing. One awaits a verb "set" or
something similar. Accordingly, Bevan goes further in suggesting
על שמם (?) "upon him that set up" (?). Ehrlich regards the phrase
as "unverständlich".

Again, a striking restoration is afforded from the Aramaic
which harmonizes excellently well with the context. For the words
ועל כנף the Aramaic had ועל גדף. Comp. כנף/גדף in the Targums

frequently, Brederek, s.v. The translator misjudged the words
ועל גדף. He should have read ועל גדף "There shall come the blasphemy of. . . .", על > עלל and גדפא "blasphemy". The translator was miscued in reading the phrase ועל גדף "and upon the
wing", making a meaningless jumble. Observe how forceful and
pertinent the last part of this difficult verse becomes: ". . . .he
shall suspend sacrifice and offering. There shall come the blasphemy
of the defiling pollution (to be discussed, see p. 40) but complete
destruction will be poured on the defilement".

10.8 is probably one of the most striking instances of mistranslation. The text reads: ואני נשארתי לבדי ואראה את המראה הגדולה הזאת
ולא נשאר בי כח והודי נהפך עלי למשחית ולא עצרתי כח. The usual
translation of the last phrase but one is "And my comeliness was
turned into corruption". The translation of הוד as "comeliness"
is really an attempt to straddle the difficulty. הוד means "glory,
majesty". Commentators have been observant to point out that
the phrase corresponds to זיוי ישתנון עלי 7.28, comp. also 5.9.
What students have failed to realize is that the Hebrew is based
upon a mistranslation. The Aramaic זיוא as well as the Hebrew
cognate זיו has two meanings 1) glory, splendor 2) (brightness of)
features, countenance. The translator thoughtlessly followed the
wrong meaning by rendering הודי instead of פני.

As the Hebrew text stands, equally perplexing is the verse of
ועמד על כנו מעביר נוגש הדר מלכות ובימים אחדים ישבר ולא 11.20
באפים ולא במלחמה. Whatever one makes of the words at the end of
the verse, the four words מעביר נוגש הדר מלכות simply do not make
sense. Possibly the best proposal was advanced by Bevan in trans-
posing the words of נוגש and הדר, with the meaning of "an exactor
who shall cause the glory of the kingdom to pass away". Graetz
would insert בלי before הדר.

One may lengthen the discussion by citing other suggestions but
the supposition of an Aramaic original provides the quick clue
to the difficulty and solution. On the basis of lexical equations in
masoretic text and the Targums, it will be found that הדר מלכות
מעביר נוגש corresponds to מהעדה שלטן יקר מלכו (נגש/שלטן as in
Zech. 9.8). Observe that the last three words are precisely those in
Dan. 7.14 שלטן ויקר ומלכו. Of the taking away of dominion and

majesty, the book of Daniel employs עדה as in 5.20 ויקרה העדיו מנה ‏
7.12 העדיו שלטנהון v. 26 ושלטנה יהעדון. The translator however
misunderstood the word שלטן. He interpreted or read the word as
"exactor, ruler" instead of "dominion," the consonants
being identical. The phrase should have been translated, with
יקר מלכו appositive to שלטן, as "sovereignty": There shall stand
in his place one who will cause sovereignty and royal majesty to
pass away. The lack of connective Waws is good idiomatic Aramaic.
These hitherto unexplained words receive a natural unforced
explanation.

The phrase in 11.23 calls for comment: ועלה ועצם במעט גוי ‏
The phrase במעט גוי is curious. The usual translation is: "And he
shall rise and become strong with a few men". Now the difference
between גוי and עם seems to be this: whereas both גוי and עם may
be used for the idea of nation as a collective unit, for the constituents
of the unit, for people, עם is the term employed but not גוי. Comp.
Brown, Driver, and Briggs, *Dictionary*, s.v. עם and גוי.

In Aramaic, however, עמא stands for both "nation" and "people".

Some awkward constructions in 11.33 and 35 are clarified
again by retroversion into Aramaic. The verse in 35 reads: ומן ‏
המשכילים יכשלו לצרוף בהם ולברר וללבן עד עת קץ כי עוד למועד.
The verse may be translated: "And (when) certain of the teachers
shall fall (it shall be) in order to purge them and cleanse and make
white until the time of the end, for it is yet for the time appointed".

The difficulties are evident: לצרף is introduced awkwardly,
and בהם seems without point, for it cannot logically refer to those
teachers that have fallen and have been exterminated.

The Aramaic equivalent of כשל in the Targums is frequently
תקל which has the meaning of "stumble, fall"; its homonym II
תקל = "be weighed". It is clear what took place, and the difficulty
of the verse is at once dispelled. The teachers are to be weighed
so as to test them, sift and make clean (really לחורא "cleanse";
ללבן "make white" is too literal, and similarly in 12.10) to the
time of the end. The Aramaic יתקלו would be the equivalent of
the passive.

The above interpretation seems to be completely borne out by
reference to v. 33 where a similar misunderstanding of an original

יתקלו took place. The latter portion of the verse runs: ונכשלו בחרב
ובלהבה בשבי ובבזה ימים "And they shall fall by sword and by flame,
by captivity and spoil, for a time". One may fall by sword and flame,
but to fall by captivity and spoil is a distortion of figure. Again the
original יתקלו points to the mistranslation. The word should
have been translated as "weighed, tested". The teachers shall be
tested by sword, flame, captivity, spoliation.

A description of Antiochus IV is given in 8.23 as עז פנים ומבין
חידות. The usual translation is "a king fierce in countenance, and
understanding stratagems". The usual meaning of חידות is of
course "riddles". Not only does the word not comport with the
preceding phrase "fierce in countenance" but the meaning adds
nothing of significance to the portrayal of Antiochus. A retroversion
to the Aramaic yields again the correct reading. The translator
considered the Aramaic אוחדן as a plural of אוחדתא "riddle",
when instead he should have taken אוחדן as an absolute singular
of אוחדנא "power". The Aramaic text before him read ומשתכל אוחדן
"crafty in *power*". This is an appropriate description of Antiochus
and an apt sequence to עז פנים. The word משתכל may take a direct
object e.g. 9.13 in the Peshitta ונסתכל הימנותך/באמתך ולהשכיל.

An example of a number of mistranslations in a single verse
is found at 9.26 where the verse reads ואחרי השבעים ששים ושנים יכרת
משיח ואין לו והעיר והקדש ישחית עם נגיד הבא וקצו בשטף ועד קץ מלחמה
נחרצת שממות.

1. שבעים as mentioned previously represents the Aramaic
שבועין instead of the normal Hebrew שבועות.

2. Both משיח and מלחמה should have been definitized with the
article. The translator understood them incorrectly though they
were determinate in Aramaic, p. 10.

3. ואין לו = ולא אתי לה "And he shall be no more", discussed on
p. 13.

4. The main difficulty to be considered here however revolves
around קצו. The word is out of order because it anticipates pre-
maturely the fall of Antiochus. In the next verse he is still active
and destructive (he shall profane the Covenant, p. 23 supra).
קצו therefore represents a difficulty and must conceal some other
meaning. I would suggest that the translator had וסיפה, which he

should have read as his *sword* rather than his "end". The meaning then would be "His sword (metonomy for his army) shall keep rushing on". Comp. 11.22.

There is a strange locution in 12.2 which likewise receives illumination via the Aramaic. The passage reads: ורבים מישני אדמת עפר יקיצו "And many of those who sleep in the ground of dust shall awake". The phrase אדמת עפר is peculiar if sense can be made of it. "The collection of the words 'ground of dust' has troubled translators since G" (Montgomery). The suggestion of Bevan, following W. Robertson Smith's proposal, is that the text had an ארמות "cairns", not found however in Hebrew or Aramaic, only in Arabic. Although cited by Montgomery, the fact that the word does not exist in Hebrew is sufficient to blight the proposed emendation.

In the Targums, the word אדמה is frequently rendered by the word ארעא, absolute ארע. It will be remembered however that the word ארע means not only "ground, earth" but is employed adverbially for "under, beneath", (Dalman, *Grammatik*,[2] par. 44). For the present Hebrew text, the translation should have been the more striking "And many of those who sleep *beneath* the dust will awake". Because the combination עפרא דארעא (Heb. עפר הארץ) occurs quite frequently in the Targums, for example, and elsewhere in Jewish Aramaic, the translator may have thought that a similar phrase was extant here.

In 11.2, examined above, where there were misunderstood a number of Aramaic Lameds accusativi, the translator mistranslated within this verse a number of other phrases as well. The passage reads: הנה עוד שלשה מלכים עמדים לפרס והרביעי יעשיר עשר גדול מכל וכחזקתו בעשרו יעיר הכל את מלכות יון. The translation usually is given as: "Behold there shall stand up three kings in Persia; and the fourth shall be far richer than they all; and when he is waxed strong through his riches, he shall stir up all against (ut supra, p. 16) the realm of Greece". There are problems of identification; the king may be Darius or Xerxes (Montgomery, 423). The wealth of this king, however, is not relevant here for in the remainder of chapter 11, in the ebb and flow of attack and counter attack, stress is constantly laid on the great number of soldiers amassed to fight the new war, vv. 10, 11, 13, 15. Since he was bilingual, the main misconception on the part of the translator was that he thought חילא "army" bears the same meaning as חיל "riches", and consequently misconstrued the whole verse. The text when retroverted to the Aramaic offers the correct meaning as to what the verse should bear: רביעאה יחיל חילא שגיא מן כלא וכדי יחיל בחילה יעיר כלא למלכותא די יוניא. To point out the difficulties and the solutions that come naturally in their wake, the translator should have rendered: והרביעי יצבא צבא גדול (רב) מכל וכי יחזק (יגבר) בצבאו יעיר הכל אל מלכות יון Evidently, 1) instead of translating "he shall gather (marshall) a great army", he mistranslated by rendering "he shall become very rich", inappropriate for the context; 2) and then instead of misrendering "he shall become strong (?) in his riches", he should have understood the phrase "when he shall become powerful in his forces". Interesting in # 2 is the circumstance that in the various meanings of חיל with which he was acquainted i.e. "wealth", "strength" and undoubtedly "army" as is evident in the rest of chapter 11, he was uncertain whether in one place or the other he was to render "wealth" for "strength" or vice versa, *so he straddled the issue*, (יעשיר, חזקתו), a further proof of translation. Translate now: The fourth king will gather an army greater than any, and when he will be powerful in his forces, he will stir up all against the kingdom of the Greeks.

In 10.9.10 we have the peculiar situation where Daniel falls to the ground at the onset of revelation, and a hand touches him and *moves* him on his hands and knees: ותניעני על ברכי וכפות ידי "Moved me" is certainly awry. We would expect that the hand would *lift* him up on his hands and knees. In the Targums, טלטל is employed for "move", but the word is used also for "lift up". Comp. also e.g. Yer. Hag. II, 77d ויטלטלינה מן ארעא "and shall lift her (sc. the witch) off the ground", Jastrow, *Dictionary*, 536 for other exx. It is this second meaning that should have been employed i.e. for ותניעני the translator should have used נשא or הרים. Daniel was lying face downward in a trance and he was raised on his knees.

In this genre of mistranslations from the Aramaic, one should mention the recovery of H. L. Ginsberg at 8.27 where the word נהייתי is meaningless (*Studies in Daniel*, 58f.) The underlying Aramaic word probably was אתוהת 'ethpaʿal of תוה "I was dazed", and similarly at 2.1 where נהיתה represents אתהות, misunderstood for אתהות "troubled".

There are two verses in the prefatory Hebrew chapter of Daniel, which likewise bear traces of mistranslation. The first verse reads: (3) The king spoke to Ashpenaz his chief officer that he should bring in certain of the children of Israel . . . . . . (4) youths in whom there was no blemish, but fair to look upon and skilful in all wisdom, and skilful in knowledge, and discerning in thought, and such as had ability (כח) to stand in the king's palace, and that he should teach them the learning and tongue of the Chaldeans. . . . . . (5) and that they should be nourished (?) ולגדלם three years. . . . . .

כח in the Hebrew here is a little off. It should have conveyed the signification of "maturity", lit. "manhood", the Aramaic being גבורתא/גבורותא "manhood, maturity". In brief, we should translate: and they should have the maturity to serve in the royal palace.

The phrase "they should be nourished three years" is not quite appropriate in the context. The Aramaic word was undoubtedly רבי, which, however, makes for a much better sense when we choose another meaning of the verb and translate "to train, rear, educate". It is evident, too, that the phrase is out of place in v. 5 (similarly Marti and Löhr, Montgomery, p. 128 who cites them for objection however; the latter's parallel, nevertheless, is not quite to the point; לגדלם here cannot be dependent on וימן) and the natural follow up and the progression of the thought should be: to teach them the literature and language of the Chaldeans, and to train them for three years.

An intriguing verse which has not received a satisfactory explanation is found at 9.21: ועוד אני מדבר בתפלה והאיש גבריאל אשר ראיתי בחזון בתחלה מֻעָף בִּיעָף נֹגֵעַ אֵלַי כְּעֵת מִנְחַת עָרֶב. The passage may be translated:

While I was speaking in prayer, the man Gabriel (word play גַבְרָא גַבְרִיאֵל) whom I had seen in the vision at the beginning being caused to fly swiftly (?), approached close to me at the time of the evening offering.

As is well known, this is the *locus classicus* in the Bible whence it is derived that angels fly with wings. The expression מֻעָף בִּיעָף however is most peculiar. 1) What is meant by the expression "was caused to fly" in the passive? 2) Why was Gabriel "caused", and collaterally why the Puʻal form? 3) ביעף "swiftly" is supposed to come from a problematic root עף > יעף "fly", hence "swiftly".

A retroversion to Aramaic yields an interesting and satisfying solution. The Aramaic read עִיף מְיַעַף "enveloped in a covering" or perhaps עִיף עֵיפָא "covered with a veil", Jastrow, 1073, Payne Smith, 406, 421; Dalman, Gram. 333, 335 which the translator simply did not recognize. עִיף as the passive participle he did comprehend as to form, though lexically he assumed it to mean "fly", and so resorted to the Puʻal ביעף/עיפא מועף. ביעף he thought to have the signification of "hasten", again not recognizing the Aramaic.

The passage now bears the meaning that the 'man' Gabriel, approaching Daniel to give him the explication of the revelation, was wrapped in a cowl of some sort (comp. Targums to Gen. 38.14) so that Daniel should not recognize the form or feature of this divine being. This is in line with the psychology of our author, and indeed with the theology of the Maccabean period: no one could see God, or the emanation of the Divine Presence. Comp. further Dan. 8.13, v. 15 "the appearance of a man", 10.8 "vision". Here the contrast is made between the "vision" of Gabriel that Daniel saw "at the beginning", and the approach of Gabriel who however at this time was enveloped with a covering.

The Aramaic further clarifies an enigmatic turn of phrase in והשבית קצין חרפתו לו בלתי חרפתו ישיב לו :11.18. The Jewish Version interprets the verse as an anacoluthon: But a captain shall cause the reproach offered by him to cease; yea he shall cause his own reproach to return upon him. This deals with the famous historic scene where the Roman general, Lucius Cornelius Scipio Asiaticus, drew a circle around Antiochus, and forced him to give a reply on the spot. והשבית is difficult. The verse would be considerably relieved if we were to assume that the Aramaic פסק, a frequent equivalent of שבת in the Targums, was present in the underlying text but was misapprehended. The Aramaic verb has a series of meanings: stop, interrupt, discontinue; give judgment, pass sentence, umpire; assign, apportion, argue. Some idiomatic usages are: if a man agrees to assign a certain amount of money to his intended son-in-law (*poseq*, Mish. Ketu. 16.2); contend, argue with God (Sanh. 44b.) (the angel Gabriel), lit. give cutting words levelled against God. For the brachylogy in this verse we may translate: The general will inflict humiliation upon him with an oath; (reading בלחי > לחי "curse, swear an oath" in Aramaic. Cf. Montgomery ad loc. and so the Greek, H.L. Ginsberg, JAOS, (59), 105 citing ZAW 1939, 140; cf. further Aaage Bentzen, *Daniel*, 80 to whom I owe the above references); his humiliation will he turn back on him (again *pōseq*).

G. *The Hebrew translator made use of standard and stock translations which conveyed but wooden and misleading renditions of the Aramaic.*

Mechanical renderings, because the Hebrew translator has a set of Hebrew and Aramaic equivalents fixed in his mind, will decidedly affect the sense of a verse. Thus when the translator sees, for example, the word שלם in his Aramaic text, he may assume (see below) that the word means "finish, complete", and if this makes for reasonable sense as it appears to him, he will put down the equivalent תמם without further cerebration. He did this in a passage discussed in another connection where it reads: (8.23) And the latter times of their kingdoms, when the transgressors will have completed their transgression, there shall stand a king of fierce countenance, and crafty in power (*ut supra*, p. 26). The phrase "when the transgressors have *completed* their transgressions" is suspicious, because there is the immediate announcement about the rise of Antiochus Epiphanes, the Arch Transgressor. The Greek and the Peshitta read הפשעים "the sins", and no doubt correctly. The word כהתם remains strange. It means properly "complete, consume, cease." The sequence that one awaits here is, "When the sins have filled up their measure". That indeed would be the prelude for the role of the arch villain, Antiochus. The root תמם is frequently represented by שלם in the Targums and the Peshitta (so here מא דשלמו חובא). The Aramaic however bears two meanings: שלם = 1) be complete 2) fill up. Comp. the Targum to Ex. 28.17; 39.10; 31.5 and comp. the use of שלם in Hebrew as well in Gen. 15.16 כי לא שלם עון האמרי עד הנה exactly the nuance and idea of שלם, which should be applied to the sense of the verse here. The translator, it appears, followed the first meaning of שלם instead of the second.

He misunderstood שלם in another passage at 9.24 which reads: שבעים שבעים נחתך על עמך ועל עיר קדשך לכלא הפשע ולחתם (ולהתם קרי)

חטאות ולכפר עון ולהביא צדק עלמים ולחתם חזון ונביא ולמשח קדש קדשים.

From the balance of the stichs in the verse it is clear that the first part portrays the clearing away of transgression and evil first to bring about a new bright future. Contrast "to finish transgression, to put an end to sin, to wipe out evildoing" with "to bring everlasting righteousness, to . . . . (?) vision and prophet, to anoint the most holy place". It is clear that *to seal up*, לחתם as the verb, does not belong here. Prophets are not out of place in the new future. The LXX reads *kai suntelsthai* reading again as the first *qere*. This does not improve matters much. An important clue however is provided. Again the substrate Aramaic was שלם "fulfill". Hence in the golden future, the prophetic vision will be *fulfilled* which is precisely what we require for the verse. It follows then that the masoretic note may have applied to the second לחתם as well. Indeed there may have been *two* masoretic notes that were reduced unwittingly to one. Not only the Greek but Aquila as an important witness reads *ton telesai* (= להתם), and so the Peshitta and the Vulgate, not לחתם. The phrase therefore has the significance "to fulfill the prophetic vision".

A characteristic expression employed by the Hebrew of Daniel is עמד על עמדך Dan. 10.11; 8.17.18 which simply means "stand on your feet", so the American translation, and Ez. 2.1; 3.24. The Aramaic lexical equivalent קימתא can very well stand for "feet" Brockelmann, *Lexicon*, 654 *pes* (*hominis*) as well as expressions בקים רגליהון, קים רגלא which may be corroboratively compared. Other examples will be found in Chronicles and Nehemiah (see the discussions in sequel). I may borrow one example from Nehemiah anticipatively where at 9.3 ויקומו על עמדם is an error for the usual ויעמדו על עמדם 2 Chron. 30.16 and elsewhere. In 11.14 להעמיד חזון should have been translated לקים חזון "to fulfill the vision". Similarly 11.11.13 העמיד המון "raise up a multitude" should have been rendered by והקים המון, *not* "cause to stand".

11.31 has the peculiar expression המקדש המעוז literally "the sanctuary, the stronghold" (?). For the various explanations cf. Montgomery on the one hand, and the exposition in the light of an Aramaic original by Ginsberg, 48, on the other. The original probably ran מקדש (די) דחסינא "the sanctuary of the Almighty".

The translator first of all followed a well recognized practice of omitting the difficult די/ד in translating, found with some frequency in Chronicles and Nehemiah, though less frequently in Daniel. See pp. 136, 144.

Then, most likely, as Ginsberg observes, חסנא "stronghold" was misunderstood. I would agree that "fortress" is out of context at this point. The concern of our author is the sanctuary proper, the abolition of the daily sacrifice, and the setting up of the strange god, as the verse indicates. חסינא is a well known term for God, comp. חסין = שדי in the Peshitta Job 8.3, most likely the Targum to Ps. 89.9, see further Payne Smith, s.v. and of course in the late Hebrew. Comp. furthermore Ben Yehudah, *Dictionary* s. v. We should therefore translate: "They will profane the sacred precinct of the Almighty". While the meaning of the word would be seemingly late, though not impossible for Daniel, it is preferable, I think, to the interpretation and retroversion of Ginsberg's מקדש חסין "sanctuary and saints" because: 1) It is precarious to emend so drastically the Aramaic text sight unseen. 2) חסין for "saints" is without parallel in Jewish Aramaic. 3) *Essenoi* or *Essaioi*, supposedly a representation of חסין and therefore equated with the Essenes is problematic, *asayya* "the healers", *ḥashayya* "the silent ones", being further possibilities as well as S. Zeitlin's view that *essen/ḥoshen* marks the propensity of the Essenes to forecast the future (comp. corroboratively Field, *Origenis Hexaplorum*, I, to Ex. 28.15, p. 131; Schleusner, *Lexicon in LXX,* I, p. 917, 1822, and comment). *Essen* = a word signifying in Greek speech *logion* ("Oracle") (Josephus). Josephus borrowed *logion* from the Greek translation (H. St. J. Thackeray), and so Ho Hebraios in Mss. in the LXX (Ex. 28.22). In our view, חִסְנָא "stronghold" and חַסְנָא (defect.) "Almighty" could easily be mistaken one for the other.

There is another verse that seems to demand more extensive probing. In 11.3 the writer of Daniel gives a brief but graphic description of the rise of Alexander the Great. Verse 4 continues with a description of his fall: וכעמדו תשבר מלכותו ותחץ לארבע רוחות השמים ולא לאחריתו ולא כמשלו אשר משל כי תנתש מלכותו ולאחרים מלבד אלה. The verse is commonly translated: "And when he shall stand up (?), his kingdom shall be broken and shall be divided toward the four winds of heaven; but not to his posterity nor according to the dominion wherewith he ruled; for his kingdom shall be plucked up even for others beside these".

Imprimis a number of observations, before we come to the main difficulty, should be made.

1. Since the verse deals with the breakup of the kingdom, the preceding "when he shall stand up" is most strange. We therefore should read *ubemo ʿodo* ובמעדו/ובעמדו "when he will totter", Ps. 26.1. See note on the semi-parallel passage and the observation on וכעצמו p. 36.

2. ותחץ properly means "it shall be divided in half" which contravenes the sense of the "four winds of heaven". Aramaic פלג means both "divide" and "divide in half". Similarly Ginsberg.

The words that seem to be awkwardly juxtaposed in the verse are ולא לאחריתו. According to the parallel of כמשלו we should expect some word with a similar connotation. Certainly, "posterity" and "dominion" are peculiarly paired off. There are two possibilities:

1. It is interesting that two of the Ancient Versions offer the correct parallel to "dominion". The Greek reads *ou kata ten alken autou* "not according to his power" and the Peshitta "and not as his sword". Some critics suppose that the Greek represents a ולא בכחו in the Hebrew, or else the Greek filtered in from 8.22.24. Aside from the fact that chapter 11 is quite removed from chapter 8, the Greek there employs the more familiar *ischus* in both verses 22 and 24. What the Greek represents here is indeed difficult to discern. Schleusner in his *Lexicon* and Hatch-Redpath in their *Concordance to the LXX* confess their inability to ascertain what the Hebrew read.

There is a possibility that the Greek may have read some form of the Aramaic אחד (comp. אחיד כל "omnipotent"; אוחדנא "power") for the Hebrew text (אחר)יתו. But that they had such a form in their Hebrew text is doubtful. As ever in so many instances familiar to the students of the LXX, it appears here that they indulged in a bit of fanciful exegesis, Aramaicizing as they do, e.g. as in Isaiah, since they spoke Aramaic. Comp. J. Fischer, *In welcher Schrift lag das LXX vor*, passim.

The point to be noticed is that the Greek interpreted or read אחריתו as "power". The verse may now be examined from the point of view of an Aramaic original. The Greek provides the lead that the original Aramaic may have had אוחדנה "his power". The Hebrew translator may not have recognized the word, and he may have tacitly corrected it with the root אחר. Unconsciously he may have been guided by the thought that, since the words immediately preceding deal with the breaking up of Alexander's kingdom and its dispersion to the four winds of heaven, the sequence should be that Alexander's posterity did not succeed him to the throne. Undoubtedly the translator was aware of that elementary historical fact. The process of his reasoning may have led him therefore to translate ולא לאחריתו "and not to his posterity".

There are other difficulties connected with this supposition that still require explanation. If one looks at this part of the verse again, it is apparent that the Hebrew construction is still strangely elliptical. After each ולא one expects some verb. This ellipsis is due to a construction in Aramaic syntax which the translator had difficulty in reproducing. The copula in Aramaic is frequently expressed by איתי, and usually with ל to express relationship. The Aramaic may have been ולא איתי לאוחדנה ולא איתי כשולטנה די שלט. The verse therefore may have been originally "And it shall not be in (to) his power, and it shall not be as his dominion that he ruled".

2. There is however another preferable alternative which should be considered. It is quite possible that the Aramaic text had the word סיפה "his sword" which the translator read as "his *end*" with the same letters. This explication has the virtue of simplicity, and may be preferred. The translator misrendered with אחריתו instead of חרבו.

Akin to the above verse is the passage at 8.8 which reads; וצפיר העזים הגדיל עד מאד וכעצמו נשברה הקרן הגדולה.... The passage is conventionally translated: And the he-goat magnified himself exceedingly; and as he was strong, the great horn was broken. . . . The verse deals with Alexander the Great again as in 11.4 above. However the verse construes a non-sequitur again. If he became strong, how then immediately and abruptly was the great horn broken? We require the sense of something like "he fell away, he died", very much like the suggestion of Hitzig who suggested *ענד (he invented the word for the Hebrew) for עמד, based upon the Arabic "he died", as the opening word in 11.4. Very

likely the Aramaic ran here במחסנה (cf. for form in the infinitive
Dan. 6.21) or כדי חסן "when he became mortally weak, ill, sick
unto death". The root *ḥsn* not only means "be strong" which
meaning the translator followed here with the customary signification, but contrastedly to "be mortally sick". Comp. the Peshitta's
translation for 2 Sam. 12.15/ויאנש and Is. 39.1/חלה. There may be
an objection that there is a confusion of symbols here and that the
big horn could not have become "ill". We should probably render
more in keeping with the figure "gave way, became faint, flagged,
collapsed" or something similar. Undoubtedly the Aramaic writer
employed a wordplay *ḥsn* too on the sudden death of Alexander.
It is well known that Alexander died suddenly from a violent fever.

H.   *The nuance of a word will escape the translator.*

There is a thin dividing line between a mistranslation and a "bad"
translation, where the verse could carry a meaning but barely, yet
the translation is obviously off center. Thus, to give some modern
examples, in the story of Ruth, the country of Moab is designated
as the *field* of Moab (Ru. 1.1.2.6, the Jewish Version translating
lit.); or the Douay version at Prov. 31.15 "she giveth *prey* to her
houschold" instead of the appropriate "food", and so indeed the
Jewish Version correctly.

Thus in 12.3 for example מצדיקי הרבים "those that justify the
many", while good Hebrew, fails to bring out the cogency and
vigor of the thought of what undoubtedly was in the Aramaic
מזכי שגיאיא "those that give *merit* to many" i.e., the teachers who
went down to the line by instruction and example, the leaders
who experienced persecution and martyrdom, not incongruously
those "who justify".

Similarly with the lead of the expression in Aramaic at 7.8 ופם
ממלל רברבן where the word is usually translated "great things"
but where the meaning obviously is "boastful things" (Ginsberg,
p. 30 citing Hölscher); at 11.36 for ועל אל אלים ידבר נפלאות the
Aramaic probably ran ימלל רברבן "he will vaunt himself against
God". On the other hand, we may perceive with the same word a
genuine mistranslation at 8.24 ורברבין יחבל/ונפלאות ישחית "he will
destroy the leaders", i.e a misunderstanding of רברבן/רברבין
rabrebin/rabraban. Cf. והשחית עצומים in the same verse, and in v. 25
ישחית רבים.

In a number of instances, too, the translator made use of a
standard rendition to reproduce the Aramaic פלח "work, do" with
the Hebrew עשה. His Hebrew translation, however, comes through
oddly in a number of phrases where to render "work, do" is inapposite. Thus in 8.24 והצליח ועשה ... ועצם כחו, 11.7 ועשה בהם והחזיק,
ועשה למבצרי מעזים 11.39, ועשה ושב לארצו 11.28, וישרים עמו ועשה 11.17,
11.32 ועם ידעי אלהיו יחזקו ועשו. In all these verses it is evident that
עשה "do" is lame and puzzling: 8.24 "And his strength shall
increase .... he shall be successful and (?)"; or 11.28 "He shall
do (?) and return to his country". The root *plḥ* in Eastern Aramaic
bears the extended meaning of "wage war, do battle", comp.
Brockelmann, 572 for the verb *militavit*, the noun *palḥa* "miles",
the adjective *palḥaya* militaris, *palḥutha* militia, *pulḥana* exercitus
(= Peshitta *ḥailawatha* 2 Chron 33.5) and even the Hebrew *paloaḥ*
"soldier", Ben Yehudah, *Dictionary*, s.v. *plḥ* p. 4943, n. 1 with
observations of S. Lieberman and N.H. Tur Sinai. We should
therefore translate the verses above seriatim:8.24 And his strength
shall increase. . . .and he will be successful; and (sic!, note syntax)
he will wage war and destroy many. 11.7: and he shall do battle
against them and overcome (an instructive example); 11.17 And
he will set his face to come with all the forces of his kingdom with
his officers (1. *wesarim*; חילא/תקף "army", not "strength") and
attack . . . ; 11.28 and he shall do battle and return to his country;
11.39 and he shall do battle against the fortified strongholds (sic!)
. . . ; 11.32: and a people, conscious of their God, will take courage
and fight back.

In two passages the Hebrew לבן, if translated literally, is awkward: 11.35 runs: and some of them that are wise shall be tested
(ut supra p. 25) to refine among them, and to purify and make
white (so JV) even to the time of the end. The Hebrew verb is
assuredly strange, and the translation "to make white" is awry. It
is an off translation of *ḥawwara'* "to wash clean, make clear" a
frequent translation of כבס in the Targums. Cf. MT and Onqelos at
Ex. 19.14; Lev. 6.20; 13.55.56; figuratively Jer. 4.14.

Then again the passage in 12.10 should read: many shall purify
themselves, and be washed clean (JV: make themselves white) and
be refined.

Finally, as another example, in a verse discussed above, we may

mention 11.17. . . . .and he shall give him the daughter of women
to destroy it (?; Hebrew להשחיתה, fem. suff.) but it shall not stand
neither be for him. "To destroy it" is very puzzling. Commentators
are nonplussed by the circumstance that if it be Cleopatra I given
in marriage, it would be most strange to say that her father
Antiochus III betrothed her to destroy her, which makes for non-
sense; others maintain that "it" refers to Egypt (cf. A. Bentzen ad
loc.), Egypt implicitly understood, although Egypt is not in the
vicinity of the verse.

The almost homonymous Aramaic *hubala*, rt. *ḥbl* I "destroy",
a frequent equivalent of שחת, was undoubtedly confused with *hubla*
rt. *ḥbl* II, like the Jewish Aramaic חבוליא, חבולא, Mandaic חבול,
Hebrew חבל, associated with Akkadian *hubullu*, Brockelmann, 211
"pledge, security". The passage should be rendered: . . . and he
shall give him the daughter of women for a surety, but she shall
not stand by him, nor be for him. This interpretation is confirmed
by the eventuality that Antiochus, by marrying off his daughter to
Ptolemy V, sought to gain a foothold and influence at the Egyptian
court. It did not turn out the way he imagined. Coele-Syria remained
a bone of contention between Syria and Egypt. See S. Zeitlin,
Rise and Fall of the Judean State, I, p. 71f. Cleopatra was too
independent a woman to be in pawnage to her father. When
Antiochus later sought Ptolemy's aid in the war he contemplated
against Rome, Cleopatra advised her husband to disavow such a
course, and continue in alliance with Rome (C.H.H. Wright,
Daniel and His Prophecies, 271.)

In passing, it may be noticed that the Hebrew text is flawed in a
number of instances. Thus in 11.14, some leaders will "be raised
up" (?) to fulfill the vision but will fail. We probably should read
ינסו "will attempt to fulfill the vision but will fail", where one word
for the other was misheard. In 11.13 שנים is a gloss to קץ העתים to
avoid taking the latter expression apocalyptically. At 11.4 וכעמדו
should be read "he shall totter", p. 34, and then in 8.24 *fine* and
25 *initio* some words fell out of order so that instead of ועל שכלו:
ועם קדשים the passage should read ושכלו על עם קדשים and note the
smooth appropriate sequel והצליח מרמה בידו.

3

The Idols in Daniel via the Aramaic

In Daniel, there are a number of references to idols, the outstanding one being the so-called "Abomination of Desolation". In the number of instances in which this idol is referred to, however, its name and attribute all differ from one another. Thus in 8.13 it is called הפשע שמם; in 9.27 simply שמם, in 12.11 שקוץ שמם, at 11.31, prefaced anomalously with the definite article on the first word only השקוץ משמם; then in 9.27 שקוצים משמם pluralized in the first element. The fact that the idol does not have a uniform standard title evidences that the expression *eo ipso* bears the mark of translation.

The usual explanation forwarded first by E. Nestle ZATW iv., 248 (1884) and his *Marginalien u. Materialien*, 35, Bevan, *Daniel* 193, is that our Hebrew generally is a caricature of בעל שמם "Lord of Heaven", found frequently indeed in inscriptions. See the important note of Cooke, *North Semitic Inscriptions*, p. 45. The variants in the Hebrew, however, remain unexplained, unless steady emendation be resorted to. If however the Hebrew of Daniel is a translation, assumed in these pages, then בעל שמם as a regular name for that deity could not have appeared in the Aramaic text. No Judean writer, certainly not by the time of Daniel, would have given that honorific appellation (Lord of Heaven!) to a strange god which he would have reserved for the God of Israel alone. Throughout the Bible, alien gods are not only mocked but ridiculed with lampooning names: תמנת חרס Jud. 2.9 is caricatured as תמנת סרח Jos. 19.50; 24.30, as well as such terms as גלולים (word-play on גללים "dung",) זנה, בשת, תועבה, שקוץ "go a-whoring after". The attributes of אלהי השמים Ezr. 1.2; אל השמים Ps. 136.26; מרא שמיא(!) Dan. 5.23 "Lord of Heaven" would be ascribed solely to the God of Israel.

I. The key to our problem in the retroversion from the Aramaic is provided with the expression first met with in הפשע שמם (8.13). The Aramaic was סורחנא דסרח. The root סרח has quite a number of distinct significations: 1) be foul, stink. 2) sin. The Aramaic noun is used regularly for פשע, חטא, עון. For the latter, comp. 1 Sam. 24.11; Job 34.6. 3) lay waste, destroy. Comp. Payne Smith, *Dictionary*, s. v.; Brockelmann, 498a, both in the noun and the verb. Among these three meanings, the translator chose one that was wrong. For the second Aramaic word, he mistakenly chose "devastate, waste" instead of the more natural and apposite sense of "befouling, defiling". פשע likewise is a mistranslation of סורחן (cf. infra).

Actually, his translation of סורחן דסרח should have conveyed something like "the defiling pollution" not the "abomination of desolation". Bringing or setting up an alien god in the Temple was like bringing pollution (טומאה) into the sanctuary. Cf. Ps. 79.1 The heathen have come into thy inheritance; they have *defiled* thy holy temple. Likewise in 11.31, Daniel uses the term וחללו "they shall profane" the sanctuary. Moreover, in 8.12, where the statue (see below) is set up at the side of the Tamid, it is with *pollution*, not פשע "sin", a mistranslation again of סורחן, because with the idol, swinesflesh was offered as well, a double pollution, so to speak (see presently). There is point then to the restored conclusion in v. 14 that the sanctuary will be cleansed, and furthermore confirmed by the passage in I Macc. 4.36 cited previously ". . . .let us go and *cleanse* the sanctuary".

More systematically, we shall endeavor to explain the different terms that the translator employed for his Aramaic rendering.

1. The first time he met with the term at 8.13 הפשע שמם he mistranslated on two counts: for סורחנא he rendered with הפשע because, not unnaturally for him, this idol was the great sin, par excellence; yet it is incorrect because הפשע is not a term for a set-up idol. He likewise rendered with the definite article because of the determinate state of סורחנא. (In the other exx. of שקוץ שומם he translated competently, even brilliantly, with the first word שקוץ because it implies not only detestation, but is a word used for an alien god in the Scriptures, as 1 Kings 11.5; 2 Kings 23.13 et passim.) For the first time, then, he made a blunder with הפשע, and with erroneous

definitizing. He should have rendered the second word with a prefixing of the definite article as well just as required in Hebrew, but there was no sign of the definite state in the second Aramaic word to signal him he left out the article (p. 10). The cardinal error was to translate סרח with שומם "wasting, devastating" instead of a defiling, contemptible sense like מטמא, or מסריח, itself being good Hebrew as well.

2. In 9.27 we find the strange שקוצים משמם. This construction the translator obviously considered a plural, i.e. סרחן a plural of סרח, pointing sirhin, as a plural of serah, for surhan, hence his שקוצים. At the end of the verse, we find שמם alone. The underlying Aramaic probably read brachylogically דסרח "the defiling one, the defiler", shortened because of the preceding designation at the beginning of the verse. Very likely the translator was straddling the issue in his rendering, because of his perplexity with the Aramaic locution as is evident from his mistranslation throughout.

3. In the light of the information presented so far, the other forms naturally fall into place. Thus 12.11 שקוץ שומם is "normal" representing סורחנא דסרח, treated indefinitely by the Hebrew translator, while on the other hand in 11.31 השקוץ משומם with the definite article is סורחנא. The verb סרח as mentioned above did not carry the article and so was unconsciously omitted.

The translation hypothesis elucidates then quite appositely the sobriquet שקוץ משומם as סורחנא דסרח "The defiling pollution". The noun with the quasi-tautological adjective serves a double purpose: there were *two* pollutions: that of the idol itself and that of the swinesflesh that was offered to it, the sin of the idol the more heinous (cf. the Golden Calf).

II. We are now in a position to examine a *crux criticorum* in Dan. 8.9–14:

V.9 ותגדל יתר does not necessarily go back to ורבת יתיר "it grew up mightily" though admittedly possible, but rather ושגיאת יתיר "it *spread*, it *traversed* mightily". A horn while growing will grow upwards not sideways, even allowing for the extension of figure in the verse. If however the horn "grows" to the south, and to the east and then to Judea the proper rendition would be "spread". Cf. moreover the common סגי "go".

V.10 צבא השמים = חיל שמיא which however I take not to mean "the host of heaven" but שמיא as simply a surrogate of God; cf. Dan. 4.23, so that the phrase means the "hosts of God". For the expression Ex. 12.41 צבאות יי׳ but here to be understood as a symbolic designation of the priests. Cf. *the Testament of the 12 Patriarchs,* Testament of Levi 16.1: . . . For 70 weeks ye shall go astray, profane the priesthood, and pollute the sacrifices. . . . , and Neh. 13.29.

V.11 שר הצבא = רב חילא metonomy for the High Priest. The "stars" v. 10 (eliminated by Ginsberg) are undoubtedly the other associated subordinated members of the priesthood, not participating directly in the sacrificial service of the sanctuary, the Levites, the Temple singers etc.

מתרים; ומנה אתרים תמידא = וממנו הרים התמיד = taken *away*, not "up", Payne Smith, 534. The expression is Aramaic like מני שים טעם Dan, 3.29; 4.3; Ezr. 4.19; 6.8. The significance is that through the agency of the horn, the Constant Sacrifice was abolished.

V.12 is most difficult. What is the meaning of צבא? Why is תנתן feminine? What does על התמיד signify, = "on the Constant Sacrifice"? Why the strange בפשע "with transgression" (?)

V.13 gives us the first clue how to treat in retrospect v. 12. The passage implies that an idol was set up in the sacred precinct where the sacrifice was offered: Then I heard a divine being say: How long will this scene continue, — the befouling pollution (see p. 40) set up, and the sanctuary and the priesthood be trampled upon? He answered: 2300 days and the sanctuary be cleansed (p. 22). Accordingly צבא = idol in some sort of way. I would suggest an underlying דחילא "idol", employed lexically for תועבה Ex. 8.22, אליל Lev. 26.1, 2 Kings 18.4 אשרה in the Peshitta, the determinate being דחלתא and so in the Targums for alien gods as in Ex. 20.23 אלהי כסף ואלהי זהב. The translator probably comprehended דחילא (feminine) as "host" (חילא). תנתן as a feminine of course agrees with על; דחילא is to be construed with תנתן "set up on high" cf. הקם על 2 Sam. 23.1; Hos. 7.16, 11.7; see Brown, Driver, Briggs, *Lexicon,* p. 752; תמידא/התמיד is in error for תדירא "continually" (following Ginsberg) inasmuch as the preceding verse alleges that

the Tamid was already abolished. בפשע is a mistranslation of
בסורחנא "pollution" as has been observed previously. The whole
passage may now be translated in its original connotation:

9. And from one of them there grew up a horn, from the small
one, and it spread mightily to the south, to the north, and to the
land of delight (Aramaic was צביתא. Cf. Mal. 3.12.) 10. And it
spread to the priest-army of the Lord; and it toppled to the ground
some of the priests, and some of the 'stars' (Levites, Temple singers)
and trampled on them. 11. And the Horn advanced on to the High-
Priest; and through it the Tamid was abolished, and its holy place
overthrown. 12. An idol was set up on high with its unending
pollution; it threw Truth to the ground, gave battle (plḥ) and was
successful. 13. And I heard a divine being talking; and the divine
being said to the one addressed (rd. *hamedubbar/hamedabber*): how
long will this scene of the Constant Sacrifice last? and the befouling
pollution be set up? and the sanctuary and the host attendants
be trampled upon? 14. Then he said to him (l. *'elaw*, with Gk.,
Theod., Syriac, BH), Until evening and morning 2300 times, then
the sanctuary will be cleansed! Note how the Aramaic retroversion
supplies the key to our difficulties throughout.

III. There is another god mentioned in Dan. 11.37, unknown,
but through the Aramaic we recover his proper identification:
Neither shall he (= Antiochus IV Epiphanes) regard the god of
his fathers, nor the desire of women (?), nor any god, for he shall
magnify himself above all. Who is this god, "the desire of women",
חמדת נשים?

There are quite a number of identifications of this god of women
as Nanai, Anaitis, Astarte, Mylitta, though Ewald's characteriza-
tion with Tammuz-Adonis has become the accepted tag. I would
suggest however another identification: Dionysios. In the spring,
the Greek women would go into the hills to meet Dionysios reborn,
drinking for two days. Led by Maenads or mad women devoted to
Dionysios, they marched in a wild procession. They danced
and drank, abandoned all restraint. At the climax, a goat, bull,
sometimes a man was seized and dismembered. The women then
drank the blood, consumed the flesh thereby imagining that the

god entered into them and they became one with the god. Comp.
J. Harrison, *Prolegomena to the Study of the Greek Religion*, c.8;
H. J. Rose, *Handbook of Greek Mythology*, c.6.

The Aramaic hypothesis seems to confirm this Dionysiac identity. חמדת נשים in Aramaic would be חמידתא די נשיא where Dinešayya
would be a mocking play on Dionysios. Other evidence from 2
Macc. 6.7 would testify to the presence of the Dionysiac rites: "And
when the Dionysiac festival was come, the Jews were compelled to
go in procession to Dionysios, carrying ivy". Noteworthy is the
statement from a different perspective in the Cambridge Ancient
History, viii, 508 that "Yahweh was perhaps identified with
Dionysios". The identity seems confirmed.

In passing, perhaps we may be able to solve another mysterious
god with a puzzling attribute in Dan. 11.38, ולאלה מעזים על כנו
יכבד, translated conventionally "But in his estate he shall honor
the god of forces" (AV), or "in his place shall he honor the god of
strongholds" (JV). Commentators find it difficult again to determine who the god was. Grotius suggested Mars, the god of war.
Others have proposed Jupiter Capitolanus, or even the goddess
Roma, "her emblem, a mural crown". For all these surmises, see
Montgomery, *Daniel*, p. 461 for full references. Montgomery himself regarded the identity of the god as "obscure".

H. L. Ginsberg contends with some justice that in v. 37 Antiochus
disavows all the gods that his ancestors knew, but, contrastedly,
in the next v. 38 he honors the god of Israel in his place, bringing
the homage of gold, silver and precious things. There is therefore
a conflict between v. 37 and 38. To tag v. 38 with the identification
of the God of Israel however Ginsberg considers 1) *yekabbed*[1] as
having nosed out some such word as *yena'eẓ* 2) 38a and 38b are just
variants to one another with the preference to be given to 38a.
3) Probably the Aramaic was *yehaqel* for the erroneous *yehoqar*.
4) *Ma'uzzim* points to *ḥisnin* error for *ḥesen* "saints", coming
through in Jewish tradition as Essaioi or Essenoi (Essenes), a
doubtful equation (see p. 33) and full of historical problems.
The analysis is probing enough, but the solution is hardly convincing. Comp. likewise Bentzen, *Daniel*, 82 for a similar, though
more general, critical conclusion.

We take the view that the portrait that the Aramaic writer wished to transmit to us has the features of Zeus, as other scholars have suggested. This identification is clear from a number of circumstances. In the issuance of his coinage, Antiochus IV displaced the god Apollo and increasingly stamped his coinage with the features of Zeus. Further 2 Macc. 6.41 records that Antiochus established Zeus Xenios at Mount Gerizim, and so Josephus similarly i.e. Zeus Hellenios, Ant. XIII, 263, (Loeb classics, ed. R. Marcus, note c) as well as Zeus Olympius in the Temple at Jerusalem. From our sources in Josephus and Macc. the reference to Zeus would in all likelihood preclude identifications from outlying quarters. In short, we may safely assume that the "god of the fortress" (Montgomery) approximates the features of Zeus. How does אלה מעזים correspond to Zeus?

Although one of his older primitive titles was Herkeios "Zeus of the Fort", the protector of the village stronghold, the altar in the courtyard of the Homeric castle as it stood later on the Acropolis in Athens and other cities (Moore, *History of Religions*, I, 414), and apparently our investigation should end here for ostensibly the Greek equivalent has been found for the problematic מעזים, we are slightly dissatisfied with the equation for we think we have not reached to the heart of the solution.

It may be strongly doubted again whether the Jewish writer at such a late date in the theology of the Judean people would credit a foreign god with the attributes of "fortress", with that qualification that he would reserve for the God of Israel alone. Comp. Ps. 27.1; 43.2; Is. 17.10. If Zeus be the god that the Danielic writer had in mind, it would only be with slight and mockery of his pretensions to godhood (p. 39).

Now one of the legends about the birth of Zeus relates that he was an infant suckled by a goat Amaltheia (H. J. Rose, *Handbook*, c.3). There are a number of coins, though later, that depict such a scene. We have a copper of M. Aurelius which has *rev.* the infant Zeus suckled by a goat (Cook, *Zeus* vol. II, ii, 961); in addition, "A copper issued by Commodus has *rev.* . . . . a goat standing to the right with head turned back suckling the infant Zeus" (ibid, p. 968, fig. 857). A trace of this legend is found in Jewish tradition where the LXX translates the name of the third daughter of Job, Keren Ha-Puch, by "Horn of Amalthea" (spelling varies), the goat that nursed Zeus. This is probably based on the idea that *puch* is to be identified with a species of antelope (so L. Ginzberg, *Legends*, V, 389) though others explain the word as "eye paint" (Levy, Jastrow, Kohut). The translator of Job would not have rendered thus unless he were aware that Jewish readers reading the Greek of Job would understand his reference. If we have a reference to this legend of Zeus and the nursing goat in our Daniel passage, it would appear that the vocalization *ma'uzzim* of the Hebrew text was incorrectly transmitted and should be pointed מֵעִזִּים "a god stemming from goats". For this usage, Comp. Brown, Driver, Briggs, 579a. Of all the legends pertaining to Zeus, this would be picked up by the popular imagination (especially from the coins of Antiochus IV who made his features resemble Zeus, the coins being especially scrutinized when newly minted, and then passed from hand to hand, see below) as it would be a not-to-be-missed opportunity to deride Zeus' origin as he developed into the more humanistic Zeus, with pretensions as the god of justice, a challenge *in posse* to the God of Israel through the philo-Hellenes. Probably the masoretic vocalization arose from the fact that מָעוֹז occurs five times before in c. 11, and there was the predisposition to vocalize the same way. It is not uncommon for rival religions to deride each other's origin, biblically, as in Gen. 19 (Lot's daughters), their gods (1 Kings 11.5), the nomenclature *gillulim* "idols" with the play on *galal* "filth, ordure", and the later rabbinic times *bet gallia/bet caria* and other exx. at Abodah Zara 46a, as well as the aspersions contrariwise cast by an Apion.

Thus a god, goat-suckled, would be another in a series bearing a contemptuous designation like סורחנא דסרח.

The discrepancy between vv. 37 and 38 may be tentatively resolved in the following fashion. Antiochus IV at the beginning of his reign favored Apollo, but gradually to unify his empire established the cult of Zeus as paramount. Why he turned his back on the earlier cult, and why this should be a point that the author of Daniel should scorn is not difficult to account for. Antiochus' theatrical character (his sobriquet *epimanes* means "crazy") undoubtedly earned him popular ridicule, but for the Danielic author, the king merited disdain because he wished to be *incarnate* (*epiphanes*). Though preceding emperors established cults for worship, and deified themselves, with Antiochus IV we have for the first time the name Theos added on to his coins and the features of Zeus contrived to approximate the face of the king. If the reader consults the third volume of Plates issued in conjunction with the *Cambridge Ancient History*, he will mark on p. 12 the early and late coins of Antiochus IV. The earlier coins(g) have the portrait of the king and *rev.* a portrait of Apollo seated on an omphalos (cir. 175–170 B.C.E.) but the later coins (167 B.C.E. or later) were impressed with the portrait of the king now bearded, resembling Zeus, and *rev.* a delineation of Zeus seated. This coin bears the long inscription Basileos Antiochou Theou Epiphanous Nikephorou. There is reason to conjecture that a statue of Zeus Olympios was set up in the Temple, a bearded Zeus with the features of Antiochus (comp. CAH, viii, 508). In sum, v. 38 is to be interpreted with a double entendre: the king honors Zeus, nursed *in origine* by a goat, who in turn is himself! The verse is ironical not "bitter", as Montgomery has it. Vv. 37–38 may now be translated:

He will not look to the gods of his ancestors,
Nor to the Darling of women nor to any god will he look; but he will vaunt himself above all.
And a god stemming from goats will he honor on his place;
But a god that his ancestors did not know he will honor (himself!) with gold, silver, precious stones, and other valuables.

4

Symbolism and Language in the
Book of Jonah

Modern scholars have found the book of Jonah to be a folk tale, "neither an account of actual happenings, nor an allegory. . . it is fiction with a beginning, a middle and an end".[1] If Jonah then is not an historical event but imaginatively contrived by the author, it is proper for us to inquire why certain episodes were included in the book, and to analyze what the purpose of the writer was in emphasizing certain incidents in his narrative. Only a number of questions can be raised in the present study, some that have been asked before, but have not received adequate or satisfactory answers, others that have not received solutions at all, and still others that have not even been raised. This investigation will attempt to examine 1) the structure of Jonah, 2) its language, 3) its symbolism, principally to focus on the role of the great fish, and finally 4) to conclude with an attempt at biography of the author, as inferred from the book.

Questions arise with the opening verses. What impelled Jonah to flee from the presence of the Lord? Was it because he did not wish to take on the prophetic office and function? There were enough precedents in such prophets as Moses and Jeremiah, who felt that they were not qualified to prophesy, and at the very first declined. A judgment that shapes up in biblical tradition is that a man does not have to be a prophet if he does not want to.[2]

---

[1] Comp. R.H. Pfeiffer, *Introduction to the Old Testament*, N.Y. 1941, p. 586; O. Eissfeldt, *The Old Testament,* trans. by P.R. Ackroyd, Oxford, 1965, p. 405.

[2] Moses for example rebuffs persistently Yahweh's call (Ex. 3.10 is not a command) by demeaning his own abilities (v. 11 "Who am I that I should go to Pharaoh. . . . . ?"), v. 13 (. . . and if they say, what is his name, what shall I tell them?"), 4.1 ("But maybe they will not believe me, and they will not hearken to my voice. . . ."), 4.10 ("I have no verbal gifts . . . I am awkward in speaking, and awkward in language."). In addition, Yahweh essayed to fortify Moses for his

48

As far as Jonah is concerned, in c. 4 he is quite ready and eager to serve. When and where did this change of heart take place? It could be maintained with some justice that no conversion actually transpired. The end of the story recounts that Jonah was petty enough to rue his function as prophet, inasmuch as all the inhabitants of Nineveh were not exterminated, much to Jonah's discomfiture.[3]

mission by the performance of two miracles; of the rod turning into the serpent, and the healing of the leprous hand. Nevertheless, after Yahweh's attempt at persuasion, Moses remained obdurate: "please send someone else" (4.13.) Yahweh then is angry (v. 14) but even then there is no peremptory compulsion but Aaron is chosen as spokesman.

At his first call, Jeremiah too is reluctant to take on his prophetic function: Alas, O Lord God, behold I do not know how to speak for I am a child. He describes at another occasion the process whereby he assumed the mantle of prophecy as "persuasion" on the part of Yahweh: "Thou hast deceived me, O lord, and I let myself be deceived; Thou hast been too strong for me and Thou hast prevailed," Jer. 20.7.

Similarly, Isaiah is not appointed for his task peremptorily. Yahweh asks first, "Whom shall I send? Who will go for us?" Then Isaiah: "Behold here am I; send me." It is to be observed that Isaiah feels some hesitation in the anticipation of his call for he regarded himself as "a man of unclean lips" (Is. 6.5) which had to be wiped away first by the glowing coal of the seraph.

Ezekiel in receiving his call betrays neither willingness nor reluctance. The sheer power of the revelation, the *yad Yahweh,* gives him no alternative, putting him into a trance where there is no escape and he must hear. Yahweh, however, very much as in the instance with Jeremiah seeks to hearten Ezekiel with the reassurance that Ezekiel need not quail for he is as strong as his opponents, Ez. 3. 8f. At any rate the point in the text is sustained by the example of Moses, Jeremiah, and Isaiah.

[3] At this point a correction may be in order. It is a frequent assertion that the purpose of the book is to show that in the conception of the author God is not only the special (tribal) god of Israel but of the whole world (comp. art. Jonah, Hastings, *Dict. of the Bible),* not only of the Jewish people but of the Gentiles as well; and that Jonah, following the current assumptions of the time, sought to escape Yahweh's jurisdiction by fleeing Palestine. Jonah, however, knows very well that God is a universal god. In 1.9 he describes God as the Lord of heaven, who created the sea and the land. He also knows that God is sending him outside of Palestine to preach against Nineveh, ergo God's power extends beyond the confines of Palestine. The primary purpose cannot be to indicate God's power outside of Palestine; this is taken for granted. Of course, Yahweh's hegemony was long recognized to extend beyond the land of Israel (i.e. Judea) as everyone would know from Deutero-Isaiah.

As one reads along, Jonah goes into the hold of the ship and falls asleep. Above him was the raging storm; the mariners were terrified; and they thought that the ship buffeted by the waves was about to be broken up.[4] Why did he fall asleep?

When the captain of the ship rouses him, and charges him to pray, Jonah strangely does not do so. Jonah did pray however in the body of the fish. Wherein and how did this change take place?

Striking is the magnanimous gesture on the part of Jonah in that he proposes (1.12) that he be cast into the sea to still the angry storm. Here the great universalistic character of the book manifests itself: a Jew offers his life to save sailors who are not Jewish. In a certain sense, this was not completely called for. Jonah could have begged for mercy; he could have remained silent; he could have tried to pray. If he were a Josephus, he could have talked his way out of it. The circumstance that he volunteered to be cast into the sea is the significant action that calls for comment. One might argue, of course, that he was required to be in the sea for the story's sake because the fish had to swallow him. But the next question in order would be, why was the fish required to swallow him?

The function that the fish assumes in the story is difficult to define. If the purpose was to show that God's power is everywhere on land and sea and that Jonah cannot escape him, then this divine power Jonah knows very well (1.9). It seems more obvious to say that the purpose of the fish is to save Jonah for the second prophetic mission. Some may take the view, however, that the means employed are far out of proportion to the circumstances required. What does the great fish really accomplish? Apparently, the fish's function in the narrative is so significant,—indeed the psalm is interpolated at this point,—that the juncture seems to be the hub on which the whole story turns.

In the second mission to Nineveh, we come to the perplexing recognition that Jonah has still not qualified spiritually to be a prophet except to deliver to the Ninevites the contents of the

---

[4] The text at 1.4 is puzzling: "and the ship thought to be broken,"—is not clear. The word *hishbah* is at the root of the trouble. It was combined out of two words *hash bah* (med. Waw): and the ship,—it was feared for her that it would be broken. The verb is impersonal.

message that God required of him. The author's ostensible objective is to bring home to the prophet (and his readers) the newer conception of what God ought to be: he is not only the god of Israel but the god of the Ninevites as well (i.e. of the mortal enemy of Israel); but if they have sinned but afterwards repented, they are deserving of forgiveness. Jonah is reproved for thinking that the Ninevites were not entitled to mercy as they were non-Jews. If we wish to examine a little more closely the intent of the story however, then the finale still remains unsatisfactory, because Jonah does not seem to be involved anymore than at the beginning. Self-centered as he turns out to be, he does not seem to merit the attribute of a great prophet although he has a most significant message to deliver. On the surface, he is but the mechanical instrument for the delivery of Yahweh's message, although he understands (against his conviction?) that Yahweh too is the god of the pagans. Perhaps a new explanation is required to resolve these problems.

1. Students of the book are divided as to whether Jonah is a unity or not. In response to many of the problems, some critics through the unearthing of inconsistencies, glosses and interpolations, especially in c.1 and 4, have taken the view that much surgery is necessary to uncover the original core of the book.[5] Other critics have denied the inconsistencies as well as the glosses and interpolations on the ground that such deletions are labored and artificial.[6] Into this controversy of what verses belong to the original core, and what are additions, I shall not enter, as it would not clarify the questions raised here. I wish to present another approach and this is the hypothesis: that the book of Jonah has gone through a longish oral tradition. However in the transmission of the story and its final written redaction, the episodes were turned down side up. The episode of the escape to Joppa, the ship and the swallowing of Jonah were originally placed second; and the actual mission to Nineveh, the fast of the Ninevites was, and should be placed first.

[5] K. Kohler, *The Original Form of the Book of Jonah*, Theol. Review, 1879, p. 139f.; W. Böhme, *Die Komposition des Buches Jonah*, ZAW, VII, 1887, p. 224–284.

[6] J. Bewer, *Commentary on Jonah*, ICC series, p. 15f.

It is evident first of all that the character of Jonah in the second episode is substantially different from the Jonah in the first. In the second episode, he appears distinctly petty, self-centered, unfeeling, and conceited. Jonah is much annoyed that God's word,—he means *his* word,—has not been fulfilled. He is quite willing that the city be destroyed and the inhabitants perish as long as he is spared humiliation. Then again he exhibits a sadistic satisfaction (*Schadenfreude*), a delight in observing the injury and even death of others, as he settles in a place east of the city to watch its overthrow and destruction (4.5). He is very much like a child who is eager to see the fireworks or the explosion without regard for the consequences. Moreover, we see that he overdramatizes himself when he declares that he seeks death more than life as if he were indeed another Elijah whose mission is frustrated (I Kings 19.4 where the language is similar.) One cannot help contrast, however, the tragic sense of failure of the gloomy but dedicated Elijah with the utter ridiculousness of Jonah's situation and his fuming because his prophecy failed to come to pass. And yet again in 4.8, in exaggerated self-importance, he begs to die because the plant withered on him and he suffered from the excessive heat.

By contrast, the Jonah in c.1–2 evinces a much more noble spirit and character. At the story level, he shrinks from being a prophet (see below) and when it is discovered by lot that he is in some manner the generator, the cause of the furious storm, he voluntarily offers his life to save the lives of the sailors. Observe that this magnanimous gesture made a powerful impression on the seamen so that they prayed to Yahweh (!) and sacrificed to him and pledged themselves with vows.

If one operates then with the hypothesis that the call to Jonah began with c.3, we will perceive a progressive heightening in Jonah's psychological development and the preparation for the prophetic calling. In c.3 at the instant that Yahweh speaks to him even without specifying what the content of the message should be (". . . the proclamation whatever I shall tell you"), Jonah is ready and eager to go. After all, a prophet is not without honor, and for this self-centered man, the office of prophecy is an eminently pleasurable one that he is very desirous of filling. Nevertheless at the end of c.4, he has not undergone any change of mind or spirit—which should presumably be the main objective of the book-beyond what we hear of the gentle admonition of Yahweh "Are you very angry?". He is still the same old Jonah. If now c.1 follows c.4 we may now comprehend Jonah *post* with his new spirit. We understand also the reason on the story level for Jonah's flight in c.1. He had suffered humiliation for a fruitless prophecy before; why should he undergo humiliation again in preaching against the Ninevites who would now account him as a false prophet? In short, he is *not* the same prophet any more in c.1 as he was in c.3–4; a certain modesty, a withdrawal, even humility, has now overtaken him.

Now a number of matters fall into place. The exchange of episodes answers a question that may have puzzled some readers: you say (c.4) that Nineveh was spared destruction and was forgiven. But after all, it *was* destroyed. What happened to the city that it was overthrown? If the episodes change fore and aft, Jonah is now instructed to go for a new reason: ". . . .for its evil has come up before me", *scilicet* it has to be destroyed.

The exchange also explains the abrupt ending in c.4 which is a puzzle to some commentators. Actually, the end of c.4 is only a way station in the narrative with the continuation of 1.1: "*Then the word of Yahweh came to Jonah. . .*"

The introduction of the great fish, which readers have always felt to be a high point in the story, now makes for appropriate sense for the fish's function to furnish the proper climax in the finale. It comes to save Jonah, not to demonstrate God's power, but to bring home to Jonah that he is worthy to be a prophet, worthy to be saved.

In brief, the story receives new illumination as the psychological requirements of the different incidents are met. Chapter 3 *starts* with the story of an eager Jonah, desirous of being a prophet, and *ends* with Jonah being ejected from the fish with the sense of being a new man, forgiven, and now without sin (elaboration below).

2. Before proceeding to discuss the symbolism at length, it is necessary to clarify how the book went through a long process of oral tradition and editing. When it came to be written in its present form, additions and changes were inserted. In 3.1 the explanatory

word *shenith* "a second time" was added as well 3.5b, cf. v.8 and the discordant 4.5b. While there seems to be a definite indication that episodes one and two exchanged places at one stage in the oral transmission, it is an equally demonstrable textual fact that at another, later stage the book was *translated*, and that the Hebrew we have before us is secondary to an underlying Aramaic. This could readily be assumed on *a priori* grounds because a novella or folk tale of this genre would most likely be cast in Aramaic, the *lingua franca* of Asia Minor in the 4th-3rd century B.C.E. Then again one may ask in all innocence, and this would naturally occur to one who was reading the book in Hebrew, how did Jonah talk to the sailors; or if he had to preach against the Ninevites and proclaim their destruction, how could the king, nobles and inhabitants understand him unless he spoke Aramaic? Matter-of-factly, and vis-a-vis the story, Aramaic as the common language of Asia Minor was understood at Nineveh.[7] The presence of Aramaic words in the text, however, gives the first clue that the book was composed in that language: 1.5 *sefinah* 1.6 *hit'ashet* 2.1; 4.6.7.8 *manah* as in Dan. 1.10.11; 3.7 *ṭa'am* in the sense of "command, ordinance" as pointed out by others. There are other examples however which show via *mistranslation,* which are the surest indication of an underlying document, that the book originally was in Aramaic.

1.7 a. בשלמי 1.8 b. באשר למי 1.12 c. בשלי

1.7 is regarded as an Aramaism by critics. Actually it is an "etymological" translation of the Aramaic reproducing בדיל מאן which however should be translated "on account of whom, because of whom". Classical Hebrew would be למען, בעבור.[8]

The further proof that the latter is a mistranslation is found at the example of 1.8 where, in reality, there are two misrenderings. In the first, it is evident that the Hebrew translator wrongly separated the Aramaic words בדיל מאן as בדי למאן translating lamely באשר למי, making for clumsy sense and syntax. Moreover the sense

---

[7] T. Nöldeke, art. Aramaic languages, *Enc. Biblica,* p. 281; *Cambridge Ancient History,* III, 423.

[8] *bedil/lema'an* Gen. 18.24; Deut. 30.6 MT and Onqelos;/*ba'abur* Gen. 8.21; 18.19.

of the verse requires that the phrase should be: They said to him, Tell us now because of *what* did this evil come upon us? not because of *whom* since they knew Jonah and were speaking to him. Apparently the unvocalized text מאן was vocalized as "who" when it should have been interpreted as "what".[9]

In 1.12 בשלי = בדילי again i.e. "because of me". The Hebrew translation however means something else: that which belongs to me *not* because of me. For the usage, comp. Qid. 57b אמרה תורה שחוט שלי בשלי ושלך בשלך מה שלי בשלך אסור אף שלך בשלי אסור. "The Torah prescribes: do the slaughtering of my animals on my grounds; and the slaughtering of your animals on your grounds. Just as the slaughtering of my animals on your grounds is forbidden, so the slaughtering of your animals on my grounds is forbidden."

In 1.8 מה מלאכתך "What is your work?" is hardly appropriate in the context. In their terror, it would be in character for them to ask where Jonah came from, of what country is he, and of what people but not what his daily occupation is. In Aramaic מא עיבידתך has the meaning of "What is your *business*, what is the purpose of your voyage?"[10] 3.7 ויזעק "cried out" is an overplay at this juncture. It is a mistranslation of the word צוח "cry out" e.g. Is. 14.31 MT and Targum. The Aramaic word, however, acquired the weakened

---

[9] Syriac preserves most clearly the difference between the two as *măn* "who" and *mān* "what", and similarly in Ethiopic, comp. W. Wright, *Comparative Grammar of the Semitic Languages*, p. 123. The Oxford *Lexicon*, 577b, argues that *măn* "what" and *mān* "who" belong to late Syriac, citing Nöldeke, *Syriac Grammar*, par. 68 who avers that *mān* is a contraction of *mā denāh* or *mā dēn*. This late hypothesis however is contraindicated, I believe, by Ex. 16.15 "And each man said to his fellow, What's its name, *mān hū*, for they did not know what it was (*mă hū*). It should not be extraordinary that at this period (Ex. 16.15: critics differ about the details of the narrative whether it belongs to E (so Bacon) or to P, *The Hexateuch,* Carpenter and Harford-Battersby, II, p. 105 man was recognized as "what". Comp. Amarna, 286.5 ma-an-na "what", and compare Böhl, *Sprache der Amarnabriefe*, 1909, cited by Gesenius-Buhl[17], 433; and Amoritic *mana* "what", Bauer Th., *Die Ostkanaanäer*, 1926; Old South Arabic *man* "what", Koehler-Baumgartner, *Lexicon*, II, 534.

[10] *'ibidta/'abidta* is elusive in meaning being employed for *mela'ka* "daily work" and *ma'aseh* "business" with the double meaning that "business" implies: 1. occupation 2. *concern*, affair, matter. Comp. the Aramaic word for *mela'ka* Ex. 20.9; Deut. 5.13 and *ma'aseh* Ex. 5.4.13, MT and Onqelos.

meaning "to call", even in the usage of giving a person his name, I Chron. 8.33 "They called him Ner" (Targum); idem. 11.7 "They called it the city of David". Note in the MT passage to the latter verse in Chron. the verb קרא is used which is probably the case in our Jonah verse, but where the Jonah translator followed through with what seemed to him the more frequent meaning. He should probably have translated by ויקרא "It was proclaimed, they proclaimed".

4.1 וירע אל יונה רעה גדולה. The Aramaic student will recognize the expression at once. The Hebrew as it is constituted, makes no sense: "A great evil came over Jonah". This is not the intent of the passage. The Aramaic obviously read ובאש ליונה בישא רבא lit.: "and Jonah was displeased with a great displeasure" (Dan. 6.15) not *bisha* "evil". The translator failed to perceive the nuance in our text.

3.8 ויקראו אל אלהים בחזקה. The phrase represents Aramaic קרא בחיל Comp. Dan. 3.4 "The herald called aloud", not "with strength".

4.4 היטב not "well", but "much, very". Cf. Aramaic *tuba*.

4.11 The construction of הרבה משתים עשרה רבו is peculiar. The translator saw before him the Aramaic *saggiy* which he thought he should render by *harbeh*. Comp. *saggi/harbeh* in Onqelos and MT in Gen. 15.1; 41.49; Dt. 3.5. *Saggi min* means *more than* which *harbeh* cannot convey syntactically.

4.5 in Aramaic would provide a word-play, i.e. סכה...בצל/. מטללתא...טולא. Note also the word-plays in the names: Yonah, Nineveh, and *nuna* "the fish".

The passage in 4.8, a problem for critics, receives a satisfying explanation via the Aramaic. The passage reads: ויהי כזרח השמש וימן אלהים רוח קדים חרישית. Presumably the translation would run: And it came to pass when the sun arose, God prepared a violent east wind and the sun beat upon the head of Jonah. . . . The overlined words are difficult to interpret. A literal translation would be scarcely comprehensible in the context: an eastern *still* (?) wind. The Peshitta reads *ruḥa deshuba* "wind of fire" which JV (1917) seems to follow: "a vehement wind". The Dictionaries, BDB, Gesenius-Buhl[17] are puzzled and leave the matter with a query.

We should expect רוח קדים עזה Ex. 14.21 "a strong east wind". One of the lexical equivalents of חרש is אלם Is. 56.10 in MT and Targum. It is clear that the underlying Aramaic text read רוח קדום אלימא. The Hebrew translator however took אלם in the sense of "silent, dumb", hence חרש. He should have taken it in the sense of "strong" Deut. 1.7, Job 9.4 in MT and Targum. The Hebrew translation should have been as Ex. 14.21 רוח קדים עזה.

Moreover in the passage at 1.16 we have the strange situation, where after their deliverance, the mariners offered their veneration to Yahweh and "They sacrificed sacrifices to God, and pledged themselves with vows" ויזבחו זבח לה׳ וידרו נדרים. Since the sailors were on a ship, where did the sacrifices come from? It is hardly possible that animals were carried along with them, and at best one would be compelled to follow the Targum and explain that only when the sailors came ashore did they offer the sacrifices. Other commentators (comp. Bewer) leave the improbability to the casual inconsistency of the folktale. It might be suggested however that the underlying Aramaic קורבנין meaning "offerings, sacrifices" had here the other meaning of "gift". Comp. Payne-Smith, *Syriac Dictionary*. The sense of the passage then becomes: the mariners brought gifts in whatever small measure they possessed at hand, and vowed others for the future.

The evidence therefore would seem to shape up that the Hebrew we have before us is secondary, at the very least, as the language testifies.

3. We revert to the significance of Jonah being swallowed by the fish. It is the contention of literary critics, both ancient and modern, that when an author composes a story or poem, he is not writing a story so much as a biography of himself reflected from his unconscious.[11] His choice of words, his repetitions, the thoughtless slips he makes in syntax and composition, the names of his charac-

---

[11] Before Freud, Hebbel had written: Every writer writes his own autobiography, and his self-portraiture is most skillful when he is unaware that he is painting his own portrait, comp. W. Stekel, *The Interpretation of Dreams*, paperback, p. 379. Anatole France says somewhere that it makes no difference whether a man writes about the eye of a fly or the life of Julius Caesar, he is fundamentally writing about himself.

ters, the plots he contrives to involve his characters, the denouement, the satisfactory or unsatisfactory resolution of the complications are all an index of the character of the author. The chief figure moreover that the author is concerned about, and around whom all the action revolves in contrast to the subsidiary *personae* is really the Doppelgänger of himself. As scholars in Shakespearean criticism aver, Hamlet is Shakespeare.

What does the swallowing and the disgorging of Jonah from the belly of the fish represent? A number of factors in the situation suggest, to borrow a concept used by the psychoanalytic method, that this is a womb fantasy. Why is this a womb fantasy?

In the first place, Jonah does not die in the body of the fish. Instead of being chewed and digested to a pulp, he is very much alive although his supply of air has been cut off. He is not hungry; he is not thirsty. Very much like a babe in his mother's womb.

Secondly, after three days, he does not swim or climb out but is disgorged (ויקא) by the fish symbolically like a birth process.

Then again it is evident that the author himself unconsciously let slip that this is a womb symbol because he starts with describing the fish as male (דג גדול 2.1) and in the next verse he forgets himself and describes the fish as female ממעי הדגה. Note that *me'ayim* means the birth canal of the female Is. 49.1, Ps. 71.6; Gen. 25.23.

This notion that a fish may symbolically represent a womb formation is of course found elsewhere. The Greek Anaximander compared the womb to a shark.[12] According to the Waspishiona and Taruma Indians the first woman had a carnivorous fish inside her vagina.[13] In Greenland the erotic symbol of the fish is so highly regarded, is so efficacious, that it not only makes the women pregnant but the men as well.[14] In popular fancy, a mermaid is half fish and half woman, i.e. the bottom part of her, her genital, is represented by a fish's body.

What now is the significance of the womb symbol? In brief, the ejection of Jonah upon the dry land means that he has been born

---

[12] Comp. O. Rank, *Art and the Artist,* Eng. trans. p. 133.

[13] Standard *Dictionary of Folklore,* ed. M. Leach and J. Fried, N.Y. 1950, II, 1152.

[14] Ibid, I, 392.

again. He was not only rescued by God, but was revived as a new man without sin, like a new-born child. God rescued him and forgave him. Here is the answer to the age-old question of Nicodemus "How can a man be born when he is old? Can he enter a second time into his mother's womb and be born? The response given by the book of Jonah is Yes; through forgiveness a man can be born again. Later Jewish and Christian thought concurred with this idea. In rabbinic thought, the idea received expression as "One who has been converted to Judaism may be likened to a new born child, and his sins are forgiven".[15] In Greek a convert was called a *neophyte*.[16] What Jonah was forgiven will be discussed shortly.

It is an acknowledged thesis that one who fantasies about an inner unresolved situation will repeat and reconceive the same fantasy again just as a writer will write the same theme, the same story again and again.[17] The writer of Jonah made use of the same concept and fantasy when Jonah boarded the ship. Again, why did he board the ship and fall asleep? The ship represents again a womb fantasy, a womb formation. This is shown by the fact that in ancient languages people associated "ship" with "womb". Thus the Latin *navis* means "ship" and "pudenda", Greek *gaster* "womb" and its undoubted associative *gastra* "hull of a ship" (the Latin *gaster*, borrowed from the Greek, means both "womb" and "ship"), Arabic *baṭnun*, Hebrew *beṭen* "belly, womb", *mubṭanah* "sailing vessel" (Arabic dialect of Syria).[18] Jonah fell asleep because he

---

[15] *ger she-nitgayyer keqatan she-nolad dameh . . . . moḥalin lo kol 'awonotav:* "A proselyte who is converted to Judaism is as a child just born: . . . . all his sins are forgiven" b. *Yebamot* 22a, b. *Bekorot* 47a yer. Bikkurim III, 3. Two passages have been combined for the proof.

[16] *neophyte* = Greek *neos* "new" and *phutos* "planting".

[17] Comp. W. Stekel, *Interpretation of Dreams*, 1967, p. 389.

[18] Comp. Lewis and Short, *Latin Dictionary*; Liddel and Scott, *Greek Dictionary*; Hava, *Arabic-English Dictionary* under the respective roots. Interesting furthermore is the complex of ideas associated with "ship" and "womb" in another direction: there are some psychoanalysts who regard the nave of the church as a womb symbol because it gives security and salvation, while the church for its part calls the body of the church "Jonah's ship". Comp. G. Jobes, *Dictionary of Mythology, Folklore and Symbols* 3 vols. 1961.

wanted to put an end to existence. Sleep is death. However, the unconscious cannot conceive of death. All other persons may die except oneself. In the face of peril, real or imagined, the unconscious retreats to the safety and protection of the womb (regression) where at one time in the amniotic fluid the fetus remained safe and secure.

The two womb fantasies, it will be recognized, are fundamentally different. In the ship fantasy, Jonah desires to die; in the fish fantasy he desires to live. When he boards ship, he flees from God and cannot pray; in the belly of the fish he has found his way back to God and prays. At first he flees from a stern Father God; in the second, he knows that God is a kind and forgiving Father. In the first, he is guilt-ridden, mulish, unrepentant, sullen, childish. In the second, he has been reborn with a new heart, a new luminosity of spirit.

4. If these conclusions be considered valid, it may be possible to reconstruct a few elements of the biography of Jonah's author. Although our resources and materials are understandably meager, an outline of some thoughts and events of his life may be limned, however imperfectly.

1. "Jonah" (the author) living among the Jewish people appears to have committed a serious crime.

2. Living in proximity with pagans, he seems to have been attracted to the rites of an alien god, probably a Greek-Syrian goddess tied in with orgiastic practices.

3. "Jonah" who made a number of voyages at sea, experienced a shipwreck, and was rescued.

4. In reflecting about his experience that God saved him, despite his crime and guilt, he felt that the "Assyrians", age old enemies of Israel, could be forgiven too. "Jonah" hoped that by asking for indulgence and pardon for the "Assyrians" and their crimes, he would be and should be forgiven too and be welcomed back into the Jewish community.

That "Jonah" committed some sort of serious crime is subtly indicated in the book. Mentioned previously on the story level was the flight because of his supposed fallen reputation,—a false prophet now supposedly discredited. More deepseated than this was his flight because of rebellion and transgression. The circumstance that he took a ship to sail to the end of the world, that he wished to die, are an index of the extreme pangs of conscience that he experienced. Further, 1.10 implies some kind of terrible misdeed on Jonah's part by the question that the sailors put to him "What have you done?"[19] The question is both an exclamation of horror (cf. Bewer ad loc.) and an inquiry about the nature of his wrongdoing for the men were already cognizant that he was a fugitive as the verse continues, "For the men had known that he was fleeing from the presence of Yahweh, for he had told them". The tense is pluperfect. And then as it seems to me, in 1.8–9 we have a sequence that calls for explanation. The sailors had asked Jonah four questions: what is your business on this voyage, where do you come from, what is your country, and what people do you belong to. Jonah answers but one, the last, that he is a Hebrew, and volunteers the information that he is afraid (sic) of Yahweh, the God of heaven, who made the ocean and the land. Thus for the most part there is no match or correspondence to the questions asked and the replies given. The LXX reads עברי/עבד יי "worshipper of Yahweh" which is in no way an improvement, for the verse then is tautological. Then some commentators aver that ירא is doubtful as it should be בורח (Kohler, Budde, cited by Bewer, 38): I am a Hebrew and I am running away from Yahweh, *not* worship. Now the word *'ibhri* seems to be either an intimation for another word, or rhetorically to carry overtones of what the later language, and Aramaic, called עברין "transgressor".[20] Or perhaps it is a mistranslation of the underlying Aramaic word עבריא by עברינא "transgressor (b. Sabb. 40a)".

---

[19] Comp. I Sam. 13.11; II Sam. 3.24; Gen. 31.26; I Sam. 14.43.

[20] An interesting monograph may still be written on Hebrew rhetoric and style, specifically Hebrew words in their implied and suggestive meanings and allusions. The work of E. König *Stilistik, Rhetorik, Poetik* (1900) needs further expansion and elaboration. On paronomasia, the work of I.M. Casanowicz *"Paronomasia in the Old Testament"* JBL, 1893, 105f. is fundamental. For general Semitic, H. Reckendorf, *Über Paronomasie i.d. semitischen Sprachen*, 1909. The two latter works deal with assonances and word-plays on like sounding letters without regard to meaning. D. Yellin advanced stylistic studies by his "Studies in biblical style" (*letorat ha-meliza betanak* is the Hebrew title) making use of the

Such an interpretation clears up a number of questions. By saying that he is a transgressor, or as we would say a criminal, Jonah responds as it were to all the questions, for the answer horrifies the listeners, and does away with the need for further

Arabic *Talḥin* (comp. Mehren, *Rhetorik der Araber,* p. 107) meaning essentially a pun, and put to excellent use by R. Gordis in his commentary on Job *"The Book of God and Man",* 1965. Comp. his remarks pp. 167, 196, 347.

Requisite for further investigation is the rhetorical device of alluding, implying a different word in the text even of a different root, but strongly suggestive, and fetching from the unconscious of the reader a response, a reminiscence of the word not there, the contrapuntal note to the main theme. A comparison with other languages for such use will illustrate this heteronymous device. In Shakespeare this "dress of thoughts" appears abundantly as part of his writing. For example:-
Hamlet, Act II, sc. 2. lines. 182f.
Hamlet (to Polonius) : "Let her not walk i' the sun: conception is a blessing but not as your daughter may conceive: Friend, look to't."
The expression "walk i' the sun" carries a fourfold meaning: "the sun as a source of madness, corruption, and decay, the King and his court, and the son (Hamlet), added to its explicit meaning of pregnancy by spontaneous generation" (S.E. Hyman, *The Armed Vision*[2], p. 399). Or *ibid,* Act IV, sc. 5, line 175, ". . . .and these are pansies, that's for thoughts" where the French *pensée* is implied. This type of conceit has persisted to the present day with the outstanding example in James Joyce, e.g. his difficulty in writing he calls "the cross of cruelfiction".
This usage may be parallelled in Hebrew: Thus Is. 60.16 *we-shod melakim tinaki,* the reading is *shod* "booty" with the rhetorical conceit of *shad* "breast", even though "breast of kings" (male) would scarcely be employed. The first part of the verse is possible, Deut. 33.19. Similarly, Is. 44.28 *ro'i* (of Cyrus) "my shepherd" implies also *re'i* "my friend". Is. 44.16 *ḥamoti ra'iti* is a play on the Aramaic *ḥami* "see".
The biblical writer in nearly all the books understands and employs this procedure in the explanation of biblical names. Thus, Adam is called so because he is an "earthling", *Hebel* because Abel came to a bad end, *Lot* which means "the cursed one" in Aramaic, *Yaboq,* because Jacob "wrestled" with the angel *('abaq).* Comp. *Dictionary and Key to . . . Proper Names in the Talmud and Midrash* by D.M. Harduf, Tel-Aviv, 1960; F. Zimmermann "Folk Etymology of Biblical Names", VT Congress Volume Geneva, 1966, 311f. With regard to *'ibri* the same fancy obtains. The use of the word in Ex. 7.16 incites the speculation on the part of the midrashim that the Israelites were called this because they passed over the Red Sea; others say that they performed God's commandments because they were written on the other side *('eber)* of the Jordan. On the other hand, pertinent to the discussion that *'ibri* intimates "a sinner", Num. 21.11 which describes how the Israelites camped at *'Iyye ha-'abarim* is interpreted to mean that the Hebrews were replete with sins as if from *'aberot.*

response as the questions now all became irrelevant and secondary. His assertion that he is a sinner stops them. In addition the verse now has the forceful significance: I am a sinner and I am afraid.

What was the nature of "Jonah's" misdeed? Upon this it is only possible to give the merest conjecture. Psychoanalytic doctrine (Freud) would predicate that "Jonah" must have been guilty of some homicide. By a spiritual law of *lex talionis*, of like for like, only one who was overwhelmed by a feeling bloodguiltiness could have offered himself as a sacrifice for others. The notorious example in the Bible of one who fled the presence of God was Cain, the first murderer (Gen. 4.14). Or "Jonah" may have been guilty of the other primal crime of mankind: incest.[21] The biblical tradition however knows of one other crime overshadowing murder and sexual perversion: apostasy, worship of an alien god.[22] Through the Hexateuch and the Prophets, the Bible never tires of warning about the swift and sure punishment of one who worships other gods aside from the god of Israel. It is the first of the Ten Commandments: Thou shalt have no other gods before me. A violation will be visited upon the third and fourth generation by an avenging Yahweh. One who sacrificed to any but Yahweh was to be exterminated (Ex. 22.19). No crime in the biblical tradition was more heinous than the Golden Calf, and the avenging Levites on orders from Moses massacred the calf worshippers. The ferocity of the punishment is seen in Deut. 13.16.17, where a whole city, if known to be beguiled to the worship of strange gods, is to be annihilated. King David despite his murders and adultery was a "good" king;

---

[21] *The Basic Writings of Sigmund Freud*, ed A.A. Brill, N.Y. 1938. Two of these crimes, murder and incest, are indicated within the book of Jonah itself. The city is to be destroyed because of *hamas* "violence, murder", and because "every one corrupted his way", exactly for the same reasons that the world was inundated in Noah's time, Gen. 6.11. The "corruption of every man his way" has the special meaning of "sexual irregularity". Comp. Jastrow, Dictionary s.v. *drk* and comp. Ehrlich, Gen. 6.11 and his comment at Jer. 2.23. Non-Jews are not punished for idol worship as they are regarded merely as foolish, benighted and objects of derision. Comp. Is. 40.18f.

[22] In later times, rabbinic law summed up the three primal crimes as *'abodah zarah, gilluy 'arayot, shepikat damim*. Tos. *Shabbat* c. 16, ed. Zuckermandel, p. 134[24], *Yoma* 82a, *Sanh.* 74a.

Jeroboam II by all signs was an energetic and vigorous ruler, but he served not Yahweh and therefore was "evil". Now "Jonah" in the course of his life lived on good and friendly terms with pagans. This is intimated by the story where, to repeat, he had seen much good in the non-Jewish sailors who were after all of the proletariat and largely slaves, but nevertheless "Jonah" was willing to give his life for them. The author moreover attributes to the mariners the Hebraic sentiments almost expressed in a liturgical formula: O Lord, let us not perish because of the life of this one man; and yet hold us not responsible for innocent blood that may be shed; but may Thou do according to thy wish (cf. Deut. 21.8). Moreover, the author of Jonah is quite concerned about Jonah's reputation as a prophet *among pagans.* 4.1f.

"Jonah"'s father undoubtedly instructed him as a young boy, not about murder and adultery which would be beyond the child's ken, but about the terrible consequences of worshipping strange gods. This I believe is also suggested by the story. In 1.6 the captain approaches Jonah to bestir himself: "Pray to your god! Perhaps he will consider us so that we do not perish!" Who is this captain that does not appear again in the book? We know who he is. In fantasies and in dreams, the person in authority, whether emperor, general, consul or captain is surrogate for the father. The voice in "Jonah"'s unconscious is the voice of his father admonishing him: Pray to the Lord your God so that he think of you so that you do not die! This however "Jonah" in his wantonness of heedless youth disregarded. Seduced by his companions, and egged on by his associates, and beguiled by the sensual rites and orgiastic practices in the pagan worship of gods and goddesses (the prophetic literature uses *zanah* "go a-whoring" with meaningful effect), "Jonah" lapsed into following "strange ways" and alien customs, much to his father's heartbreak. Cf. Prov. 30.11.17.

Be that as it may, whether "Jonah" was guilty of murder, incest, or idol worship, this last which I favor, it was a transgression, or rebellion or disobedience of the Father about which "Jonah" had the most serious overwhelming guilt feelings that he could not wipe away or expiate. He could not live in the society of his fellow-Jews; he may have actually experienced public disgrace. He could have gone over the border to a neighboring territory, but no, he chose a ship[23] going to Tarshish, to the end of the world, leaving his country. He offered, too, his life in expiation.

It is quite clear that "Jonah" was familiar with sea-faring. He knows technical terms and marine procedure. The fury of the storm is quite graphically described. The seamen throw ballast overboard to give buoyancy to the ship. Jonah goes to the hull of the ship to sleep *(yarkete hassefinah* 1.5). The word *shataq* (1.11.12) means the subsidence of the storm (Ps. 107.30. This psalmist too knows of sea perils). The attempt on the part of the sailors to return to the land is indicated by the word *wayahteru* "they dug in their oars". Such terminology seems to point to the circumstance and to warrant the conclusion that "Jonah" travelled on the sea and made a number of voyages. He knows that Joppa is a seaport, although a heathen town up to the time of the Maccabees, from which to make his departure.

On one of these voyages "Jonah" experienced a real shipwreck. This is not only suggested by the background of the story, but by the interpolated psalm in c. 2. This chapter has been a debating ground for critics, but I would follow those who maintain that the psalm is older than the narrative. Comp. O. Eissfeldt, *Introduction.* Eng. Trans. 406. The psalm was deliberately introduced because of that experience: (v. 4) For Thou hadst cast me into the deep, into the depths of seas, and currents overwhelmed me. . . . (6) The waters closed in over my body; the great deep encompassed me; seaweed entwined around my head . . . (7) But Thou didst bring my life safely from the Abyss . . . (v.8) When I lost consciousness,

---

[23] It should be observed that symbols, and this would be the case in the figure of the ship here, combine within themselves splinters of other motives, unconscious distortions, blends, and displacements which merge within the same unconscious symbol. Undoubtedly the ship, for example, represents the world at large, as well as a happy prosperous means of voyaging through life. This hope for a new life on the part of Jonah and at the same time a desire to end one's existence is a logical inconsistency in the conscious mind; but the unconscious disregards inconsistencies and tolerates both impulses and inclinations, negative and positive, at the same time. ". . . . . The word 'No' does not seem to exist for a dream. Dreams show a special tendency to reduce two opposites to a unity, or to represent them as one thing". Comp. Freud, *Collected Papers,* IV, 184.

I remembered the Lord . . ." The author of Jonah incorporated this psalm as a reminiscence of the shipwreck. The ship had gone down, and by all ancient probabilities "Jonah" should have been consigned to a watery grave, to be devoured by fantastical monsters of the deep as the ancients so vividly thought. A miraculous thing happened. Perhaps by clinging to a raft for three days and three nights,[24] and aided perhaps by other sailors who survived, "Jonah" was cast up in wondrous fashion on the dry land. This miraculous saving of his life was a revelation to "Jonah". Certainly, if he were to be punished, his life should have been extinguished then and there. Here was the natural inevitable occasion for his life to come to an end. But on the contrary he was rescued, and this meant that his sin was no more, and that God forgave him. Whereas in the ship-womb fantasy he could not pray, now he was forgiven and reconciled to his God and so he could pray (2.2: And Jonah prayed to the Lord his God from the entrails of the fish). As he matured he recognized that God was not the stern vengeful Father of his younger days, hounding his life, but the kind forgiving parent who loves his son.

While "Jonah" had a liberal non-chauvinistic attitude towards pagans, because, living with and among them, he found that some had religious and ethical ideas similar to his own, he drew the line at the "Assyrians" (and this was the occasion for the "prophecy" and the writing of the book), the old arch-enemies of Israel, who

---

[24] Jonah's stay in the body of the fish for three days and three nights is to emphasize the great miracle that Yahweh performed for him, for it was universal knowledge that Jonah would have certainly expired. The three days and three nights symbolize a recovery from illness after one has been in the limbo of life and death. This use of "three" is exemplified elsewhere. Apparently in a medical "crisis" where the patient was very weak or semi-comatose but who managed to survive, a rule-of-thumb of two days, or certainly by the third day, the patient recovered or he did not. Comp. Hos. 6.2: He will bring us to life after two days, and on the third day he will have us stand erect. Similarly, Hezekiah questions Isaiah (II Kings 20.8): "What is the sign that Yahweh will heal me and that I will ascend to the House of the Lord *on the third day*?" A later associative development maintained that the soul clung around the corpse for three days in the attempt to revive, but then mournfully departed when putrefaction set in. Comp. y. *Mo'ed Qatan*, 3, 82b. Comp. L. Ginzberg, *Legends of the Jews*, V, 78.

destroyed and pillaged the land, decimated the people, and led into captivity the best of nobility and royalty. The "Assyrians" were extremely brutal.[25] "Jonah" felt that they should have scant mercy, and as the eternal foes of Israel, he thought, they did not belong in the pale of God's creatures. He entertained the thought that if he were a prophet, or had the powers of a prophet, he would allow no compassion for them, and in three days[26] they would be overturned, annihilated. They would naturally be given warning (1.2); they must be given warning beforehand, because God cannot act whimsically.[27]

Another thought crossed his mind: what if the people of "Nineveh" should heed God's warning and actually repent, and put

[25] Who the "Assyrians" are (they are not mentioned as such in Jonah) and what city "Nineveh" is intended seems difficult to pinpoint. "King of Nineveh" (3.6) is an absurdity. A contemporary would have said "King of Asshur" Is. 37.21.37. In the apocryphal books it seems likely that Nineveh (Tob. 1.3.22), was a surrogate in Hellenistic times for a capital city, identified with some degree of probability as Antioch, the third largest city in the Hellenistic world after Rome and Alexandria (Zimmermann, *Book of Tobit*, p. 20.) The author of Judith who identifies Nebuchadnezzar as he who reigned over the Assyrians in Nineveh "the great city" is not ignorant of history but seeks to flag the reader that the work is fiction. Comp. Torrey, *The Apocryphal Literature*, 89. It seems unlikely however that "Nineveh" is to be identified with any Hellenistic city. Antioch was first founded in 300 B.C.E.; Seleucia on the Tigris about the same time and Jonah was already canonized by 200 B.C.E. as evidenced by Ben Sira (49.10). "Nineveh" may have been typologically conceived. On the other hand, since the writer of Jonah assigned his hero the name of Jonah ben Amittai, identical with the prophet of Gat Ḥefer (II Kings 14.25) of the 8th Century, he could not for historical verisimilitude employ Babylon as the hated enemy. This would have been chronologically and circumstantially impossible. But "King of Nineveh" as an historically monstrous combination may have been intended by the author for King of Babylon, the equation however being wrong for "King of Babylon" means king of the realm, not of the city. Comp. Is. 39.1. It is possible that Jonah had in mind the ruination of Babylon on a number of occasions: Seleucus lost it, but won it again as his territory; it was lost by Antigonus partially; and in 275 Antiochus ended Babylon's civil existence. Vide *The Cambridge Ancient History*, III, 93.

[26] So the LXX. Ehrlich proposes 'arb'ah as being graphically closer.

[27] This is in accordance with the biblical tradition (more specifically the prophetic tradition of Ezekiel) where no enemy may be exterminated without a warning. Comp. Ez. 33.3.7; II Chron. 19.10

on ashes and sackcloth, and even on their animals (3.8) as they were foolishly reported to do? What if the kings and his nobles were to hearken and order a fast, and call on everyone to repent (3.7)? God surely would forgive people who repented. Here "Jonah" was uncertain, torn between his thoughts and emotions. Could their nature change? Could they become good pagans? On the other hand, the atrocities that they committed against Israel (Lam. 1–2) could these ever be forgiven and forgotten? His mind veered to his rescue: You once committed a great crime in the eyes of God and man. If God forgave you, why cannot you forgive them?

With this train of thought, "Jonah" was prepared to write his story, a message to his contemporaries, and an indirect apologia pro vita sua.

5

Esther: Original Language, Locale, Date, and Purpose

The linguistic character and the Aramaic origin of Esther cannot be considered by itself except in its relation to the so-called "Rest of the Chapters of the Book of Esther", a loose but mechanically conjoined number of sections in Greek placed among the apocryphal books. Because these chapters were not found in the Hebrew, Jerome put them in a jumbled fashion after the canonical Esther, called by him "deuterocanonical", and so regarded by Catholic scholars. These *disjecta membra* have been re-arranged by students in a more logical order, to synchronize and complement the progress of the Esther story in the following arrangement, with letter designations of A to F:[1]

A. Mordecai's Dream, and the forecast of the great attack of the nations against Israel. The contest of the two dragons; see sec. F. The casting of lots before God, and the salvation of the Jews, 1.1–18.

B. Ordinance for the destruction of the Jews issued by the Persian king, 2.1–6.

C. The Prayer of Mordecai (3.1–10) and that of Esther (4.1–16). It should be noted that in these prayers the name of God is mentioned some 20 times in marked contrast to the canonical book where God's name is not mentioned at all.

---

[1] The designations of A to F are the conventional tags assigned by scholars to the sectional arrangements, synchronized with the progress of the story in Esther. It is hypothesized that the jumbled state in which the sections are currently extant, e.g. as in the Authorized Versions of the Apocrypha, was occasioned by the Latin Father Jerome, who considered only those chapters canonical that he found in the Hebrew. Comp. Torrey, *The Apocryphal Literature*, 58; Pfeiffer, *History of New Testament Times*, 305.

D. Esther in the presence of the king. Radiant with her beauty, but with heart full of fear, Esther comes uninvited to the king. He is angry; her action entails a death penalty, and under stress she faints. The king is moved, and leaping from his throne, holds her in his arms, and restores her. She swoons again (5.1–4).

E. Reversal of the decree against the Jews and the condemnation of Haman. The Jews may observe their laws, observe Purim, and avenge themselves on their enemies (6.1–9).

F. The fulfillment of the dream and its interpretation by Mordecai (cf. sec. A). The little fountain that became a river is Esther; the two dragons are Mordecai and Haman; the many waters are the nations that sought to destroy Israel. The casting of the lots and the decision in favor of Israel was made by God (7.1–10).

There are a number of problems that have been posed by scholars: were these sections once a part of the canonical Esther? If so, why were they excluded? Or to the contrary, is the book of Esther, perhaps, an abridgement of a longer story? Were these apocryphal sections written in Greek originally, or is there an underlying document composed in Hebrew, or Aramaic?

As will be shown, there can hardly be any question that these sections were in the main, (sections B and E excepted, written in Greek, and referred to below), a part of the original Esther tale. First evidence is that there are a minimum of six different versions of the same story. The conventional Greek version B (the "LXX"), containing the additions, is not one that follows the Hebrew text line by line, where the student will sporadically find divergencies between his Greek and Hebrew. Torrey will go so far as to say that there is no Greek translation at all to the extant Hebrew. It is but one *version* of the Esther tale from Aramaic. The second version A, printed by some editors page by page confronting B (so e.g. by O. F. Fritzsche and Lagarde), published separately in smaller type in the small Cambridge edition by H. B. Swete, but in large type and separately by the larger Cambridge edition (1940), is certainly not to be declassed as a secondary version, as the editors themselves indicate.

This A version is commonly called "Lucianic" (codd. 19, 93a, 108b, Athos 513; comp. p.vi of the larger Cambridge) but as will be shown was translated too from a Semitic original.[2] Josephus apparently follows a "Lucianic" text though he too has his own version, omitting sections A and F (*Antiquities* 11.6). Then again in F. Field's *Origenis Hexaplorum quae supersunt* under the general heading of *alia exemplaria*, but where in the notes the variant mss. are cited and are a close approximation of the Hebrew, nonetheless these *exemplaria* have some amplifications, as at 5.14 (p. 799); 6.8.9 (p. 800); 6.11; which indicate again another recension. In Aramaic, there are two Targumim to Esther (7–8 cent. C.E., so P. Cassel, "Zweites Targum zum Buche Esther", 1885, but for Dalman, *Grammatik*[2], p. 35 even later) as well as a mediaeval Aramaic text "The Dream of Mordecai", A. Merx, *Chrestomathia Targumica*, 1888, 154–64. There are daughter versions of the Greek,—the Old Latin in Sabatier, *Bibliorum Sacrorum Latinae Versiones Antiquae*, Remis, 1743, I, 791f. supposedly "Lucianic" in character (B.R. Mozo, *La versiona latina di Ester secondo* in LXX, 1928), and Jerome's Vulgate,—altogether with the canonical Hebrew a minimum of 6 versions.[2a]

Not only do we have different recensions of the tale, but secondly in a number of important particulars they contradict the canonical

[2] Comp. Torrey's article, "The Older Book of Esther", HTR, 37 (1944), pp. 1–40; idem, *The Apocryphal Literature*, 58.

[2a] Although the "Rest of the Chapters of the Book of Esther" has been edited a number of times as in P. de Lagarde's *Librorum Veteris Testamenti canicorum pars prior graece*, 1883 and in A Scholz, *Commentar uber das Buch Esther*, 1892 as well as by A. E. Brooke, N. McLean, and H. St. John Thackeray, *The Old Testament in Greek*, vol. III, Part 1: *Esther, Judith, Tobit*, 1940, I have preferred the edition of O. F. Fritzsche, *Libri apocryphi Veteris Testamenti graece*, 1871 as being more serviceable: 1. The B text and the "Lucianic" text (A) confront one another page by page, and make for easy comparison. 2. Fritzsche offers an edited text with corrections and restorations of his own. 3. The numbering of the verses, especially those of A and F make for easy referral. While Fritzsche made a number of inevitable slips as pointed out by Torrey, and the Cambridge edition newly brings readings from the Athos codex (y), see p. vi of their prefatory note, and as a matter of course I have referred to the latter edition for any substantial variants, for the few times that I had to quote from both the Greek versions, Fritzsche's edition answered my needs competently enough. Where variants seemed required, I have cited them. Comp. further Carvey A. Moore's *Esther*, pp. 51 f.

Esther. All the names of the personae, for example, with the exception of Mordecai, Esther and Haman are variously reproduced. Even Esther is the daughter of Amminadab (2.7.15; 9.29B) and not Abihail. Abiel of the Old Latin however is not a corruption of Abihail; Abiel figures as the grandfather of Saul, 1 Sam. 9.1; 14.51, an ancestor of Esther. The two conspirators Bigtan and Teresh, who sought to murder the king Ahashwerosh (Artaxerxes in B, Asueros in A), are Gabatha and Thara in B, Artagos and Thedeutos in A. In 1.10, the 7 chamberlains are denominated in Hebrew and Greek as: Mehuman by Aman, Bizta by Bazan, Harbona by Thara, Bigta by Barazi, Abagta by Zatholtha, Zetar by Abatataza, Karkas by Tharaba. The astrologers in Esth. 1.14 named Carshena, Shetar, Admatha, Tarshish, Meres, Marsena and Memuchan are given as three in B: Arkesios, Sarsathaios and Malisear with four names missing (or omitted) with hardly any approximate identification with the names in the Hebrew. Version A does not mention any names at all. The eunuch Hatak (4.10) is Achrathion in B; A has in its version "one of the eunuchs". Zeresh, wife of Haman, is Zosara (5.10.14 and elsewhere both in A and B). Harbona at 7.9 is Bugathan. The ten sons of Haman likewise vary (9.7): in Hebrew they are Parshandata, Dalphon, Aspata, Porata, Adalia, Aridata, Parmashta, Arisai, Aridai, Vaizata which Greek B represents as Pharsan, (kai ton adelphon autou is error for Delphon), Pharna, Gazaphardatha, Marmasaima, Izathouth, ending up confusedly " . . . and the ten sons of Haman, son of Amadatha Bougaios". It might be argued that these discrepancies between the Greek and Hebrew names may be explained on the basis that the Greek transliterations are inner-Greek corruptions, and that in contrast the well known names of Mordecai and Esther were reproduced with fidelity (but as Nöldeke remarks in his article "Esther" in the Encyclopedia Biblica, 1404, n.3 the Greek Mardochaios is philologically more defensible from Marduk than the vocalization Mordecai) because they are well known, whereas the names of chamberlains, the astrologers, and the sons of Haman could be flawed with corruptions. Mordecai's genealogy, for example, is represented with some degree of verisimilitude, with no disturbing corruptions to speak of. Hatak, on the other hand, as reproduced by Achthraios mentioned above, and Harbona reflected by Bugathan as well as the above mentioned examples,— all demonstrate that the divergencies are authentic. No, we have true variants here stemming from a different source, or sources.

Thirdly, the chronological and episodic discrepancies between the Greek versions (largely B) and the canonical Esther call for notice and examination.

Whereas in Greek B 1.17 (Fritzsche, p. 32; his enumeration seems confusedly duplicated) Mordecai is recognized to have an honored place at the royal court in the second year of Artaxerxes, (in A he is assigned "to guard the palace portals well"), in the biblical Esther 2.16.19, Mordecai only arrives at court after Esther has been made queen in the seventh year of Aḥashwerosh.

In 1.14 (*ibid.* 32) Mordecai himself reveals to the king the machinations of the conspirators, as he heard their plans when he lodged with them in the palace; in canonical Esther 2.21–23 it is Esther who tells the king about the conspiracy, having been told of it by Mordecai who had as yet no access to the king.

In 1.17 (*ibid.* 32) Mordecai receives a munificent reward for his loyalty in disclosing the conspiracy; in the biblical Esther Mordecai receives promotion and reward at the end of the account (8.1 f.). The honor given to Mordecai in C.6 is of a different character, a foiling of Haman.

In 1.18 (*ibid.* 32) in cod. B, but even more explicitly in A, Haman seeks to harm Mordecai because Mordecai denounced the conspirators to the king; in Esther, Haman is provoked because Mordecai would not bow to him.

At 4.11.12 Esther declares that she looks with horror at the overweening glory of evildoers and at the bed of the uncircumeised, and despises as a "menstruous cloth" her crown and fine apparel. The Hebrew gives no such impression. Thus—

While 4.14 declares that she has not eaten at the table of Haman (*sic*), nor drunk the wine of the heathenish libations, the Hebrew reports how Esther invited the king *twice* (and Haman) for a banquet, 5.4.8.

In sec. 6.9, Haman is declared to be a Macedonian (!); in the Hebrew at 3.1, Haman's father is Persian.

It is clear that divergencies in details, episodes, chronologies, and motivations are of some moment.

Fourthly, in exploring further the relationship between the biblical Esther and the Greek versions of A and B, it is interesting that the Greek versions, in the narrative portions, are detected to be translations from Aramaic, but the prayers of Mordecai and Esther are manifestly from Hebrew. It has been previously asserted by such scholars as Fuller, Nöldeke, André, Gregg, Hartom and Eissfeldt[3] that the Greek is the original language, and that it need not be assumed to be translated from Hebrew, and that if there seem to be Hebraisms, they are the conventional type of phrases used by a Hellenistic Jew. This type of argument has long been challenged, ever since there has been a complete turnabout and re-examination in the analysis of the original languages of the apocryphal and pseudepigraphic books. A majority of the books thought to be originally Greek have been recognized to be Hebrew or Aramaic.[4]

The case is no different with the Greek versions of Esther. Thus, the first section A, Mordecai's Dream, manifests itself to have been written in Aramaic (rather than Hebrew). Note first the word-order: in v.2 *enupnion eide Mardochaios* exactly as in Dan. 7.1, *ḥelem ḥazah*, accusative, verb, subject. The phrase is strictly Aramaic, not Hebrew, as one may say *ḥalam ḥalom* Gen. 40.8; Deut. 13.2; Joel 3.1; Jud. 7.13, or *ra'ah ba-ḥalom* Gen. 31.10; 1 Kings 3.5; Gen. 41.22 but not *ra'ah ḥalom*. There are also other distinctly Aramaic locutions: Mordecai was *anthropos megas* (v. 3) i.e. *gabra rabba* in the sense of "great, important man" as in the

[3] Comp. O. F. *Fritzsche, Kurzgefasstes exegetisches Handbuch zu den Apokryphen des A.T.*, 1851, S.71; J. M. Fuller in *The Rest of Esther* in H. Wace's *Holy Bible: Apocrypha*, I, p. 365; T. Nöldeke, EB, col. 1406 (perhaps Hebrew, "but the hypothesis is not probable"); L. E. T. André, *Les Apocryphes*, 1903, p. 203; J. A. F. Gregg, in Charles' *Apocrypha and Pseudepigrapha*, I, p. 666; W. O. E. Oesterley, *An Introduction to the Books of the Apocrypha*, 1953, p. 191; also B. Jacob, *Das Buch Esther bei den LXX*, ZAW 10, 241–98 (1890); C. Siegfried in *Apocryphal Book of Esther*, JE, V, 237f.

[4] R. H. Pfeiffer, *History of New Testament Times*, p. 60f., 769; C. C. Torrey, *The Apocryphal Literature*, vi, and p. 4; F. Zimmermann, *Book of Tobit*, p. 145f.

frequent talmudic usage e.g. "See what a great man testifies about him" *Hul.* 7a and elsewhere. A Hebrew *'ish gadol*, in the sense of "important man", is not found in the Hebrew Bible though *gadol* "great, important" as an adjective or predicate naturally is found. Then again in v.12 the verse recounts that Mordecai, awake, having "seen" the dream (Aramaic as above) sought by every means to understand it "until night time", *eos tes nuktos* B; version A diverges by saying "until daytime", *eos tes hemeras*. The two verses through the translators portray two different circumstances. B implies that Mordecai, awake from his dream, sought all during the day to discover its interpretation; A states in effect that Mordecai, wakened, tried to understand the dream all through the night, from every angle, till daylight. The latter seems to be the more natural circumstance. Both ascend to the same Aramaic text *'ad nogha*. *Nogha*, like its congener *'urta*, may mean both "daylight" and "night time". Payne Smith, Brockelmann; Levy, Chaldäisches *Wörterbuch*, Pes.3a, G. F. Moore, *Journal of the American Oriental Society*, 26 (1905), pp. 323–29. It is obvious that the B translator took *nogah* as "night time" while the A translator interpreted *nogah* as "daylight". The same word was misunderstood again in v.11 where the verse in B reads "And light and the sun arose" (*kai phos kai ho helios aneteile*) while A even more enigmatically omits the "and": light, sun arose. It must be evident that the translators misapprehended *negah* the verb as *nogah* the noun. We should translate: the daylight came and the sun arose. The error came through misvocalizing, the letters being the same.

As further evidence that A had an Aramaic text before him, we may notice 3.6 where the verse declares that Haman sought to destroy Mordecai and all his people in one day; and Haman was provoked to wrath, and proceeding in all his anger he became red (?), (*eruthros egeneto*), ordering him out of his presence. The latter phrase literally "turning him aside from his eyes" gives us the clue what the original reading was. The translator had in mind the verb *seqar* "to redden, mark with red, paint with red" (cf. the noun as well *siqra* "red paint"). He should have read however *seqar* in the sense of "look at with enmity, or hostile eyes", with "brennendem, feindlichem, neidischem Auge" as Levy, "Chaldäisches Wörterbuch", p. 185 has it. The translation should have conveyed the sense: Haman, with baleful eye, ordered Mordecai out of his sight.

Then in v. 12, where Haman goes to his gods to ascertain the day of destruction of the Jews, and to cast lots for the month of Adar-Nisan, the passage continues, " . . . to murder all the Jews, from male to female, and to plunder the children (?)", *kai diarpazein ta nepia*. "To plunder the children" is an incongruous phrase; plunder does not apply to them, and uselessly epexigetical to "male and female" preceding. In Aramaic איקרא signifies 1) *children* (cf. analogously the Latin *impedimenta* "baggage, children") and 2) honor, *wealth*; *'iqara* is a standard equivalent in the Targums for the Hebrew *kabod*. The translator was mistaken in his rendering. He should have translated: and to despoil all the *wealth*. This corresponds to the familiar "to despoil all their wealth" of Esther 3.13; 8.11.

Parenthetically, section B of the above mentioned displaced apocryphal sections contains the noted broadcast by the king to all his subjects for the fatal annihilation of the Jewish communitics. It is agreed on all hands, by virtue of the florid, verbose style that B was originally written in Greek. The same observation holds true with regard to apocryphal section E proclaiming the revocation of the B section, i.e. an edict now for the rescue of the Jews. Undoubtedly at an early date B and E were interpolated into the Greek translations of Esther for influencing Hellenistic readers. Josephus in his account knows already of these two sections.

In section C we come into a wholly different atmosphere with the two prayers of Mordecai and Esther. There can hardly be any question, as it seems to me, that the prayers of Mordecai and Esther must have been written in Hebrew. The tradition in biblical and Jewish liturgical composition strongly supports this view. Although Aramaic was widespread, prayers were written in Hebrew even in strongly Aramaic milieus, Dan. 9.4–19; Neh. 1.4–11, extending through the *'Amidah* and the compositions of Rab down to mediaeval poets (comp. *Anthologia Hebraica* by H. Brody, 1922). A number of exceptions are the *Qaddish, Yequm Purqan* and certain cabbalistic pieces, but the Jewish prayer book, as an anthology of prayers, is almost completely Hebrew. Moreover in section C the passages themselves give the evidence of their Hebrew origin. Thus in 3,2 B we read " . . . there is none who shall speak against thee in thy wish to save Israel" *(kai ouk estin ho antidokson soi)*; *antidokseo = dissentio, resisto*, and so Vulgate here, comp. Schleusner, *Lexicon*, I, 242; there are no Hebrew equivalents. On the other hand, A reads ". . . there is none who shall set himself in array against thee *(kai ouk estin hos antitaksetai soi)*". Both versions are translating the Hebrew root ערך, with B choosing the Hebrew sense of setting words in array against God (Ps. 5.4; Job 32.14) while A picks up the Hebrew sense of drawing up an army in array, as in battle.

One may note too some Hebraic constructions and locutions. In the same verse, the beginning reads: Lord, Lord, because *(hoti)* all is in his power. . . . (B), while A runs: Lord Almighty in whose power *(ou)* all is . . ." show different conceptions of the word אשר. I would venture to say, too, that the doubled apostrophe *kurie kurie*, like *Dominator, domine* in 4 Ezra 5.23; 7.17 and elsewhere, = Yahweh Yahweh, as in Ex. 34.6, except that the pronunciation had already come through as *Adonai, Adonai*, and similarly A's *despota* which implies the same *Adonai*. V.3 likewise contains a Hebraism wherein the translator, it can be observed, followed his text literally, "For Thou hast made the heaven and the earth and every wonderful thing *in it* under heaven . . ." i.e. *en te=bah* "in her" literally, feminine, and resumptive of "earth".

The argument of C. C. Torrey, on the other hand, that in this Prayer of Mordecai, where B reads *en huperephania* "in vaunting, in boast", but A reads *en peirasmo* "in testing, in trial", and therefore both readings ascend to an Aramaic *'ithnas' ah* is not decisive. As Torrey indicates, there are two words involved, one with Samek, and therefore "trial, temptation", and one with Sin "haughtiness". The retroversion must be questioned on other grounds in the misinterpretation, namely via the Hebrew. The word may have been בהתנשא with word and construction exactly as in Prov. 30.32, which A however sought to interpret as if from the root נסה, a

familiar enough procedure, cf. Symmachus and Theodotion to
Job 4.2, G. Beer, *Der Text des Buches Hiob*, 1895, p. 22.

After the prayer, as the narrative resumes again though briefly, the
Aramaic comes through again as the distinct language (4.8).
Thus, "And Esther the queen resorted, lit. fled (*katephugen*,
Vulgate *confugit*) unto the Lord, caught up by the fear of death"
kateilemene, Aramaic probably אחידה באימתא דמותא). In its simple
meaning, the Greek verb is employed primitively for the sense of
"flee down, take flight". Cf. *kataphuge* lexically for *nus* "flee", 2
Sam. 22.3; Jer. 16.19 (Heb.); Deut. 19.3, and Schleusner, *Lexicon*,
II, 228f. I am inclined to single out the reading *'apket* = she turned
to, supplied by the mediaeval "Dream of Mordecai" in Aramaic,
which deploys side by side in the text three verbs, really variants to
one another: *'aq* (1. *'aqat* "it distressed her"), *'araq* (1. *'arqat* "she
fled") and interestingly *'apket* "she turned to, she fled". *'Aq* and
'araq are simply variants of one another, the latter being the more
original. It is also clear that *'arqat* and *'apket* are doublets in
translation to *katephugen* in the mediaeval "Dream of Mordecai",
itself a translation from the Greek. This secondary Aramaic translator incorporated the two renderings as he was uncertain about the
Greek word: 1) she fled 2) she turned to. Since the latter meaning is
the more natural one, it would appear that an original *'apket* was in
the original underlying Aramaic text which the Greek translator
misunderstood. We should translate: And Queen Esther turned
unto God.

When the prayer resumes however, the language again is un-
mistakably Hebrew. In v. 5 the text runs: For I have heard
from my birth in the tribe of my father (*ek genetes mou en phule
patrias mou*) that you O Lord have taken Israel from all the nations
etc. First, "tribe of my father" is the familiar *matteh 'ab/'abot*
Ex. 31.2, Lev. 24.11; Num. 1.4 et seq. "Birth" moreover seems to
be an off translation of מולדת, not "birth" really, but "kindred".
The better sense would be: I have heard from my *kindred*, in the
tribe of my father. Esther, as the book recounts, was orphaned
early. Version A however gives in parallel a striking example of
this mistranslation: *ego de ekousa patrikes mou biblou* "I have
heard from the *book* of my father" = *shama'ti misefer 'abi* which

the translator misconstrued; he should have read *mesapper* the verb. He should have rendered *shama' ti 'abi mesapper* "I heard my father tell." That there was this reading is confirmed by the corresponding passage in the "Dream of Mordecai" which runs *ulhod ishte' i li* "Moreover it was told to me".

Furthermore in the passage at v. 8 there is another indication of the Hebraic character of the prayer: "... turn their plans against themselves, and make an example of him who has begun (?; *arksamenon*) upon us" (B). Similarly A. The translator confused the root *hll* "begin" with *hwl* "fall, fall upon, attack", e.g., Hos. 11.6 (attack with the sword: the parallels are *'akal, killah* in the verse). The translation should have run: make an example of him who has fallen upon us (precisely with the preposition Jer. 23.19 and elsewhere).

The underlying Hebrew evidently continues in v. 13 where Esther, speaking of her contempt for the imperial crown that she wears, declares: I abhor it as a menstruous cloth (*hos rakos katamenion*. See the note of Fritzsche, *Libri Apocryphi*, p. 48); on the other hand, A reads *hos rakos apokathemenes*, lit. as a "cloth that is set apart" and by extended meaning apparently as the equivalent of *aimorrousa* "bloodstained". Comp. Liddell and Scott, *Greek Dictionary*[8] p. 200, Schleusner, I, 293. It is quite evident however that between the two readings of A and B, and the use of *apokathemenes/niddah* in the LXX at Lam. 1.17; Ez. 22.10; 36.17 that they both saw *niddah* in their text with the not too felicitous reproduction on the part of A of *apokathemenes* for *niddah*, root *ndd*, as "that which is thrust aside". The text probably had *beged niddah*, either the clothes a woman wore at her impurity or the bloodstained cloth itself.

With chapter 5 the narrative resumes again, and in Aramaic as one could now expect rather than Hebrew. Torrey has pointed out[5] that in 5.13 there was a misreading of *re'utha* "the king's countenance was filled with goodwill" while Esther's face (A gives the correct sequence here) was suffused with perspiration, *de'utha* i.e. Aramaic. One may add that in v. 8, where the king alarmed,

---

[5] Comp. his article "The Older Book of Esther" in HTR, 37, (1944), p. 8.

(*agonisas*), rose from his throne, the Vulgate reads *festinus ac metuens*, a doublet, pointing to the Aramaic *'itbehal* which has both the meanings of "be hurried" and "be alarmed".

And finally we may look at 7.17, corresponding to the Hebrew Esther 8.17 ורבים מעמי הארץ מתיהדים where the passage in A reads: And many of the Jews were circumcised (!), *kai polloi ton Ioudaion peritemnonto*. The translator failed to understand this Aramaic construction which ran ושגיאין ליהודיא גזירין. This is the familiar passive participle with the Lamed of agent. The translation should have run: and many were circumcised *by* the Jews i.e. many who sought refuge from the revolution's excesses sought out the Jews to circumcise them, see below p. 98. It is quite possible that MT's מתיהדים represents an original *'etpa'al* form, i.e. the passive "were made Jews".

Summarizing, it is now possible to establish provisionally some of the findings that we have arrived at. 1) In the third century B.C.E., a number of the versions of the Esther story were in circulation. 2) These stories were written in the language of the people, in Aramaic. 3) The prayers in the original recension were written in Hebrew following a traditional pattern of praying in that language. 4) These versions motivate episodes in the story differently than in the Hebrew Esther. 5) The several Aramaic versions were translated into Greek. Analogously, the book of Tobit has been transmitted through three Greek versions, two separate Hebrew versions, a Syriac version, an Aramaic version, all derived however from an original Aramaic version (not extant) which in turn was translated into Hebrew.[5a]
Our Hebrew Esther is an abridgement of one of these Aramaic versions.

The evidence, first of all, that the Hebrew Esther is *abridged* is indicated by the following circumstances.

1. Scholars remark that Mordecai, in not bowing to Haman, is indulging in an inexcusable action as there was no reason for Mordecai not to show elementary courtesy to a high official, that from time immemorial the Hebrews have given obeisance to

---

[5a] Zimmermann, op. cit. 138.

superiors. Where now is this hubris of Mordecai and in addition
the seeming hypocrisy in that he declares that he would be content
to lick the feet of Haman to save Israel?[6] The midrashic *Aggadat
Esther* faults Mordecai for this attitude (ed. S. Buber, p. 14). The
Midrash to Esther, sensing something is wrong, fancifully suggests
that Haman had put a picture of an idol on his garment to be
worshipped. However, Mordecai in saying that he would not
worship anyone except God (3.5–6 B) was acting in accordance
with his religious conviction. The king's order was that everyone
should bend his knees (3.2); the term is *kara'*. The Bible records that
the Hebrew never hesitated for ordinary civilities "to bend one's
head, or bow one's body" as for example Abraham to Ephron and
the Hittites (*wayishtahu*, Gen. 23.7.12; elsewhere combined with
qdd Gen. 43.28; I Kings 1.16; and as a gesture of acknowledgement
and thanksgiving Gen. 24.26; Ex. 12.27; 34.8; Num. 22.31). However, *kara'* is distinctively used for the worship of God, is a posture
of worship or prayer, never for a human being, Ezra 9.5; Is. 45.23;
Ps. 95.6, even 2 Kings 1.13 wherein Elijah has assumed for the
royal officer the terrible numen of an avenging instrument of
Yahweh. Only our apocryphal passage supplies the adequate
reason for Mordecai's refusal to fall on his knees ("For I will
not worship—*proskyneso*—[7]anyone but Thee, O my God . . ."),
which the canonical Hebrew fails to furnish.

2. Scholars are puzzled moreover by the fact that lots were
cast (who cast the lots? Hebrew is ambiguous) for the 13th day of
Adar as the day of destruction, a delay of a full eleven months.
In the first place, we may query, why were these lots needed to be
cast altogether, when an executive order, say, could have been
issued and carried through in a few weeks? And then again, how
is it that the day had been put off for such a long time? Apocryphal
version A supplies the correct reason. The verse runs: Haman
went to his gods to ascertain the day of their death (of the Jews),
and to cast lots for the 13th day of the month of Adar-Nisan to

---

[6] 3.5–6; comp. Pfeiffer, op. cit. 312

[7] *Proskynesis* is a religious act. Comp. W. F. Arndt and F. W. Gingrich, *A
Greek-English Lexicon of the N.T.*, 1957, p. 722.; Liddell and Scott, s.v. "make
obeisance to the gods or their images"; Schleusner, *Lexicon*, II, 288 (partially).

destroy all the Jews, from male to female, and to despoil their children (1. *wealth* as above p. 76; A 3.12). For a project to exterminate all the Jewish people which might run amiss, be mishandled and backfire, Haman went to his gods who settled on Adar, a favorable month (cf. *The Assyrian Dictionary*, Chicago, p. 111) and a favorable day,—one that would not be unlucky like the Roman *nefas*. The apocryphal verse motivates and clarifies with the required explanation: the lots were cast before the gods, and the gods decided it both for the month and the day.[8]

3. In 2.21 Bigtan and Teresh get "angry" and seek to murder the king, though no explanation is given which should prompt their action. However Versions A and B furnish some interesting reasons that seemed to have played a significant role. Mordecai had lodged in the court with the two eunuch conspirators. In B. 2.21 they became angry because Mordecai was promoted. Unquestionably this advancement stirred up their jealousy and envy, and their anger was displaced onto the king. No doubt their hostility started with Mordecai's appointment as recorded in B 1.3; and subsequently, at their execution, when Mordecai was further advanced and was told by the king "to guard the royal gates well", A 1.17, the appointment aroused the fury of Haman who had his plans thwarted by this new stumbling block. At any rate, we are informed by B 1.18 that "Haman sought to do evil to Mordecai and his people *because* of the two guardsmen". Haman thought that his conspiracy was discovered. Canonical Esther relates none of this,— an illuminating part of the story.

4. In Hebrew 5.1 f. we read that Esther, having donned the royal robes, proceeded to the palace. "She stood in the inner courtyard of the king's palace, opposite the palace; and the king was sitting

---

[8] Comp. J. Lewy, "The Feast of the 14th Day of Adar", HUCA, 14, (1939) p. 145. As to how important a lucky or unlucky day may be, one may refer analogously to the Roman superstition that every even day in the calendar was of ill omen, to say nothing about the days that were regarded as *nefas*, in which one could not do business at all, that were devoted to lustrations, to worship of the dead, or to purification such as February 1–14, April 5–22, June 5–14, July 1–9, and still others amounting to 57. Comp. W. Warde Fowler, *Roman Festivals*, 1899, pp. 3 and 9.

on his throne opposite the entrance. (2) And when the king saw Queen Esther standing in the courtyard, she won his favor; and the king extended the golden scepter in his hand, and Esther approached and touched the tip of the scepter". The queen had stopped in the middle of the courtyard before the king noticed her, if indeed he could clearly discern that far. Comp. 6.4 where he inquires as to who is in the courtyard and his pages have to report to him that it is Haman. Moreover, he did not have a scepter like a long rod to extend to Esther in the courtyard; something is missing. Comp. Carey A. Moore's translation of *wa-yehi* at v. 2 "finally". Either the king rose from his seat to meet Esther, or Esther came into the throne room into the royal presence. The Greek A and B supply the natural lively scene: Esther came in with two handmaids, one preceding her, and another carrying her train. (Esther certainly would not come in all by herself). She passed through all the doors *and stood before the king* (3.6 B,A). Now the proximity and presence could win the heart of the king. At the sight of the king, resplendent in his majesty, Esther swooned. He sprang from his throne, caught her in his arms, and said "What is it, Esther? I am your brother (?)[9]; be of good cheer; you shall not die; for the law applies to the public; there is no danger to you". It is obvious that the Hebrew cut drastically, but, on the other hand, the Greek version furnishes a much needed dialogue, lively action, natural responses between Esther and the king.

5. In c.6 the monarch, sleepless, having had his journal read to him, discovered that Mordecai had not been rewarded for his loyalty. V.4 starts abruptly "And the king said, 'Who is in the courtyard?' Now Haman had come to the outer royal courtyard to tell the king to hang Mordecai . . . " The epitomizer, however, forgot that this was in the middle of the night so that Haman's activity was premature. Greek A, at least, denotes the passage

[9] It is apparent that "brother" in the context is odd. The Greek misread or confused some such form as אחיך, probably the Pa'el (Margolis, *Grammar*, p. 60; S. Baer, *Libri Danielis Ezrae et Nehemiae*, 1882, p. lvi for the shorter and longer forms) to mean "your brother" making for bizarrerie in the sentence. He should have read or interpreted the word as "I shall keep you alive, I shall *save* you". Note the sequence "You will not die".

of time by stating that morning came, and that Haman had risen early in the morning to request Mordecai's execution.

6. There are also a number of touches in the Greek versions that seem indispensable for the Hebrew narrative. No description is given of the feelings and apprehensions of the personae involved. Was not Esther gripped with fear as she advanced uninvited, a mortal transgression, to seek audience with the monarch? Aside from the prayers she offered, and the days of fasting, Greek B asserts that while her face was cheerful, her heart was full of fear, as wonder we might. Nor does the Hebrew express any surprise of Mordecai wherein he was to be led around the city dressed in the royal robes, and on the king's horse, nor the sentiments of Haman when the tables are turned and he has to lead the horse. Greek A describes Haman's depressed spirit; how he has to persuade Mordecai to change his sackcloth for the kingly robes; how Mordecai, no less incredulous and suspicious, looks for a sign from God, and at a favorable omen accepts Haman's urging (6.11 A).

Granted that the Hebrew is vivid and dramatic, the fact is that there is a noticeable faltering and letdown at critical junctures (cf. 5.1–2). In c.4 there is little dialogue furnished for the circumstances. In the speed-up, everyone comes, goes, tells, especially vv. 9–10, and similarly 8.4. The omission of the name of God will be discussed below (p. 102).

We have seen then how the Greek versions supply and fill in notable lacks in the narrative. The fact that the abridged Hebrew is a translation from a substrate Aramaic version confirms the thesis that the canonical Esther is the latest version of the story. We may now proceed to show how the Hebrew Esther was *translated* from an underlying Aramaic document. Verses that have been inexplicable receive a new illumination and vigor.

The prima facie evidence of translation is the presence of some thirty Aramaic words in the text listed by S. R. Driver in his *Introduction to the Literature of the Old Testament*, p. 485. We may add the word שנה too (2.9) as a reflection of the same word in the Aramaic text with the sense of "he transferred". The meaning "alter, transform, change" makes no sense in the passage. Comp. Payne Smith, *Dictionary*, 586. The expression אחת דתו להמית (4.11),

with the numeral preceding, is undoubtedly an Aramaic retroversion. Cf. Dan. 2.9 חדה היא דתכון. Then too the persistent
deployment of the passive construction as in 2.6 "who was
exiled from Jerusalem with the Golah that was exiled. . . .";
2.16 "And Esther was taken"; 2.8 "And when it was heard . . . then
she was taken . . . "; 2.23 "And it was investigated . . . . it was
found . . . . and they were hanged . . . and it was written . . . .";
3.13 "And there was sent . . ."; 3.14 "The writing to be given . . . ."
be published . . . "; 3.15 "And the decree was given . . . "; 2.19
"And the girls were gathered . . . "; 8.9 "And they were called . . .
and it was written . . . "; 8.13 "to be given . . . ";— all a distinct
characteristic of Aramaic style (cf. J. A. Montgomery, *Daniel*,
91, n. 9; 92). Other Aramaic constructions manifest themselves
as in the characteristic passive participle with Lamed of Agent,
(and in a most singular one that is a mistranslation (p. 80)) as in the
following examples. Thus, 4.3 (*saq*) *wa-'efer yuzza' larabbim* =
many bedded down in ashes; 5.12 *'ani qaru' lah* = she invited me.;
3.11 is a mistranslation: *ha-kesef natun lak* is usually interpreted
to mean "Let the money be given to you" = keep the money, says
the witless king to Haman. Paul Haupt in his monograph *Purim*
(p. 6) declares that no Oriental monarch would ever do anything
like the surrender of such money, and rightly so. The Aramaic
construction read: *we-kaspa yehib lak* meaning lit. "Let the money
be given *by* you" i.e. "You give me the money! And as for the people
do what you will." The Hebrew misconstrued the expression, and
the proof is that in 4.7 Mordecai does mention that the money
is to be given to the king's treasury.

Students of Esther have also noted the inverted word order,
the object first and then the verb, a mark of Aramaic, discussed
above as a characteristic in the Greek versions. In the Hebrew
Esther we may note ושללם לבז 3.13; 8.11. It may be observed too
that the Hebrew translator mistook the temporal mode of the verse
in a number of examples. The Aramaic participle highly elastic,
independent of the main verb, may surprisingly mark time past,
present, or future (cf. Margolis, *Grammar*, par. 58.). So in the very
first verse: And it was in the days of Aḥashwerosh, *the* Ahashwerosh (RSV the *hu'* is the demonstrative Aramaic, see p. 107)

who *rules* from India to Cush . . . Obviously one should understand "who ruled". The translator read either *malek/melak* in the
Aramaic, or mechanically rendered the Aramaic participle (preterite) by the unacceptable Hebrew participle. In 2.5 the translator,
unconsciously influenced by the Aramaic text *hawa'* before him,
rendered *hayah* instead of *wayehi* which he usually did elsewhere
(cf. 1.1; 2.8; 5.1.2). On the other hand he confused *hawa'* with *hu'*
at 9.1 where the Aramaic read the idiomatic natural *et-hapek hawa'*
"it was transformed", but where he translated with *we-nahapok hu'*
awkwardly.

There are a number of instances, moreover, where the determinate
and indeterminate state of the Aramaic was not comprehended
properly by the translator. At 2.14, the rejected candidate for the
queenship, as the verse avers, would be brought back to the second
harem, *bet ha-nashim sheni*, peculiarly without the article.
Probably the Aramaic read *baita denashin tinyana* where the latter
word was taken indeterminately (see p. 10). Similarly 2.19 where
one should read *ha-betulot*. On the other hand, because he copied
mechanically the text before him, he unconsciously transgressed
a grammatical rule at 7.6, where Esther, pointing to Haman,
exclaimed: this enemy and adversary, this wicked Haman המן הרע
הזה. As Ehrlich remarked, a proper name cannot carry with it an
adjective definitized. In Aramaic, however, this is perfectly possible.
Comp. e.g. חנן בישא "This bad man Hanan", Baba Qama 115a,
Jastrow, *Dictionary*, 167.

C. C. Torrey was the first to argue for the hypothesis that Hebrew
Esther was translated from Aramaic. His argument is convincing
and cogent. I accept his restoration at 2.13 ובזה as a mistranslation
of the Aramaic באדין "And then", cf. Greek *tote* "then". His restoration at 7.4 מעיקא as "oppression" rather than the Hebrew "oppressor" is well taken (but cf. further suggestions below, p. 91).
At 9.25 "her entrance" is a misreading of Aramaic ובמעללה "at
his entrance". About others I have mixed feelings. I maintain that
it is a shaky procedure if, after one recovers the retroversion to the
Aramaic, one proceeds further to emend the restoration, a risky
methodology. And this is what Torrey did at 1.22; he is correct
though in assuming that מדבר ascends to the Aramaic "lead,

conduct" although the emended restoration כלשון/כל לשן does not clarify too much (see p. 90). Doubts about his corrected restoration at 7.8 also hold: אתחפיאו is not a retroversion of חפו.

I would like to add a number of examples that appear to be mistranslations in Esther. Mention was made that in 2.9 the root שני was incorporated into the Hebrew text as וישנה where in the latter part of the verse the literal translation would run, "And he changed her and her maidens to the best place in the harem". The language, however, is a little strange. One would expect the verb עבר in the Hif'il with the meaning "He transferred her", the only logical verb. The Aramaic verb שני, however, signifying "transfer" in the Pa'el looked so much like a Hebrew verb that the Hebrew translator without further thought inserted this Aramaic into his Hebrew.

In 1.8 there is a peculiar use of the word יסד in the passage וְהַשְּׁתִיָּה כַדָּת אֵין אֹנֵס כִּי כֵן יִסַּד הַמֶּלֶךְ עַל כָּל רַב בֵּיתוֹ לַעֲשׂוֹת כִּרְצוֹן אִישׁ וָאִישׁ.

For יסד we must translate ad hoc, "For so did the king charge, order." A standard equivalent in the Aramaic is תקן which, elusively, for the translator had a number of meanings: establish, arrange, ordain, improve, straighten, set in order. The translator, in his dilemma, settled upon יסד inappropriately in the verse. The Hebrew paqad, ziwwah, would have been the more usual, and perhaps the more suitable. Translate: for so did the king ordain.

The whole verse in fact requires reconstruction. If the first part of the verse means that the drinking was according to law (when the king drank, everyone had to drink with him[10]), then the sequel that "there was no compulsion" is puzzling. The third part of the verse is no less mystifying, for if the king did command to do the wish of every man, then this contravenes the first part again that states "The drinking was according to law". Greek B reads[11] intriguingly, "The drinking was not according to the set law" which would harmonize the different members of the verse appropriately. The difficulty seems to revolve around the word *ka-dat*. Scholars would emend to *kaddot*, with the sense that drinking was

[10] Comp. Herodotus, I, 33; Xenophon, *Cyropaedia*, VIII, 8 cited by Moore, *Esther*, p. 7.

[11] *ho de potos outos ou kata proskeimenon nomon egeneto.*

done by flagons i.e. unrestrainedly. This proposal has its difficulties.[12] The Aramaic substratum would seem to offer the correct
alternative. The Hebrew translator saw in his text כדנא which
he thought was *ke-dina* "according to law", because of his consciousness of *dat* and *din* as a thematic thread running through
the first chapter of Esther (vv. 13.15.19). This reading made for
the thought confusion in the coherence of the first and second parts
of the text. His reading should have been *u-mishtaya kidna* "And
the drinking was thus". For the construction, cf. *millah kidna*
Dan. 2.10 "A matter like this". *Dena* is spelled with *Alef* as well,
cf. Targum Ez. 38.12 and elsewhere, Kohut, *Aruk*, III, 94 (of
course, his idea that *dena* is feminine is incorrect); Dalman,
Dialektproben,[2] p. 3. The translation should have conveyed the
sense: The drinking was thus: there was no compulsion, for so did
the monarch order each chief steward to do the wish of every man.

Evidence for Aramaic translation shows up again at 9.29. The
passage reads peculiarly ותכתב אסתר המלכה בת אביחיל ומרדכי
היהודי את כל תקף לקים את אגרת הפורים הזאת השנית. "And Queen
Esther and Mordecai the Jew wrote the full strength (?) to confirm
this second letter of Purim". There are two well known questions:
what is meant by "full strength"? and what is this "second letter
of Purim?" The syntax of את כל תקף is likewise most peculiar. No
proper exegesis has been presented. The underlying Aramaic text
read לכל גבורתא which the translator assumed to be "strength".
The Aramaic word however, like the semantically associated חילא,
has the signification of "marvellous event, miracle" which is the
required sense here. Esther wrote up the marvellous event of Purim,
the fitting sense to the passage. The "second" letter of Purim raises
the question of the "first" letter: where, what is the "first" letter?
Torrey[13] contended that the "second" letter is the Hebrew that
we possess, while the "first" letter was the Aramaic one from which

---

[12] The suggestion of John Gray, *Legacy of Canaan*[2], p. 226 that we should
read *kaddot* i.e. drinking was by flagons is ingenious, yet fails to ring true, as *kad*
is a pitcher, large in size, which for example Rebecca carried on her shoulder to
water the camels Gen. 24.15–16. Anyway the plural of *kad* is uniformly *kaddim*,
1 Kings 18.34; Jud. 7.16.19.20.

[13] Torrey, "Older Book of Esther", 31–34.

the Hebrew was translated. I am inclined to follow him but not on these grounds (see below p. 102). The word השנית = תנינא(ד) or תנינא which in Aramaic not only means "second" and hence the mistranslation, but *again*. תנינא/דתנינא should not have taken as an adjective to 'iggeret but as an adverb "again". The significance of the verse now becomes clear: Esther wrote up the whole miracle of Purim to confirm again this letter of Purim (cf. 9.20.26.).

The translator made a somewhat similar error at 2.19. The text runs: ובהקבץ בתולות שנית ומרדכי יושב בשער המלך. Commentators cannot fathom the import of the phrase "And the maidens were gathered a *second* time". After all, Esther was already crowned queen (2.17). Some assume that the king continued to require girls for his harem, but then this item seemingly has no connection with the sequel. We should consider this verse and the following verse 20 as a *retrogressio*, perhaps a summing up for emphasis of vv. 8–10 (Moore, 30). The translator misapprehended the phrase מדריש, מן דריש which has two meanings in Aramaic, 1) again and 2) from the first, from the beginning. Comp. Brockelmann, *Lexicon*, 728 b; L. Ginzberg, *Geonica*, I, 82. The second meaning clears up matters correctly. The passage should run: Now when the maidens were gathered from the *first*, Esther told not of her kindred or people, as Mordecai commanded her etc.

One verse troublesome to commentators has a number of mistranslations in it. The text reads (10.3): כי מרדכי היהודי משנה למלך אחשורוש וגדול ליהודים ורצוי לרב אחיו דרש טוב לעמו ודבר שלום לכל זרעו. The problems are: 1) What is the phrase גדול ליהודים precisely to mean? 2) Why is Mordecai designated as "pleasing" to *most* of his brethren"? It is not likely that there was opposition to him. 3) Then again, why only "pleasing?"

The word גדול is indefinite, unfocused. When we retrovert to the Aramaic, the word acquires the essential point. רב not only means "great" but "leader". Cf. analogously רב כהניא, רב כנישתא רב חילא and other determinants with רב. Note now the proper contrast: Mordecai was not only second to the king but a leader of the Jews. Cf. Targums to Esther!

The next phrase contains the enigmatic word רב. The Aramaic most likely had סוגאה. While the Hebrew expresses the sense of "majority, most", Aramaic goes its own way with *suga'a* to denote "multitude, throng". Comp. similarly Lat. *multitudo* and Brockelmann, 457. However, רצוי represents a misreading. The text in the Aramaic had רעי which the translator read as pe'il form i.e. re'e, hence his רצוי "pleasing, acceptable". He should have read the different Aramaic root II רעי as an active participle meaning "He was concerned for the welfare of . . . . " The passage should bear the significance: Mordecai was the leader of the Jews, and concerned for the welfare of his brothers". Note the follow-up: seeking the good of his people.

The last phrase ודבר שלום לכל זרעו is probably to be taken in the sense of "He brought peace to all his kindred" i.e. Aramaic דבר "conduct, lead, bring", and זרעו reproduces the Aramaic זרעיתה "his family" and so indeed the translation of the Targums. Similarly in the difficult passage in 1.22 להיות כל איש שרר בביתן ומדבר כלשון עמו. דבר = "conduct, conduct oneself" as Torrey suggested. However לשן does not only mean "tongue, language" but with an extension of meaning "interpretation, version" e.g. *lishna qamma* and *lishna batra* "the first version and/or the second interpretation," Pes. 45 a; Ta'anit 30 a, and cf. Greek *glossa* and our English *gloss* = interpretation. The translation should run: that every man be ruler in his house, and be leader according to the fashion of his people.

When Esther had made her accusation against Haman, 7.7 states that the king in his anger arose from the banquet and went out into the garden. Commentators have called into question the anger of the king. There is no proper reason for anger at this point in the narrative (cf. Ehrlich ad loc.) He may have been surprised, stunned, without a plan of what to do, but scarcely angry. The Hebrew *ḥamato* however represents the Aramaic *rugzeh* which in its fundamental meaning has the import of "agitation". Cf. 2 Sam. 19.1 where David at the loss of Absalom was "agitated, moved, grief stricken" (*rgz*). Translate here: and the king arose in his agitation.

We may mention, in conclusion, the passage at 7.4 which ends with כי אין הצר שוה בנזק המלך. As remarked, Torrey proposed מעיקא which was misinterpreted as "the oppressor" whereas it should have been taken as the feminine determinate "oppression".

The interpretation does not seem completely satisfactory i.e. oppression is not worth the king's endamagement. My own proposal is that the two words have been interchanged. The Hebrew should have read כי אין הנזק שוה בצר המלך "Because the injury is not worthy in the distress of the king". This makes for a suitable sequel to the prior statement of Esther that if she and her people were sold into slavery, she would have kept silent for the damage involved would not be worthwhile to distress the king.

Greek B however has the reading "For the enemy is not worthy of the *palace* (aules) of the king". This reading may provide a clue as an alternate to the Hebrew above: "So that distress be not *put* in the palace of the king." שוי was probably misunderstood by the Hebrew translator as "worthy" rather than "put, place" in one of the grammatical forms; note the following Bet. "Palace of the king" is politeness for the king himself. "Palace" cues however the whole reading. The unusual reading "palace of the king" for which the Hebrew has נזק suggests that "damage" is a translation of the Aramaic i.e. חיבולא "injury, damage", which the Greek however read as היכלא, again Aramaic.

In sum, the Aramaic translation provides a satisfying synoptic explanation of some puzzles in the book's structure and composition. A number of basic problems associated with the Aramaic hypothesis spring to mind, however, which deserve investigation and discussion.

What was the purpose of the story?

Why was the book translated from Aramaic?

Why was it curtailed?

How is it that the name of God was eliminated, as well as the prayers of Mordecai and Esther?

What real relevance has the name Purim to the story?

When was the book written and where?

To discuss these questions adequately, a different perspective on the story, as well as a newer understanding of the motives of the dramatis personae, together with an account of the backdrop and milieu of the book's composition need to be presented.

The reader of this Megillah gets the impression that Ahashwerosh was a simpleton and braggart who liked his wine and women.

He gave a party for 180 days (6 months!) for all the governors and administrative officials. In the capital Susa, he gave an extra party for 7 days. The drinking was wide and unrestrained, according to everyone's wish and capacity. At the culmination, he ordered Queen Vashti to come before the throng to show off her beauty, but Vashti would not come. The king in a petulant huff consulted with the astrologers, and she was deposed. The astrologers suggested that beautiful girls be mustered for the king's pleasure, and so in the course of events, Esther was brought to the harem. The book blandly states that in the evening a girl would come, and in the morning depart; and if she qualified as a sex object as the implication is, she might be called again. The king, falling in love with Esther, crowned her queen. Disjointedly, a conspiracy is mentioned at this point where two guardsmen sought to murder the king; Mordecai found out about this, and told Esther, who reported the conspiracy to the king. On examination, the conspirators confessed and were executed.

The monarch was so naive that he appointed crafty Haman to be his vizier, who broached a proposition to the king to annihilate the Jews. The order for the extermination proceeded; at the instance of Mordecai, Esther went to the king, uninvited against law and protocol, and in mortal peril. He graciously pardoned her, and she invited him and Haman to a party. That night the king was sleepless, and learned from his journal about Mordecai's faithful service. In the denouement of the story, Haman, invited to a second party by Esther with the king, was deposed and summarily executed.

Since Haman's edict could not be reversed according to Persian law (1.19; 8.8), Esther begged that the Jews be allowed to defend themselves which Aḥashwerosh granted. We are told that the Jews in defending themselves killed 75,000 persons (Greek 15,000), in Susa 500, and 300 on the next day, as well as the 10 sons of Haman. In celebration of the deliverance, Esther and Mordecai proclaimed Purim a holiday, and declared that its observance was never to cease. Mordecai became vizier.

Such is the recount of the Esther story on the surface. The Jewish writer composed this historical novel from the vantage point of what was important to him. He stressed: 1) The deliverance of Jews from annihilation. 2) How this was accomplished by Esther and Mordecai. 3) How Purim was established as a celebration of this event. The book must be looked at however from a different prospect, to arrive at a truer picture of events. The Jewish writer failed in his enthusiasm to tell his story to convey the dramatic power-play and revolution that occurred.

When the king had been on the throne for three years, he became aware of dissident elements and restless conspirators that were at large in his kingdom, as he subsequently learned from the conspiracy of the two guardsmen in the royal palace. To win over everyone, and to create an aura of good feeling, he made lavish parties for 180 days, so that all could come and participate, together with the aristocracy, the governors and the army commanders (1.3.4.). Again, to win everyone's good will and loyalty, one could drink wine at will, and out of the king's golden beakers. If you drink the king's wine out of the king's cups, you unconsciously make a pledge of loyalty to him with the wine. A special party of 7 days was made for the Shushan inhabitants, as the capital would have more of the dangerous revolutionaries hatching plots, who might carry through a palace revolution more quickly and effectively than the rest of the country. Aḥashwerosh, moreover, requested Queen Vashti to appear so that his beautiful queen would gain male admiration, ardent chivalry, and an unhesitating pledge of loyalty, to fight for her and not against him. A rift appeared in the lute. Vashti refused to appear before the drunken mob. This was a stunning refusal for the king, not a tiff in private quarters. The king needed someone to talk to for a long time, to confide in. It took 4 years to decide on a new queen (Esther 2.16). The refusal of Vashti was disgraceful and public, and caused a weakening of the loyal ties that the king so wished to deepen and confirm.

The procession of girls to the king was not a series of sex exploits, since he could have any girl in the kingdom regardless. It was mostly conversation and interview, implied in 2.14. Was the prospective new queen one whom he could trust absolutely, one who was astute and responsive? We know from the book that Esther, his final choice, was courageous (4.16f.), politically astute (5.4), with a fine sense of timing (5.8: two parties); she organized the counter revolution, and yet was femininely charming.

With regard to the conspiracy of the guardsmen, the episode is truncated in the Hebrew. Greek B and A (1.14) have it that Mordecai had lodged in the courtyard of the king, and overheard the plans of the conspirators (they were angry because Mordecai was promoted (2.21 B), and Mordecai had informed the king (not Esther as in the Hebrew). Ahashwerosh "examined" them (put them to the torture) and had them executed. He therefore must have learned of the spreading conspiracy, for the monarch told Mordecai to guard the doors securely (1.17 A). Greek B moreover asserts (1.18)[14] that Haman sought to do evil to Mordecai because of his two guardsmen. Apparently Haman suspected that the guardsmen confessed and implicated him. Consequently he sought to destroy Mordecai; and not because Mordecai would not bow down to him as the Hebrew has it, but because the plans now might be known to the king.

Uncertain as yet, the monarch settled on a bold move. He appointed Haman vizier to watch him. Haman *per contra* was in a position to make a lunge for royal power. The suggestion to give 10,000 talents so that he could destroy the Jewish people was playing for high stakes. The money would satisfy and buy off the king, he thought, but really at no loss to himself, as he would confiscate Jewish property anyway (3.13). Further, it would be a grasp and control of police power. For the nonce, the king would sign the order. This would parallel the actions of a Stalin, a Beria, a Himmler whose power was augmented through the control of the police.

Lots were cast for the Jewish liquidation. Greek A (3.12) clarifies matters a good deal by stating that Haman went to his gods, and the gods, not he, determined the month and date, very much

---

[14] The passage in A has a lacuna. It should run as follows: *kai edoken auto domata peri touton.* v. 18. *kai en Aman amadathou Makedona endoksos kata prosopon tou Basileos.* Cf. Greek B.

like the old Babylonian assize at which the gods at New Year cast lots for the fate of men. The awesome date was put off for 11 months, for it will be recalled that very much like the Romans who had more unlucky days in the year than lucky ones,[14a] so in Babylonia a propitious day was sought for any enterprise. In his day in Persian history, Pseudo-Smerdis seized the throne on the 14th of Adar[15].

At the instance of Mordecai, Esther went to the king unbidden thereby breaking the law. The king was angry at first, but God moved him, as the Greek states, to extend the royal scepter, thereby saving her life. Inferentially, the king must have realized that she would not have come risking her life unless it was something vital and important. Esther moved courageously, "Let the king and Haman come to a party today". The monarch was intrigued. There was something going on. Not only did Esther risk her life, *but why invite Haman*? At the party the question was asked again; yes, the monarch would give her half the kingdom. Esther faltered: if the king and Haman would come tomorrow to a second party, she would respond to the request of the king. Commentators are puzzled. Why did Esther put off the party, and petition for another day? Some say that at the last moment her heart failed her. Others say that there had to be the intervening night, wherein the king learns of Mordecai's faithful service, and wherein he decides to honor Mordecai. The book however suggests another explanation though we have to "ferret and sniffle it out". Esther had not "seen" the king for thirty days (4.11), and therefore was unsure of the king's continuing affection. After an absence of thirty days, a certain estrangement develops between husband and wife. A newer bond and intimacy has to be established. Although the king had reprieved her, Esther with feminine intuition considered that if the king made love to her that night, and she gave him sexual satisfaction, she would have the more assurance in the triangle at the party. The king did not do so.

He was restless that night. God took away his sleep (Greek A).

Q[4] W. Warde Fowler, *Roman Festivals*, pp. 3, 9.
[15] J. Hoschander, *Book of Esther in the Light of History*, 168.

The monarch ordered that his journal be read to him. An anti-Haman attendant deliberately chose to read how Mordecai saved the king's life. Greek A continues: There was an argument among the attendants as to what benefaction Mordecai had performed. The king fixed his mind closely to this, saying "Mordecai was trustworthy in guarding my life. He enabled me to live from then to now, and I sit this day upon my throne. I have not done anything for him. I did not do rightly". Then the king said to his attendants, "What shall we do for Mordecai, my savior, in this affair?" The young men were wily enough to excite[16] ill will against him, for the fear of Haman lay upon their minds; *and the king understood this* (italics mine). This is the crucial moment and the pivot in the whole story. It began to dawn on the king that his servants and guardsmen had already been corrupted by conspiracy; that Mordecai was a man whom he might trust, and Haman contrastedly might be a key conspirator. Meanwhile Haman had laid his plans to execute Mordecai on the advice of his "friends" (i.e. his fellow-conspirators) and appeared at court to have his request granted. The king now was looking at Haman differently. He put a test question: what should be done for the man whom the king delights to honor? Haman answered, Such a man should wear the royal robes that the king himself wore, and ride the horse that the king has ridden, with the royal crest upon its head, and a governor or prince leading the horse with bridle. Haman did not care which prince or governor; he had the whole thing sewed up. Thus the procession would move through the city. The populace would have the strong impression "Why that man is like a king!" Aḥash-werosh grasped the implications immediately: if someone wears your kingly robes, and rides on the horse with the royal crest, then this is a thrust and surge for power. Very shortly, Haman would be king in fact. There was but one step more for the king to be displaced (regicide). The ruler acted decisively, "Dress Mordecai in the king's robes, and *you* lead Mordecai around the city on the king's horse". In swiftness and resolution, Aḥashwerosh

---

[16] There is a slight misunderstanding of the underlying Aramaic. חכימו means "They were wily"; the Greek translator took it in the sense of "They knew".

came out on top momentarily. Mordecai, at least, was one to be trusted; he had loyally saved the king's life before. Haman's heart grew faint within him (6.11 A) as we might well imagine, and he reluctantly carried out the king's command.

That Haman was under suspicion now is indicated by the fact that at this second attendance at Esther's party he did not come quite as the honored guest but under the accompaniment of the king's soldiers, a different state of affairs (6.14). Esther came, still apprehensive, but reinforced and armed with a powerful argument which however she did not have to use. If Esther should petition for her life, the ruler might say, "The decree has been issued; it cannot be reversed; but I will save you". Then Esther would let loose the second countercharge, "If that be the case, then the man Mordecai whom you dressed in royal robes *today*, and proclaimed that such is the man whom you delight to honor, will have to be killed too. He is my cousin". As it was, Esther pointed to Haman as the villain who wished to murder her and her kinsmen. The monarch, in his agitation, went out to the garden to think things over, as he was overwhelmed not only by the perfidy of Haman so much as the suddenness of the confrontation without a plan to proceed. He returned and found Haman lying prone by the divan of Esther[17] supplicating for his life. The king seized his opportunity; he *pretended* that Haman had assaulted the queen! The ruler ordered Haman summarily executed. The counter revolution had started.

Haman was toppled, but the Hamanites were still many, alive and dangerous, and bent on genocide. Esther begged that a decree be issued that the Jews be allowed to defend themselves. This was the organized counter revolution. The king assented. This is instructive. Actually the ruler should have taken a hand in the suppression; this is a function of the state, an obligation of the army. On the one hand he was ready to sell the Jews for money (3.11 see p. 85 for the construction); on the other hand, he did not want to risk unpopularity; but since executions were an imperative, he decided to let the Jews do the nefarious work.

---

[17] על המטה means "by the divan" not "on". Cf. Ex. 2.15 "by the well".

The counter revolution took sizeable proportions, 75,000 killed in the realm, 500 in the capital and 300 on the next day. Many of the people pretended to be Jews "because the fear of the Jews fell upon them" (8.17). Mordecai took over Haman's official function with the king's signet ring "in royal apparel of blue and white, and with a great crown of gold, and with a robe of fine linen and purple". With the tables turned, the royal officials began to extol the Jews (9.3).

We have now to inquire when, where, and why was this book written?

The present writer cannot follow Pfeiffer[18] in thinking that the book was written in Palestine, ca. 125 B.C.E. as a reflection of the new self-conscious, nationalistic spirit of the Jews, with their new independence, royal dynasty, and the victorious afterglow of the Maccabbean struggle. I would rather place the writing of the Aramaic version(s) in the Diaspora, for the book contains a distinct exilic atmosphere where neither sacrifice, nor Temple, nor Torah, nor Prophets nor tithes, nor first fruits are referred to.[19] Moreover the fact that the book was written in Aramaic shows likewise its origin, to the north of Palestine, in Seleucid Syria, and specifically in Babylonia as the restoration of the Aramaic shows it to be Eastern Aramaic.[20]

Now a striking feature of the book is the fact that Mordecai is referred to as "Mordecai the Jew". To a Jew reading this book, this attribute is meaningless and perplexing. He would know that Mordecai was Judean from the genealogy in 2.5. Why then Mordecai the Jew (5.13; 6.10; 8.7; 9.31; 10.3)? This only makes sense if directed to a *pagan* reading the Book of Esther. The author would be constantly reminding his reader that Mordecai was a Jew. We may state then in our view that the book of Esther in the shortened form, and the antecedent of our Hebrew version, was written to publicize certain ideas.

Cyrus and his successors were generally favorable to the Jews.

---

[18] Pfeiffer, op. cit. 745–46.
[19] Cf. the writer's *Tobit*, p. 49.
[20] איקרא, שני, מן דריש. See pp. 76, 87, 89.

He encouraged the rebuilding of the Temple. Darius II as we learn from the Elephantine papyri authorized the celebration of the Passover by the Jewish military troops in Egypt. However, after the conquest of the Persian Empire by Alexander the Great (d. 323 B.C.E.) who set up city after city after the model of the Greek polis with city councils, magistrates, prefects and whatever, the favorable climate in which the Jews flourished underwent a change. In the city of Babylon, and afterwards in Seleucia on the Tigris, the twin capital with Antioch on the Orontes, the latter the third largest city in the world after Rome and Alexandria, great numbers of Jews, —some 200,000 in Antioch alone—and tens of thousands in Mesopotamia as reported by Josephus, flourished side by side with large numbers of Syrians and Greeks. Incidentally, Josephus wrote the first version of his history in Aramaic for his co-religionists in Mesopotamia (*Wars,* preface, sec. 1).

Now the rivalry between the groups seeking Hellenistic favors was keen. One group, if favored, could command the blessings of political, economic and social advantage. The Jewish fall from favor undoubtedly caused dismay and concern among the people. We know of Jewish hatred in the Elephantine papyri[21]; and our book of Esther has an authentic note in one of the verses: There is a certain people scattered and dispersed among the population of the royal provinces; their laws are different from every other people; they don't observe the king's laws; it does not pay for the king to suffer them . . . it is all right to despoil them (3.8.13). Propaganda, a book was needed. So under the guise of history, a series of events were outlined and set forth to show:

1. The Jews had been in Babylon for the longest time, "natives" since Nebuchadnezzar (2.6).

2. The Jews were tied to the royal Persian family by ties of blood through Queen Esther.

3. The Macedonians married 10,000 Persian women at the instance of Alexander. He himself and 80 of his officers married Persian princesses. Alexander married Barsine, a daughter of the

---

[21] A. E. Cowley, *Aramaic Papyri of the Fifth Century B.C.,* # 27 dated about 410 B.C.E.

last Persian king, Darius. He married another, Roxanna of the aristocracy, with whom he had a son. The Jews and Macedonians were therefore related. In 1. Macc. 12.7 the Jews refer to the Spartans as "our kinsmen". See Zeitlin, *Book of Maccabees* ad loc. for this belief commonly held in Asia Minor.

4. Moreover, the Jews occupied high position in the government (Mordecai as vizier).

5. Loyally, the Jews helped to preserve the state *ex parte* the king.

6. After the revolution, Mordecai organized the state and put it on a sound fiscal basis, subtly suggested by the fact that Aḥash-werosh remitted taxes (2.18; to gain popularity) but they were restored under the aegis of Mordecai (10.1).

7. The populace and the administration extolled the Jews because of the authority of Mordecai; his reputation went far and wide; the power and the prestige of the Jews increased (9.2–4).

8. This signal success on the part of the Jews in carrying through the counter-revolution was always to be celebrated by the Jews as a national deliverance in the Persian Empire, as a perennial reminder to successive governments.

9. Through "executive order" Purim was to be observed as a national holiday by the *Persians* as well. The king in his edict proclaimed, according to the Greek: Do you therefore among your notable holidays keep a distinct day with all festivity that now and hereafter it may be a [day of] deliverance to us . . . Every city and province that shall not do accordingly shall be consumed with vengeance by spear and fire . . . (6.17–19 B).

The book then was written in Aramaic so that the Syrians, and not only the Jews, could read it as well, and then the book was trans-lated into Greek for the Hellenes.

It seems unlikely that the writing of the book was meant to introduce the celebration of Purim. As Paton remarked, observance always precedes the historical document. Purim has been traced by J. Lewy to the word *pur* in Akkadian, signifying "lot" originally "pebble".[22] However it is erroneous to assume that because the

---

[22] J. Lewy, op. cit. p. 138f. "Purim" is considered by him to be based upon פרוריא meaning "destruction" which the Jews by folk etymology associated with *puru(m)* "lot".

word is found in Akkadian, the source of the word is to be found in that language. *Pur* is a good Aramaic word (*pura*) meaning "lot, destiny" (Jastrow, *dictionary* p. 1146), and yet is associated with *prr*, as so many Ayin Waws are fraternal to the geminates as *bz/bzz*; *sb/sbb* and frequently. It is hardly possible that the Hebrew holiday would have a foreign borrowed name, either from Akkadian or Persian, an unparalleled procedure, as well as the psychologically strange name of Holiday of Destruction/Destiny, or even Lots. All holidays are Hebrew: Rosh Ha-shanah, Yom Kippur, Pesaḥ, Shabuot, Sukkot, Ḥanukkah. The root *prr/pur* has the signification of "annul, frustrate" e.g. Ps. 33.10: God *annuls* the counsel of nations; He frustrates the thoughts of people. While it would be a serious step to contravene the traditional interpretation *pur hu' ha-goral* = pur means 'lot' (3.7; 9.24), the fact is that most of the etymologies in the Bible are folkloristic, fanciful, or wrong. Eve's name *Ḥawwah* does not come from *ḥay*, nor Cain from *qanah*, nor Noah from *naḥam*, nor Reuben from "See! a son!", nor Yehudah from "Give thanks" and so on down the line. The Jewish writer thought that the holiday came from *pur* because lots were actually cast, although rather secondarily to the whole story. My suggestion is that Purim (cf. for the form, *ṭur*, *ẓur*) signifies the holiday of the Plot that Failed, or the Overturned Plot, where *pur* would have that connotation of "overturn, frustrate", plural *purim* "The Overturned Events", an appropriate designation for the unfolding of the plot.

It is interesting that Mordecai and Esther have non-Jewish names. In itself this would be nothing unusual as we learn from Ezra c.2 about the Aramaic, Babylonian and Elamite names, as well as later of the Greek names that the Jews assumed in the Hellenistic period. The unJewish names of Mordecai and Esther have led Jensen, Winckler and others[23] to hypothesize that we have a mythological pattern in which Mordecai represents the Babylonian Marduk, Esther is Ishtar, while arrayed on the opposite flank is Haman representing the Elamite god Humman, so that the Purim struggle represents an old mythological contest

---

[23] Lewy, op. cit. p. 127 and the literature there cited.

wherein the gods of Babylonia overthrew the Elamite gods. Others find parallels in the Arabian nights. Scheherazade, who sought to protect her family and herself, was a Jewish girl according to the Arabic writer Masudi[24]. This symbolization has taken on other forms in Jewish tradition. Haman the Agagite had already been identified by Josephus in the first century as an Amalekite, and therefore Mordecai, descended from Kish, was carrying through the old war between King Saul and Agag (1 Samuel 15) king of the Amalekites, and some scholars uphold this theory. I would take a different view. Haman is a good Aramaic word meaning "death", as well as a collective term for "denizens of the underworld"[25]. In old Babylonian tradition there was the well known classic struggle, ending with the destruction of Tiamat and her cohorts by Marduk, the supreme god appointed by the gods to overcome her at the beginning of creation. Marduk was successful. What we have in the biblical book therefore, and in an unconscious pattern followed by the writer, is the classic struggle between the forces of light and darkness, with the forces of light victorious. Nevertheless, from the insight we have gained from the revolution and power-play in the book, it is quite evident that the book contains a genuine historical core even though there are problems in a number of names and dates. The first draft of the book was composed probably in the latter half of the 3rd century B.C.E.

The Aramaic document antecedent to our Hebrew text was shortened designedly to show how important the Jews were in the life of the state. The name of God, and the prayers to him by Mordecai and Esther were deliberately omitted. It is well known how rival factions deride one another with regard to origins, gods, customs etc. The epitomizer considered that the book should be read as "pure" history without the name of God to be ridiculed by pagans, or prayers to be derided. And so there was added the

[24] al-Tabari, ed. de Goeje, I, 688.

[25] Brockelmann, *Lexicon*, eds. 1 and 2. The hypothesis that I have advanced that Haman means "noise maker", which the popular imagination formulated as a contemptuous term for Israel's arch enemy is on a different level of popular etymology. Comp. the writer's *Folk Etymology of Biblical Names*, VT Congress Volume, Geneva, 1965.

statement that you could read the whole history in the annals of the Persian kings (10.2). This shortened Aramaic version gained wide dissemination. Since the Jews were enjoined to celebrate Purim at stated intervals (9.27), a demand arose that the book be read in Hebrew in the synagogue. *It was the abbreviated version that was translated into Hebrew. Habent sua fata libelli,* or in paraphrase: Little history books have their own history.

6

Chronicles as a Partially Translated Book

1. As one reads the Book of Chronicles, one is constantly struck and puzzled by the marked contrast and variety in the style. No book in the Hebrew Bible presents such variegated markings in idiom, syntax and word-usage. As we progress from one section to another, one part will breathe on the one hand a distinct archaic atmosphere which we recognize to be that of Samuel-Kings, and is indeed a clear copy of the earlier work, and on the other hand, we find ourselves in sections which are recognizably late, which give such awkward turns to the ideas expressed, and such obscure phrasing to the thought, that we look in vain elsewhere for parallels and usages in the language. The peculiar diction in the late sections has been pointedly dwelt upon by other writers. Thus Driver:[1] "The style of the Chronicles is singular. Not only does it display the general novelties of vocabulary and syntax indicated on p. 505f. 'pages that contain a list of the peculiar Hebraic words and phrases of Daniel] showing that either the language itself is in decadence, or that the author has an imperfect command of it; but it has in addition numerous peculiarities and mannerisms of its own, not found in other post-exilic writings, which are often, if the Book be read carefully, perceptible in a translation. In some instances they appear in germ, of *occasionally* (italics S.R.D.) at an earlier period in the language; in others they consist of a peculiar application of old words." On p. 539 he adds the following significantly enough: "In the addition to the idioms that have been noted, hardly a verse occurs, written by the Chronicler himself, which do not present singularities of style *though they are frequently of a kind that refuses to be tabulated*" (italics mine).

---

[1] *Introduction to the Literature of the Old Testament*, rev. ed. 1913, reprinted N.Y. 1942, p. 535 f.

The last words I have intentionally italicized to indicate that a new frame of reference may be necessary to account for many of the peculiarities.

2. Our difficulties in dealing with the linguistic problems of Chronicles are complicated by the circumstance that at times the Chronicler can make himself seemingly clear and intelligible, and on the other hand, his obscurity seems to lie frequently in such passages, not where there are rare Hebrew words the sense of which may escape us, but on the contrary where they are perfectly understood, but do not add up to any sense. Let the reader glance through the last five chapters of II Chron. and he will see the point of my remarks. Observe such verses as II Chron. 30.5, 10, 12 (גַם), 15 (נִכְלְמוּ), 18, 22, in steady sequence. Textual emendation, be it added in passing, does not avail much; and indeed one must be chary of correcting in the text in Chronicles, especially since these peculiarities abound, and for aught we know are indigenous to the Chronicler, and not mistakes at all. Comp. Curtis, who though he expresses himself somewhat differently, utters the same caution: "No doubt many of the marks of slovenly and careless composition which are so common are due to copyists' errors, but so many of them are certainly original . . . "[2] Note the conservative treatment accorded the books in Kittel's *Biblia Hebraica*, and rightly so.

3. Is there another explanation, an hypothesis from a different approach, that can illumine these difficulties? In 1907, Sir Henry Howorth offered an ingenious and plausible explanation of the difficulties in Chronicles. He urged that the linguistic and syntactical difficulties owe their existence to the mediation of a translation: the Chronicler translated his material from Aramaic into Hebrew.[3] The proposition of Sir Henry is well taken, and I concur in the hypothesis. His argument, however, is faulty from a number of fundamental aspects: the hypothesis to be valid has

[2] Curtis, E. L., *Books of Chronicles*, in the ICC series, N.Y. 1910, p. 27.

[3] H. H. Howorth, *Some Unconventional Views on the Text of the Bible*. VII *Daniel and Chronicles*, in *Proceedings of the Society of Biblical Archaeology* XXIX (1907) pp. 31–38, 61–69.

to rest upon linguistic data and proof. Surmises without demonstration remain but surmises. The Aramaic words and syntax cited by Sir Henry as general evidence, but not actually particularized by him in chapter and verse, might well be exampled elsewhere in the later development of the language as in the Mishnic tradition. What we shall have to look for in Chronicles are distinctions that are characteristically Aramaic, if we seek proof for translation, and which cannot be duplicated in the Hebrew.

4. If the reader will go along with me in assuming this hypothesis that there are sections (not all sections) in the Chronicler that have been translated from the Aramaic, I think that I can summon enough evidence to show that it is his translation that sponsored the unique Hebrew; that many "difficulties" disappear; that verses will be infused with new meaning through reference to the Aramaic; and many times what seems peculiar is merely a translation of a natural Aramaic idiom.

5. Since the Chronicler did make use of other sources to compose his work, whether or not we follow him in his claim to use those books that he cites as his authorities, the fact is that it would be perfectly natural for him to translate material from a popular history if he found such grist for his mill. In the late period of his *fluorit*, Aramaic would be the natural language in which he could find such histories. More, a significant *a priori* presumption in favor of the Aramaic hypothesis lies in the fact that Chronicles and Ezra, in reality one book, have a bilingual character of Hebrew and Aramaic alternating sections very much like in Daniel.[4] It is axiomatic that an author would write in one language. When the Chronicler came to write his history, piecing passages as he did from Samuel-Kings, he had to translate his Aramaic into Hebrew to lend an appearance of truth and coherence, perhaps indeed to lend sanctity and canonicity for what he had to say, *via* the language of religious memory,—Hebrew. Hebrew would weave the pieces into whole cloth.[5]

6. *A priori* assumptions aside, it is to the linguistic evidence that we must now turn. With a strange Hebraic idiom at hand at almost

---

[4] See above pp. 7–9.

every turn, the first suspicion of a translation was aroused through the presence of Aramaic words and expressions. The occurrence of Aramaic words and idioms in themselves would not constitute grounds for an Aramaic *Vorlage* as intimated above. In Chronicles, however, although Aramaic idioms, expressions and constructions abound, there is a sizeable group, of a sort that have not been Hebraized, that have not found a niche so to speak, in the Hebrew, that are so distinctly Aramaic that the evidence, cumulative as it gets to be, must invoke the hypothesis of a translated document.

7. Thus אַרְגְּוָן in II, 2.6 is really Aramaic. The Chronicler should have used אַרְגָּמָן, which in fact he does use elsewhere, but he unconsciously followed his Aramaic text אַרְגְּוָנָא (Dan. 5.7; 16.29). In I Chron, 13.12 we are struck by the strict Aramaic form הֵיךְ, "how," where Hebrew would have used אֵיךְ. הֵיךְ is found significantly enough in Dan. 10.17, a striking reference and parallel because it bears out the same tendency of the translator in the Hebrew of Daniel where he likewise transcribed the הֵיךְ of his underlying text. ‖ Note the form אֶתְחַבַּר in II, 20.35 and, by the way, the left-handed usage of חבר in the next two verses. ‖ Observe the expression יום ביום I, 12.22, II, 8.13, 24.11, 30.21 where the earlier Hebrew would be יום יום. Our expression however is a reproduction of the Aramaic phrase יום ביום Ezr. 6.9‖ The Chronicler failed to translate with עָזַר "help" I, 12.33.38 into Hebrew, the עָדַר from his Aramaic text. ‖ צפירי עזים II, 29.21 is instructive: on the one hand, it is Aramaic צפירי עזין Ezr. 6.17; on the other hand, it is like the translation Hebrew of Daniel again צפיר העזים Dan. 8.5, 8. Actually the Chronicler should have rendered שְׂעִיר הָעִזִּים, the latter regularly translated by the Targums צפיר בר עזין comp. Num. c. 7 *passim*. and especially Lev. 16.5 without בר.

‖ Note also such extremely Aramaic colorings as מְכָרְבָּל I, 15.27 (Aram. כרבלא Dan. 3.2); עַתִּיק I, 4.22, comp. Dan. 7.9.13.22.

8. Many words, specifically grammatical forms, appear strange in the Hebrew, but become cleared up when we recall the Aramaic. I can note three instances where the Chronicler, through the suggestiveness of his Aramaic, prefixed a *Mem* to his Hebrew form

---

[5] For the reasons why Aramaic Ezra was not translated into Hebrew see p. 141.

superfluously because his Aramaic word had it. Thus מַחֲלֻיִּים
"sufferings" II, 24.25, *a hapax legomenon* simply reproduced or
was suggested by מַרְעִין. ‖ In II, 30.10 וַיִּהְיוּ מַשְׁחִיקִים in the strange
Hif'il with the prefixed מ was cued by the underlying Aramaic
Haf'el (מְחַיְּכִין). A similar example is found in II, 28.23 מַעְזְרִים (!)
which could have only arisen from the suggestion of מסייעין. ‖
The most peculiar הָעַרְבִיאִים II, 17.11, where the Chronicler uses
elsewhere הָעַרְבִים II, 21.16; 22.1 when he did not forget himself
in translating, can only come from an underlying עַרְבָאִין, det.
עַרְבָאֵי,עַרְבָיֵּא.

a. Some examples require a fuller explanation. In II, 20.34 the
Aramaic suggestion accounts for a peculiar grammatical form
puzzling to many commentators. The passage reads: ויתר דברי
יהושפט הראשונים והאחרונים הנם כתובים בדברי יהוא בן חנני אשר הֹעֲלָה
על ספר מלכי ישראל. The word הֹעֲלָה as a *Hof'al* of עלה, "go up,"
is certainly strange. Without entering into a lengthy pro and con
discussion, we may confidently assume that we have a vestige of
the Aramaic text. Even the vocalization harks back to a *vox
memoriae* of an original הֹעֲלָה, Aramaic *Hof'al*, 3rd person, fem.
plural, of עלל "enter into," *Hof'al* "brought into" — our *inserted*.
The feminine plural is accounted for because הֹעֲלָה agrees with
the previous דברי, which in Aramaic was מִלַּיָּא, a feminine plural.
על is simply ל. Translate: . . . "behold they are written in the
words of J. son of H. which are inserted in The History of the
Kings of Israel."

9. The Aramaic suggestiveness of the text provides the key to
a number of other problems.[6] In I, 26.17 we have the peculiar
malformation לַצָּפוֹנָה where we should expect either צָפוֹנָה or
לַצָּפוֹן. Where does this לַצָּפוֹנָה come from? Very clearly from his
Aramaic text לְצָפוּנָא which in Aramaic is simply the determinate
case, Hebrew לַצָּפוֹן.

When we look at the passage which the Chronicler was trans-

---

[6] Since I use "suggestiveness" and "suggestion" frequently, I ought to make
it clear how the words are employed. Because Hebrew and Aramaic are so close,
it was but natural for the Chronicler to be unconsciously influenced by the words
he saw before him. Thus, as will be shown, if the Chronicler saw the word קם

lating, it is easy to see how he made the error. In I, 26.14 he translated למדנחא, לצפונא correctly with מזרחה, צפונה; v. 15 נגבה; then v. 16 varying his style למערב; v. 17 למזרח: but because he had varied his style of translation, he fell into error with the next word, unconsciously remembering what he did in V. 14: hence לַצָּפוֹנָה(!), and the next one לַגֶּגְבָּה(!); but in v. 16 where he translated with למערב he unconsciously carried over the memory of his translation, hence v. 18 has למערב.

a. With these facts and explanations in our mind's eye, a similar interpretation satisfies us for II, 29.16 ויבאו הכהנים לפְנִימָה. Notice that if the Chronicler is wary and alert, he translates correctly v. 18 ויבאו פנימה. In II 31.14 he slipped again (למדנחה) לַמְזְרָחָה.

10. A habit of the translator, wherein again we detect the translation process, is to render in a standard, almost rule-of-thumb fashion the same Aramaic word with the same Hebrew one. It saves time and effort in thinking about nuances: he reproduces the word in a sort of stock dictionary definition: he is under the impression that he is literally rendering the word before him. He may have adopted consciously a consistent procedure. For a large part of the time he would be correct; occasionally he would fall into a peculiar Hebrew through which we recognize his (mis)translation. To give an example from modern translators: the Jewish Version in Ruth c. 1 translates שְׂדֵה מוֹאָב (vv. 1, 2, 6 etc.) as the "field" of Moab. Now there is no "field" of Moab; it is either "land" or "country." But because שדה is largely "field,"

---

in his Aramaic text, he would tend to reproduce the word in his translation Hebrew, although Hebrew differentiates between קם and עמד, while the Aramaic uses קם for "rise" and "stand." See p. 111.

This process takes place all along in translation from other languages. To give an example: those who read *The Ingenious Exploits of Don Quixote* may wonder what is so ingenious about the scatter-brained hero's chasing windmills, for instance, and his other fantastic adventures. The answer is, that for centuries translators have been rendering the word *ingenioso* in the title by the similar English *ingenious*, when the proper translation should be that of Robinson Smith's "imaginative, visionary." Margaret J. Bates has written a complete dissertation on *discreción* in the works of Cervantes on "his large number of fine shadings" (Washington, 1945).

or more probably the translators wished to render word by word, we get the strange English "the field of Moab."

a. It will appear that our translator in a similar spirit applied himself to his text in much the same way. Thus the lexical counterpart of שְׁבַק, in Aramaic meaning "leave, allow, abandon, forgive," is the Hebrew עָזַב. But the meaning of שבק goes its own way in Aramaic to signify "leave behind, bequeath, pardon, forgive, send away, divorce," some meanings that עזב will not have. In the light of these observations, it will be obvious, peculiar as the following texts appear to be, how the solution goes in hand with the difficulty.

II, 32.31 וכן במליצי שרי בבל המשלחים עליו לדרש המופת אשר היה בארץ עֲזָבוֹ הָאֱלֹהִים לנסותו לדעת כל בלבבו. The intent of the verse is fairly clear. Hezekiah (in the Chronicler's eyes) especially enjoyed God's favor and protection; with regard however to this particular circumstance, wherein the envoys came to inquire about the marvel that was done in the land, עזבו אלהים. The Aramaic original probably ran שַׁבְקֵהּ אֱלָהָא "God let him alone" i.e. allowed him to be his own, so to speak: permitted him to act as he wished without Divine guidance. God did not abandon him, forsake him, as עזב implies. The translator failed to catch the correct meaning, and rendered mechanically. A good *quid pro quo* here would be הִנִּיחוֹ אֱלֹהִים:. שבק is used for הניח in the Targums as in Gen. 42.33, Judg. 16.26, Ezek. 41.9, 11 and elsewhere.

b. The same mistranslation with the same word עזב takes place in II, 28.14. The passage reads: וַיַּעֲזֹב הֶחָלוּץ את השביה ואת הבזה לפני השרים וכל הקהל:. The armed force left the prisoners and the spoil before the princes and assembly to determine the next step for disposal. But again עזב לפני is most strange. Once more we expect וַיַּנִּיחוּ "and they set down." עזב "forsake, abandon" is most inappropriate. Accordingly what must have happened may be repeated from above. עָזַב, a stock rendering, is nevertheless a mistranslation of שבק. The translation should have reflected the thought: they put down the prisoners and spoil before the princes and people for decision.

c. A third example of stock rendering-mistranslation appears in I, 16.37 וַיַּעֲזָב־שָׁם לפני ארון ברית יי לאסף ולאחיו לשרת לפני

הארון תמיד לדבר יום ביומו: As may be seen from the context, David assigned the Levites and priests their positions about the Ark and the Tabernacle. But as the reader will now object, ויעזב is most inapposite. Plainly, David let them function, permitted them to minister before the Ark of the Covenant. He did not abandon them. לאסף as a mistranslation for את אסף will be discussed further on.

11. A second word that the Chronicler misuses as a stock word is אֱמוּנָה "faithfulness." Apparently, as will be evident from the passages below, he felt that the Aramaic הימנותא should always be translated this way. For the most part, he would be correct. But הימנותא bears the allied and special signification of "stewardship, office," and so indeed in Syriac. Hence אמונה will be misplaced in a verse that tried to convey, for instance, what the levitical or priestly office was. Examine now the following passages: I 9.22 כלם הברורים לשערים בספים מאתים ושנים עשר המה בחצריהם באמונתם. התיחשם המה יסד דויד ושמואל הראה בֶּאֱמוּנָתָם: must mean "in their office" mistranslated from הימנותהון. Comp. v. 31 ומתתיהו מן הלוים הוא הבכור לשלם הקרחי בֶּאֱמוּנָה עַל מַעֲשֵׂה הַחֲבִתִּים: Likewise II, 31.15 ועל ידו עדן ומנימן וישוע ושמעיהו אמריהו ושכניהו בערי הכהנים בֶּאֱמוּנָה לתת לאחיהם במחלקות כגדול כקטן: Comp. also v. 18.

In short, it is very wooden to follow the dictionary here (comp. BDB s.v. אמונה) and render "in trust over;" obviously again אמונה must mirror the Aramaic הימנותא.

12.a. Another pair of lexical equivalents, which proved a snare to the Chronicler, is the Hebrew עָזַר = Aramaic סִיַע, Pa'el סַיַּע, Ithpa'el אִסְתַּיַּע. Very interestingly for our study, and again a manifestation how the Chronicler mistranslated his Aramaic, the word אִסְתַּיַּע in the Ithpa'el has the meaning of "join in troops, form troops," סִיעָא, סִיעֲתָא "company, troop." עָזַר obviously does not possess the meaning "form a troop." Yet mysteriously, and with a peculiar awkwardness, the Chronicler makes use of עזר in this sense: I, 12.22 כי לעת יום ביום יבאו על דויד לְעָזְרוֹ עד למחנה גדול כמחנה אלהים: The context deals with the numbers of the "gibborim" who joined David in the formation of his army. לעזרו cannot mean "to help him." Clearly, they came to conscript the army for David.

Observe the point of עד למחנה גדול כמחנה אלהים. The logical deduction that we are to make is that we have here a use of עזר which harks back to the Aramaic סיע, and is indeed a translation of the word, except that to the Hebrew reader, the verse conveys a sense entirely different from what he knows of עזר. It follows that in v. 21 והמה עָזְרוּ עם דויד על הגדוד should be interpreted in the same way. Translate: "They formed a troop with David against the (enemy) army" or "they conscripted with David" etc.

b. II, 26.15 ויעש בירושלים חשבנות מחשבת חושב להיות על המגדלים ... ויצא שמו למרחוק כי הפליא לְהֵעָזֵר עד כי חזק: Practically the whole chapter up to this verse deals with the military powers of Uzziah, his exploits, campaigns, and military preparations. He assembled an extraordinary number of men for the army, 307, 500 (v. 13) with officers (v. 11–12) as well as equipment (v. 14) until, as our verse under discussion has it, "his reputation went far," not because as the AV and the JV have it "he was marvellously helped until he was strong" but because he had conscripted so many troops until he was militarily strong. Again there seems to be a stock rendering of אסתייע by the *Nif'al* of עזר. In v. 13 לעזר למלך על האויב should be translated similarly: "to be mobilized for the king against the enemy" not to help him. It looks too as if I, Chron. 12.1 עזרי המלחמה should be explained similarly.

13. Driver (*ILOT*, 535) has remarked upon the weakened usage of העמיד in Chronicles with the clear meaning of "establish, appoint" whereas in the earlier books the meaning is "station."[7] Actually the exx. of העמיד reproduce הקים of the Aramaic "establish, appoint." To put it another way, the Aramaic קָם is not completely parallel to the Hebrew קָם. The Hebrew differentiates "rising" and "standing" by the separate words of קָם and עָמַד. The Aramaic uses but one: קָם. The sense of the passage should have determined for the Chronicler which one word he should use קם or עמד. But sometimes he failed to distinguish them, and a peculiar Hebrew results. ‖ Moreover קַיֵּם in the Pa'el has the meaning

[7] Comp. I 6.16, 15.16.17, 17.14, 22.2; II 8.14, 9.8, 11.15. For II 33.8 (II Kings נתתי) see below.

"adjure, administer an oath" nearly always a lexical equivalent of הִשְׁבִּיעַ ,נִשְׁבַּע in the Targums. העמיד does not mean "administer an oath."

a. Let us take a number of examples. Thus II, 13.4 וַיָּקָם אביה מעל להר צמרים אשר בהר אפרים ויאמר וגו'. Now Abijah did not "arise" from on the mountain,—that would be a most extraordinary feat—but plainly he "stood." The Chronicler translated correctly II, 24.20. The Hebrew should have been ויעמד making much better sense. The Chronicler obviously rendered in a mechanical fashion as the Aramaic וקם started the sentence.

b. In II, 34.32 the passage reads וַיַּעֲמֵד את כל הנמצא בירושלים ובנימן ויעשו יושבי ירושלים כברית אלהים אלהי אבותיהם: The context has to do with the *berit* that Josiah covenanted with the people (v. 31). Now it is ridiculous to say that Josiah caused all those in Jerusalem and Benjamin to stand up. Rather we shall have to admit that ויעמד is a mistranslation of וְקַיֵם which in Aramaic means to "have one swear." This is exactly what is required for the verse and the Hebrew should have read וַיַּשְׁבַּע את כל הנמצא וגו'.

c. More. The questionable reading in v. 33 וַיַּעֲבֵד את כל הנמצא בישראל לעבד את יי אלהיהנ is most assuredly to be interpreted the same way. ויעבד is error for ויעמד which in turn is a mistranslation for וְקַיֵם. Again וַיַּשְׁבַּע should have been the rendering. Our verse then receives pertinent meaning and clarification: he adjured all those present in Jerusalem to worship the Lord their God.[8]

14. An unusual expression with the Chronicler, which he uses frequently, but which hitherto has defied explanation, is the

---

[8] I do not want to admit this as part of the argument but in II, 33.8 ולא אוסיף להסיר את רגל ישראל מעל האדמה אשר הֶעֱמַדְתִּי לאבותיכם wherein the parallel in II Kings 21.8 has הֶעֱמַדְתִּי / נָתַתִּי, I strongly suspect a lapse of memory on the part of the Chronicler. He had in his mind's eye a familiar Aramaic phrase די קיימת לאבהתכון "which I swore to your fathers. . . ," found frequently as translation in the Targums e.g. Deut. 6.10.18.23; 7.8 has the fuller expression קימא די קיים לאבהתכון. העמדתי is a mistranslation of קיימת. Otherwise how can we explain such a striking variant to נתתי? Comp. F. Perles, *Analekten*, Neue Folge, Leipzig, 1922, 88 for a similar idea. He had but another step to take, to say that העמדתי is a mistranslation.

combination עָצַר כֹּחַ = be able, have power to do something.
The phrase occurs significantly enough elsewhere only in trans-
lation-Hebrew of Dan. 10.8, 16; 11.6. Where does this expression
come from? Observe the following passages:

I 29.14 .וְכִי מִי אֲנִי וּמִי עַמִּי כִּי נַעְצֹר כֹּחַ לְהִתְנַדֵּב כָּזֹאת

II 2.5   .וּמִי יַעֲצָר־כֹּחַ לִבְנוֹת לוֹ בַיִת

II 13.20   .וְלֹא עָצַר כֹּחַ יָרָבְעָם עוֹד בִּימֵי אֲבִיָּהוּ

II 22.9   .וְאֵין לְבֵית אֲחַזְיָהוּ לַעְצֹר כֹּחַ לַמַּמְלָכָה

Omitting כֹּחַ:

II 14.10   יְיָ אֱלֹהֵינוּ אַתָּה אַל יַעְצֹר עִמְּךָ אֱנוֹשׁ

II 20.37   .וַיִּשָּׁבְרוּ אֳנִיּוֹת וְלֹא עָצְרוּ לָלֶכֶת אֶל תַּרְשִׁישׁ

The only serviceable explanation that can be offered, it seems to me
is the supposition that the Aramaic phrase מְצֵי חַיְלָא "be able,"
which may be employed with or without חַיְלָא, was present in the
Aramaic text.[9] There are two other observations that are to be
made about מצי חילא which are quite pertinent. In the first place,
we observe that the Chronicler translator has the tendency (and
with other translators, too,) consciously and sophisticatedly to
translate by *two* Hebrew words, because he had two words in
his Aramaic text.[10] In the second place, we observe that עצר is a
mistranslation of the underlying מצי. For what does עצר mean?
In the way the Chronicler uses the word, it cannot bear the dictionary definition of "restrain;" it is clear that in some instances
the meaning should be "summon strength" but עצר never means
that, nor "increase" which is usually ascribed to it. Where does
עצר come from? In looking at this phrase מצי חילא the Chronicler

---

[9] The expression is found in the extant sources of the Eastern Aramaic alone.
Comp. Payne-Smith, *Thesaurus* s. v. *mezi*: without חילא in Jewish Aramaic as
well, Jastrow, Dictionary s. v. מצי.

[10] This tendency to translate words as they are, to be cued by the suggestiveness
of his text in front of him without regard for their idiomatic meaning, is constantly
evidenced by translators. Thus for עצר כח I 29.14 we have the targumic נסגי חילא,
Luther's *vermögen Kraft*, while other translators give "be able," the LXX, V,
AV, JV, Smith-Goodspeed.

failed to distinguish between I מצי and II מצי. The former has the meaning "be able" while the latter has the signification of "squeeze, press." That is the signification that the Chronicler irrationally picked up as translation with his עצר! The word both in Hebrew, and in Aramaic, through which medium the Chronicler would be most familiar with the word has the meaning of "press, squeeze."[11] In short, the Chronicler failed to recognize מצי as "be able" and adopted the only מצי that he knew "squeeze, press," hence עצר. Again we see a mechanical rendering, without understanding that עצר כח as an expression is without sense. Of course, without כח, the Chronicler still maintained his lexical equivalent עצר, hence, II Chron. 14.10; 20.37.

15. Another set of standard equivalents is found in the equation of רָבָה "increase, grow great, be many" and the Aramaic סְגִי which has practically the same signification. But not always. רָבַב, רָבָה may mean "grow, increase" but they do not have the signification of "spread over an area" which סְגִי would have. Thus when the Targum wishes to describe how leprosy spreads out, it will use סגי. Comp. Onkelos Lev. 13.12, 20.25, 39. Probably the Aramaic סגי "go, go one place to another" is so derived (Levy, *Wörterbuch*). At all events, notice how inappropriate the Hebrew is in the following two verses. In the first instance סגי as "spread" is the only apposite meaning. The translator again just equated רבה with סגי with an unwieldy result. I, 5.23 ובני חצי שבט מנשה ישבו בארץ מִבָּשָׁן עד בעל חרמון ושניר והר חרמון הֵמָּה רָבוּ. They "spread out" (סגי), not they increased. Differently in I, 4.27 ולשמעי בנים ששה עשר ובנות שש ולאחיו אין בנים רבים וכל משפחתם לא הרבו עד בני יהודה. הִרְבּוּ in the Hif'il is a mechanical transcription of אַסְגִּיאוּ "increased". Comp. the Targum to this verse.

16. Finally, to conclude this discussion of lexical equations, and how the Chronicler by using stock translations made awkward Hebrew, I should like to mention the equation of חוּשְׁבָּן = מִסְפָּר

---

[11] For the Hebrew עצר comp., עוצר בספוג המים יורדים, פותח ידו ואין המים יורדים Yalkut to Job, p. 1009 of ed. Horeb "If one squeezes a sponge, the water goes out; if one opens his hand the water does not go out." For the Aramaic, see Jastrow s. v.

Num. 3.40, 14.29 and Targums. It will be clear that the Chronicler gave through his mechanical translation a thoughtless twist to the Hebrew. The passage reads: I, 22.16 לזהב לכסף ולנחשת ולברזל אֵין מִסְפָּר. The word מִסְפָּר "number" cannot apply to bronze and iron. In the preceding v. 14 מִשְׁקָל, לנחשת ולברזל אין מִשְׁקָל is obviously the correct word for describing bronze and iron, not as in v. 16 מִסְפָּר. What the Chronicler had in v. 16, in the underlying Aramaic, was according to the lexical equation above דְּלָא חוּשְׁבָּן "without reckoning" which he translated lamely by אין מספר. He would have scarcely written so in an original Hebrew.

17. One who undertakes to study a foreign language knows that it is the small particles in the sentence, so to speak, that are the most difficult to master. They seemingly have but little meaning, and appear but to be surplusage. One picks up, more or less easily, the nouns, the verbs, the adjectives and adverbs. But the little particles, unless one has entered into the recesses and intimacies of the language, its character and idiom, may nevertheless continue to defy one to the very last. In German it is *hin, ab, zu, her* that continually baffle; in Hebrew it is אֲשֶׁר, כִּי, גַּם and the prefixes ל . . . , ב . . . ; in Aramaic, it is the particle דְ or דִי which may mean "who, which, that," also "in order that" and may serve as well for a sign of the construct. Another word לְחַד, לְחוֹד the forms as found are variable, have the meaning of "also" *and* "only," two opposites in the same word. Whether this word as it appears in an Aramaic sentence means an intention to include or exclude could be of considerable pertinence to the ultimate meaning.

a. The Chronicler understood Aramaic well enough; but perhaps because he translated at times word for word, or because a word started a sentence for example and therefore he failed to explore the import and sequence of the sentence, or because he read into the text at times that which was not there,—at all events it seems quite clear that he misunderstood these small particles, because as will appear the sentence does not make sense in context, and when we retrovert to Aramaic, the passage then becomes clear and strikingly intelligible. Our conclusion will have to be that the Chronicler must be translating. II, 11.22 ויעמד לראש רחבעם את אֲבִיָּה בן מעכה לנגיד באחיו כִּי לְהַמְלִיכוֹ is certainly most extra-

ordinary. The meaning must be "in order to make him king"
but כִּי never bears that meaning and is unparalleled. How did
כִּי come into the text?

Again the Aramaic supplies the key. The most obvious explanation is that the Aramaic particle דִּי, or perhaps in one of its compounds is the source of the trouble. In the simplest constructions,
דִּי has the meaning of *because* (כִּי) and also, at the beginning of a
subordinate clause, the meaning of *in order to, in order that*. That
is what is required for our verse. It is possible that the underlying
Aramaic text ran (יַמְלְכָה) דִּי "in order to make him king." The
דִּי was mistaken as "because," hence כִּי or else the Chronicler
could not think of the Hebrew for "in order that." It may be argued,
however, that our Hebrew text implies an infinitive. Another
alternative could be offered בְּדִיל דְּ or בְּגִין דְּ both meaning "because."[12]

For the construction of בדיל with the infinitive, comp. Onkelos
Ex. 1.11 בדיל לעֲנוּאיהון. Whatever alternative we wish to hypothesize, it is clear that some form of דִּ as a conjunction of purpose
was misuderstood as דִּי the causal conjunction. The Hebrew
should have been probably בעבור להמליכו or בַּעֲבוּר הַמְלִיכוֹ, לְמַעַן
הַמְלִיכוֹ which I Chron. 19.3 allows.

b. A second example where the mistranslation of this single
particle דִּי invoked a series of grammatical difficulties is found
in II, 8.11 ואת בת פרעה העלה שלמה מעיר דויד לבית אשר בנה לה כי
אמר לא תשב אשה לי בבית דויד מלך ישראל כִּי קֹדֶשׁ הֵמָּה אֲשֶׁר בָּאָה
אֲלֵיהֶם אֲרוֹן יי׳. The words כי קדש המה form a *non-sequitur* to the
preceding Hebrew words. Moreover, to what does המה, as plural,
refer to? And how did the ark come to *them*?

Suppose we retrovert into Aramaic the clause beginning with
the words בבית דויד מלך ישראל. The Aramaic ran: בְּבַיְתָא דִּי דָוִד
The phrase מַלְכָּא דִּי יִשְׂרָאֵל דִּי קוּדְשָׁא דִּי אֵנּוּן דִּי עַל לְוָתְהוֹן אֲרוֹנָא דִּי יי׳

---

[12] Comp. as an instance where both are used synonymously in Tal. Jer. Ta'an.
69a.... בגין דשמעינן עלך דאת בעי מתעבדה ארכינטס ובולבוטס ....בדיל דשמענך.
עלך דאת בעי מזבנה איסייא דיליך בדיל ד. is found in Onkelos 6.3, and on Palmyrene
inscriptions: comp. Cooke, *North-Semitic Inscriptions*, 265, 320, while בגין ד
is confined to Palestinian Talmud, Midrash, and Targum of Jerusalem,—Dalman,
Grammatik des jüdisch-palästinischen Aramäisch.

די דויד מלכא די ישראל looked like a familiar phrase: of David the king of Israel. The translator was mistaken. A caesura should have been placed at מלכא; די ישראל begins a new clause. In the phrase די קודשא אנון is the equivalent of קדישין אנון. The expression will have the analogy in such usages as דְּאַבָּא עֲדִיפָא מִדְּבְרָא "that of the father is better than that of the son" because "the genitive designated by means of ד may stand by itself, without an antecedent noun" Margolis, *Babylonian Talmud-Grammar*, 65. T. Nöldeke, *Syriac Grammar*, par. 209. Our verse should be translated then: But the daughter of Paraoh Solomon removed from the city of David to the palace which he built for her, because he said, my wife shall not dwell in the palace of David the king; because the people of Israel are holy lit. of holiness, as the ark of the lord had come unto them. The mistranslation of the first די, in taking it as a construct instead of a subordinating conjunction, led vice-versa to the mistranslation of the second as a subordinating conjunction instead of the sign of the construct.

c. As mentioned above, the Aramaic לְחַד,לְחוֹד, has the meaning of "also," and the delimiting sense of "only" as well. In the Targums it is used for גַּם, and on the other hand for לְבַד, רַק, אַךְ etc. As will be shown, if at times we substitute גַּם for רַק and even vice versa, the true sense of the verse will be disclosed.

II, 28.10. To understand this verse, we should realize the circumstances that prompted the accusation. Because Judah had sinned (v. 2), Aram in alliance with Israel had attacked and defeated Judah. Israel took captive 100,000 Judahites, women and children and booty and brought the spoil to Samaria (v. 8). Oded the prophet protests and says: ועתה בני יהודה וירושלים אתם אמרים לכבש לעבדים ולשפחות לכם הֲלֹא רַק אַתֶּם עִמָּכֶם אֲשָׁמוֹת לַיי' אֱלֹהֵיכֶם: What the prophet clearly implies is this: not only is Judah a sinful people, but Israel is not to consider itself blameless: "And now you think to subdue the Judahites and Jerusalem to be bondmen and bondwomen to you; behold only with you are crimes before the Lord your God." So the Hebrew. Something seems to be wrong. Notice that the sentence cannot mean: only you are guilty before the Lord. Such a statement is clearly against the charge that the prophet wants to make. Although Israel had sinned, and was punished, Judah was equally blameworthy. We must conclude with the suggestion expressed above that the Chronicler had mistranslated לְחוֹד with רַק instead of גַּם, "also you" not "only you."

d. This state of affairs may be recognized again in another passage, albeit invertedly, where the Chronicler put down גַּם instead of רַק. Chapter 30 in II Chron. begins with an appeal sent by Hezekiah to all of Israel and Judah to reconsider their ways and return to their Lord, God of their fathers (v. 7). The messengers bringing the appeal are met with jeers and insults in Ephraim (v. 10), although some responded and came from Manasseh and Zebulun (v. 11). Then v. 12 continues: גַּם בִּיהוּדָה הָיְתָה יד האלהים לתת לָהֶם לב אחד לעשות מצות המלך והשרים כדבר יי. The translation should not be "Also in Judah was the hand of God to give them one heart, to carry out the commandment of the king and the princes by the word of the Lord." The purport of this verse plainly is that only, *only* in Judah was there singleheartedness (לב אחד) to comply with the king's command. Only with such interpretation does the context make sense.

18. Another small particle that can be troublesome and misleading in an Aramaic sentence is the prefix ל. This *Lamed* may serve all the uses of the *Lamed* in Hebrew, but in Aramaic it serves an additional function as the sign of the accusative (Hebrew את). This distinctive usage may prove a continual embarrassment and confusion to one who finds an Aramaic sentence swarming with a plethora of *Lameds*: if the translator is not wary he might mistake one usage of a *Lamed* for another. That the Chronicler did exactly this is proved, I think, from the following passages:

a. I 16.37 ויעזב שם לפני ארון ברית יי לְאָסָף וּלְאֶחָיו לשרת לפני הארון תמיד לדבר יום ביומו. As the text stands, the verse can only mean: David left there before the Ark of the Lord to Asaph and his brothers to minister before the Ark always, for the affairs of each day. Now, David did not leave it *to* Asaph and his brothers, but left (direct object) Asaph and his brothers to minister. The translator should have rendered את אסף ואת אחיו. The proof: in

v. 39 where the names continue, we have וְאֶת צָדוֹק הכהן ואחיו.
Hence we recognize a misconstruction here of the Lamed. The
translator was misled by . . . ל שבק in the Aramaic, a frequent
construction. Note moreover that ויעזב "abandon, forsake" fails
to catch the nuance of שבק meaning "leave to."

b. II, 28.13 (For the introduction to this verse, see above on
II, 28.10): The passage which runs: ויאמרו להם לא תביאו את השביה הנה
לאשמת כִּי לְאַשְׁמַת יי עלינו אתם אמרים להסיף על חטאתינו וגו' is difficult.
The whole matter is cleared up if we assume that the Chronicler
read ל wrongly; we should read אשמת את.

c. The following passages illustrate other kinds of mistranslations
of the ל:

I 26.14 ויפל הגורל מִזְרָחָה לשלמיהו וזכריהו בנו יועץ בשכל הפילו גורלות
ויצא גורלו צָפוֹנָה.
V. 15 לעובד אדום נֶגְבָּה וגו'.
V. 16 לשופים ולחסה לַמַעֲרָב.
V. 17 לְמִזְרָח הלוים שִׁשָׁה לַצָּפוֹנָה(!) ליום ארבעה לַנֶגְבָּה(!) ליום ארבעה וגו'.

There is a subtle distinction in the use of the ל here which the
Chronicler translator failed to perceive. When I say that I am
casting lots (e. g. arrows) in a certain direction, I can properly
use the terms מזרחה, צפונה etc. But when I say that I am casting
lots for a certain purpose, for the north gate, for the south gate
etc., I cannot use מזרחה, צפונה "direction towards," with the
locative ה—, but only לַצָּפוֹן, לַמִזְרָח. Now in v. 13 it is distinctly
said ויפילו גורלות . . . לשער ושער "And they cast lots . . . for each
and every gate." Further proof: when the Chronicler did not
forget himself, he translated correctly. Note v. 16 למערב, and in
v. 17 למזרח. An unavoidable conclusion is that the Chronicler
was translating an Aramaic passage. Observe also, in line with
what was said at the beginning of this paper (in re צפונה, נגבה
etc.) some new examples of impossible grammatical constructions
in v. 17 לצפונה, לנגבה (suggested by לצפונא etc. of the Aramaic)
instead of לנגב or נגבה, לצפון and צפונה.

d. In another instance where the Chronicler failed to keep the usage of the *Lamed* steadfastly in mind, he lapsed in taking the prefixed *Lamed* in the Hithpaᶜel, specifically the word להתיחש, as a direct object! To understand this fully, some preliminary explanations are necessary. In II, 31.15 we are told that certain men, apparently Levites (so v. 14) were stationed in cities of the priests (בערי הכהנים) to give portions by lots to their brothers (v. 15). This "giving of the portions" (לתת לאחיהם) extends throughout v. 19 enumeratively as follows: in v. 16 לכל הבא בית יי, in v. 18 "to all who claimed connection in children, wives, sons and daughters" וּלְהִתְיַחֵשׂ בכל טפם נשיהם ובניהם ובנותיהם in v. 19 to "the sons of Aaron, the priests who were in the suburbs of cities." In v. 19 there is a final summation לתת מנות לכל זכר בכהנים וּלְכָל הִתְיַחֵשׂ בלוים. The last phrase וּלְכָל הִתְיַחֵשׂ בלוים is especially instructive. The reader will notice that we have omitted in v. 17 וְאֵת הִתְיַחֵשׂ הכהנים לבית אבותיהם והלוים מבן עשרים שנה ומעלה וגו׳. This construction now comes under consideration. In view of the fact that portions were reckoned by genealogy in v. 18 ולהתיחש בכל וגו׳, and in v. 19 ולכל התיחש בלוים, it follows that in v. 17 where we have ואת התיחש, this is likewise dependent upon the previous ולתת, and that את התיחש must be incorrect. אֶת is a mistranslation and a misapprehension of ל, and the Hebrew translation should have been ולהתיחש like the others. Translate: and for those Kohanim that were connected through the fathers houses, and the Levites from twenty years and over etc.

e. *Per contra*, a case where the *Lamed* was retained when it should have been translated by את is seen in II, 23.1 ובשנה השביעית התחזק יהוידע ויקח את שרי המאות ולעזריהו בן ירוחם ולישמעאל בן יהוחנן ולעזריהו בן עובד. To be brief, all the *Lameds* prefixed to the proper names should have been translated with את. The proof; note first of all the anticipating את שרי המאות and then significantly, in the same sentence, the sequence of names with את: ואת מעשיהו בן עדיהו ואת אלישפט בן זכרי. It is clear that the Chronicler indecisively kept the ל in the first batch of names, then reversed himself and translated with את. This is in complete consonance with the psychology of a translator (comp. the circumstances of התיחש just previously) who, thinking that neither renderings are exactly wrong, will try to incorporate both, without realizing that his resulting text is peculiar, and is a give-away that he is translating. In our present text, if the Chronicler would have kept consistently with ל throughout, or with את throughout, his translation would have been admissible. It is his inconsistency that betrays him. To paraphrase a well known proverb, to translate is to betray, not the author, but oneself.

f. Finally, in this group of *Lameds* misinterpreted and confused must be placed the passage in II, 30.20: וישמע יי אל חזקיה וַיִּרְפָּא אֶת הָעָם. Hezekiah had prayed that Yahweh should not punish the people for having eaten the passover offering without having been purified according to ritual. Now we should *not* translate "And the Lord hearkened to Hezekiah, and healed the people." There was no healing required. The answer to our problem lies in the fact that the Chronicler mistranslated. The Aramaic ran וְאַרְפֵּי לְעַמָּא *And He let the people alone*. He did not punish them. With the wrong cue of רפי = *heal* in his mind already, the Chronicler further mistranslated לעמא as = את העם. For the construction, comp. Jastrow, *Dictionary*, s.v. רפי e.g. ארפון להון "Let them alone".

19. Another category of phenomena that indicates the Aramaic origin of large sections of the Chronicler is a number of grammatical *monstra* that are cleared away only by reference to an underlying Aramaic. In passing, it may be noticed that emendation is of no avail; commentators refrain from correcting the text, content with debiting the Chronicler with "a late Hebrew style." Consider the following passages:

I 29.17: וְעַתָּה עַמְּךָ הַנִּמְצְאוּ פֹה רָאִיתִי בְשִׂמְחָה לְהִתְנַדֶּב לָךְ. David in this public prayer of thanksgiving indirectly compliments the people for having brought such abundant gifts. The phraseology however is surpassingly strange. הנמצאו certainly is queer with עמך although plural/singular is possible. ראיתי is impossible; but רָאוּ or רָאָה as an emendation is altogether unlikely. To be brief in discussion, if we turn to the Aramaic for retroversion, we see how the peculiarities arose: וּכְעַן אוּמְתָךְ דִּי שְׁכִיחָה כָּא חֲזֵת בַּחֲדוּתָא לְהִתְנַדָּבָה לָךְ. I shall not press the point, but I think that the translator took שְׁכִיחָה as 3rd feminine plural of the perfect, when he should have taken the word as the feminine passive participle which would agree more concordantly with the feminine אוּמָתֵךְ. The forms of course are identical. However, most certainly חָזָת[13] feminine singular of the perfect was misread as חָזִית "I saw;" hence רָאִיתִי which as a personal interjection on the part of David in the verse makes for non-sense. The verse should have been probably rendered: וְעַתָּה עַמֵּךְ הַנִּמְצָא פֹּה רָאָה בְּשִׂמְחָה לְהִתְנַדֶּב לָךְ.

a. II, 25.8 כִּי אִם בֹּא אַתָּה עֲשֵׂה חֲזַק לַמִּלְחָמָה יַכְשִׁילְךָ הָאֱלֹהִים לִפְנֵי אוֹיֵב כִּי יֶשׁ כֹּחַ בֵּאלֹהִים לַעְזוֹר וּלְהַכְשִׁיל. The circumstances leading up to this verse are as follows: Amaziah, to strengthen his military forces, mustered 300,000 troops from Judah (v. 5); and further hired mercenaries from Israel to the extent of 100,000 more (v. 6). But a man of God came to him saying, O King,[14] let not the military force (צבא) of Israel come with you; God is not with Israel, all the sons of Ephraim (v. 7). The next verse is the one under discussion.

It will strike the reader at once that עשה חזק למלחמה is most peculiar syntactically. Where could this phrase come from? For emendation we are offered on the basis of the LXX and other versions אִם אַתָּה תַחְשֹׁב לַחֲזֹק בָּזֹאת, hardly very happy. Moreover יכשילך האלהים לפני אויב forms a *non-sequitur*. Assuredly the prophet does not mean to say that the king is to mobilize for war as it would be implied in the first part of this verse, because the words beginning יכשילך וג' threaten, on the contrary, punishment for a transgression of that sort.

Retrovert to the Aramaic and the difficulty clears up. The Aramaic probably ran as follows: דִי הֵן אַנְתְּ אָזֵל עֲבֵד חַיֵּל לִקְרָבָא which is what the translator read, and which produced our awkward Hebrew. He should have read much more simply: דִי הֵן אַנְתְּ אָזֵל

---

[13] Or, even a rarer form, חֲזַת as in Babylonian Aramaic (Epstein, *Dikduk* p. 95; Dalman, 342; Nöldeke, Syriac Grammar, par. 176).

[14] Incidentally, note the position of הַמֶּלֶךְ in the sentence. The Hebrew would put the word at the last e.g. II Sam. 14.4 הושיעה המלך, Jud. 3.19 דבר סתר לי אליך המלך, while the Aramaic would put המלך first in the discourse Dan. 2.4 מלכא לעלמין חיי.

עֲבֵד חַיִל לְקְרָבָא "Because if you are going to marshall an army for war, etc." אֲזַל עֲבֵד is excellent Aramaic, and by the by, another indirect index of our Aramaic hypothesis, in place of the expected אֲזַל לְמֶעְבַד. Comp. Nöldeke, *Syriac Grammar*, par. 272. It is clear that the translator took the first verb wrongly as an imperative, and likewise the second; and by virtue of taking the first two as imperatives, he fell most naturally into taking the third as an imperative as well חַיִל/חֵיל. The proof that our interpretation is correct is evidenced by the presence of צָבָא in the preceding verse; more significantly, יכשילך וגו' forms *now* a telling apodosis: "then God will cause you to fall before the enemy, because God has the power to help." Note the word כֹּחַ which in Aramaic (חֵילָא) would make a word-play on the preceding חֵיל. The whole sentence now becomes lighted up with new meaning. It becomes characteristic of prophetic utterance in advising monarchs not to depend upon military power and formation. For the idea in Chronicles, comp. II, 14.10. Translate therefore: "Because if you are going to collect an army for war, God will have you stumble before the enemy, because it is in the power of God to help or cause to stumble." The restoration yields excellent sense and continuity.

20. In this discussion of grammatical peculiarities wherein recourse must be had to the Aramaic for a satisfying explanation, we may mention the extraordinary chronology that appears in Chronicles. The appearance of the participle, for example, where we should expect the perfect or the imperfect, undoubtedly arises from the circumstances that the Aramaic participle has the enormous elasticity to be employed for the past, present, and future. The Aramaic participle possesses this character to such a degree that a narrative can be interrupted anywhere to be continued with a participle. E. g. ואתאו שטריא וְתָפְסִין לְרַבָּא. Margolis, *op. cit.*, 80; biblically, comp. Dan. 5.23 where the verbs are changed a number of times in the verse. Now to express the imperfect, the Aramaic will combine הֲוָא with the participle. There is at least one reflection of this in I, 15.25 where we read וַיְהִי דָוִיד וְזִקְנֵי יִשְׂרָאֵל וְשָׂרֵי הָאֲלָפִים הַהֹלְכִים לְהַעֲלוֹת אֶת אֲרוֹן בְּרִית יי' מִן בֵּית עֹבֵד אֱדוֹם בְּשִׂמְחָה: For the purpose of our discussion we shall treat הַהֹלְכִים = הוֹלְכִים. The

combination of וַיְהִי....הֹלְכִים must be admitted to be awry. Yet all it does is to reproduce a well authenticated Aramaic construction. While as a rule, הוא agrees with the verb, there are enough examples to show that הוא does not necessarily change; e. g. Ber. 23a כי הוה אזלינן almost exactly parallel to our instance.[15] The point is that no author would have composed such Hebrew *ab origine*.

21. Quite important for the understanding and reconstruction of the Hebrew text, and equally as a demonstration for the underlying Aramaic, are the mistranslations that are quite evident through the veil of the Hebrew. A mistranslation can be of the greatest significance because as H. L. Ginsberg has remarked on occasion "the translator's errors are not confined to inept renderings of the author's Aramaic, but extend to renderings of Aramaic expressions other than those intended by the author.[16]

a. II, 17.13 is very instructive in this regard. The preceding passage as introduction reads as follows: "And Jehoshaphat waxed great exceedingly: and he built in Judah castles and cities of store". The next verse continues: וּמְלָאכָה רַבָּה הָיָה לוֹ בְּעָרֵי יְהוּדָה ואנשי מלחמה גבורי חיל בירושלים. It is idle to translate "much work" or "many works." What kind of works were they? מלאכה as such is vague, pointless. We have to revert to the Aramaic. The *Vorlage* ran ופלחותא סגיאה הות לה בקרוי יהודה. The word פלחותא is ambiguous. To the Chronicler it looked like the familiar word for "work," hence his מלאכה. However another meaning of the word, especially in the eastern Aramaic, is "army, host;" בני פלחותא are *fellow soldiers*; רב חילא = רב פלחותא Payne-Smith, *Syriac dictionary*, s. v. פלחותא and חילא. Our verse now picks up significant pertinence and meaning, with the second part of the verse lending proper complement:

[15] Comp. Levias C., *Dikduk Aramit Bablit* [*A Grammar of Babylonian Aramaic*, N.Y. 1930], p. 288 for further exx.; also Nöldeke, *Mandäische Grammatik*, p. 284, n. 3.

[16] H. L. Ginsberg, *Studies in Koheleth*, N.Y. 1950, p. 21.

A large military he had in the cities of Judah,
And men of war, picked men, in Jerusalem.

היה may appear slightly difficult. BH[4] reports that 5 mss. read הָיְתָה.

b. Another passage that evidently does reflect an Aramaic underlying document is found in II, 26.19: "Then Uzziah was wroth; and he had a censer in his hand to burn incense; and while he was wroth with the priests, the leprosy shined forth on his forehead (וְהַצָּרַעַת זָרְחָה בְמִצְחוֹ) before the priests in the House of the Lord beside the altar of incense." In a prosy text such as Chronicles, the word זרחה seems to be most unusual and exaggerated. By this time, the reader will have surmised that the source of our difficulty comes from a mistaking of the Aramaic. And rightly so. The Aramaic ran וְצַרְעָתָא צְמַחַת בְּבֵית אַפּוֹהִי. The verb צמח in Aramaic means "grow" and "*shine*." In fact, "shine" is the more frequent meaning for the word in the Aramaic, and undoubtedly this misled our translator.

That צמח could easily be mistaken as "shine" is demonstrated by the fact that the LXX takes צמח as "shine" in a Hebrew text. Comp. Is. 4.2 צֶמַח, ʼεπιλάμψει.

Our Chronicles text should have conveyed the thought "and leprosy *sprouted* on his forehead." The unusual determinate הצרעת for צרעת (Contrast Lev. 13.9,11,12.f.) is likewise a mistranslation— a confusion of the absolute and determinate states of the Aramaic, a matter which will receive attention below.

c. In I, 22.14 we have a peculiar statement on the part of King David concerning his preparation for the building of the Temple. He says: וְהִנֵּה בְעָנְיִי הֲכִינוֹתִי לְבֵית יי׳ זָהָב כִּכָּרִים מֵאָה אֶלֶף וְכֶסֶף אֶלֶף אֲלָפִים כִּכָּרִים וְלַנְּחֹשֶׁת וְלַבַּרְזֶל אֵין מִשְׁקָל כִּי לָרֹב הָיָה וְעֵצִים וַאֲבָנִים הֲכִינוֹתִי וַעֲלֵיהֶם תּוֹסִיף: The difficulty revolves around one word בעניי. The word forms a contradiction in terms to what follows. It is grandiose humility to say that one has prepared for the house of the Lord 100,000 talents of gold, and a million talents of silver, and bronze and iron beyond weight,—all this being done בעניי "in my affliction," or "poverty" or "distress."

I think that the Chronicler translator misread here a שׂ for a שׁ i. e. בַּחֲשׁוֹכִי for בַּחֲשׂוֹכִי. In the Targums חשך in various formations is used for עָנָה, עָנִי etc. The translator was misled in his translation by the position of the word at the beginning of the verse. He should have read בַּחֲשׂוֹכִי meaning "in my conserving, in my saving." This meaning becomes most appropriate for the content of the verse that follows: through his conserving, he was able to prepare 100,000 gold talents etc.

For the peculiarity כִּי לָרֹב הָיָה, see below in the discussion of the misreadings of הוּא and הַוָא on the part of the Chronicler.

d. The text of II, 30.15, most remarkable as it is, receives elucidation when reference is made to Aramaic. The text runs; וישחטו הפסח בארבעה עשר לחדש השני והכהנים והלוים נכלמו ויתקדשו ויביאו עולות בית יי. That word נכלמו is certainly perculiar. What were the Levites and the Priests ashamed of?

Now according to II, 30.3, the reason that the Passover sacrifice had not been offered was that the priests had not prepared themselves (לא התקדשו) on *time*. This is a sore point with the Chronicler; he reverts to it on another occasion crediting the Levites for being more zealous and scrupulous in their preparations (II, 29.34). Note his remarks also about the people not being ready, and thence subsequently Hezekiah's intercession (II, 30.17 20 and v. 24!). It seems likely therefore that the Chronicler confused two roots here, חרף "do a thing early" and חפר "be ashamed," Jastrow, *Dictionary* s. v. in one or another of the grammatical forms. Our verse then is restored to its earlier and correct meaning.

e. A curious case of mistranslation, only because the Chronicler got in the habit of translating words without regard to context, and, in the present verse to be discussed because the word started the sentence, is instanced in II, 13.21 ויתחזק אביהו וישא לו נשים ארבע עשרה ויולד עשרים ושנים בנים ושש עשרה בנות:. The term התחזק in Chronicles, and indeed elsewhere, implies always that the king in question had mastered his internal difficulties, and was on his way to have his kingdom firmly established. So II, 1.1, 12.13, 17.1; II, 21.4. In what way did Abiyahu "strengthen" himself? Unless you are ready to say that he certainly must have been "strong" if he married fourteen women and had thirty-eight children!

The Aramaic had here הִתְגַּבַּר which in one of its meanings (Payne-Smith, *Dictionary* s. v. גבר) has the signification "grow to manhood, have the status of manhood," perhaps denominatively from גֶּבֶר "man." The Chronicler translated according to the more usual, frequent meaning וַיִּתְחַזֵּק. Our verse on the contrary should run: When Abiyahu grew to manhood, he married fourteen women etc.

f. Another instance of mistranslation is afforded in II, 17.3. The Chronicler describes Jehoshaphat that "God was with him, and that he walked in the first ways of David, his ancestor" כִּי הָלַךְ בְּדַרְכֵי דָוִיד אָבִיו הָרִאשֹׁנִים. It is idle to say that we should make a distinction between the "first" ways and "last" ways of David (Rashi, Ḳimḥi); such a distinction does not hold water. It is further argued that the LXX does not read here like our MT and omits "David," and therefore the "first" and "last" ways refer to the change of heart of Asa his father. The reading of the LXX might be considered significant were it not for the fact that the omission is confined to B and A recensions alone: true, the Aldina, the Complutensian, and the minor mss. do not rank with the uncials, but the reading "David" is there. Far more important is the recurrent formula wherein "David" is an integral part of the text e. g. II, 28.1 וְלֹא עָשָׂה הַיָּשָׁר בְּעֵינֵי יי כְּדָוִיד אָבִיו, II, 29.2 וַיַּעַשׂ הַיָּשָׁר בְּעֵינֵי יי כְּכֹל אֲשֶׁר עָשָׂה דָּוִיד אָבִיו:. What really took place is this: the Chronicler misvocalized his text. The Aramaic was דִי אֲזַל בְּאָרְחָתָא דִי דָוִיד אֲבוֹהִי קַדְמָיָא. He misread קַדְמָיָא singular as קַדְמָיֵא plural, making קדמיא agree with ארחתא and a peculiar text. אֲבוֹהִי קַדְמָיָא means *his ancestral father*. For the expression comp. Targum Is. 43.27 אָבִיךְ הָרִאשׁוֹן/אֲבוּךְ קַדְמָאָה. Our verse accordingly receives the natural explanation *via* the translation hypothesis: for he walked in the ways of David, his ancestral father.

g. In I, 13.2 we run into an instance where the Chronicler confused two Aramaic roots. The Hebrew passage where David opens his address to his staff of administrators reads אִם עֲלֵיכֶם טוֹב וּמִן יי אֱלֹהֵינוּ נִפְרְצָה נִשְׁלְחָה אֶל אַחֵינוּ הַנִּשְׁאָרִים. . . .וְיִקָּבְצוּ אֵלֵינוּ:. In general, the word פרץ is used very peculiarly throughout Chronicles (comp. for instance II, 20.37; 31.5; 11.23) but certainly so here. The passage must mean: if it is agreeable to you, and is acceptable with the Lord our God—; but how does נפרצה come to mean acceptable? For the word פרץ "break through, smash, shatter," the Targums use, more or less consistently, תרע. The latter was

confused with רעי (Hebrew רצה); that is to say with מִתְרָעָא and
מִתְרָעֵא as the most probable forms. The Hebrew should have been
רָצוּי.

h. Finally, in this category of mistranslations, there should be
considered the passage in I, 26.31 which deals with military conscription. Of a certain group it is said בשנת הארבעים למלכות דויד
נִדְרָשׁוּ וימצא בהם גבורי חיל ביעזיר גלעד:. The problem word is נדרשו.
It must mean in the context "they were conscripted for military
service." Note the previous verse that deals with פקדת ישראל, and
even as pointedly v. 32 וַיפקידם דויד, again demostrating the military
context.

פקד both in Hebrew and eastern Aramaic bears the signification
"inquire, seek," BDB, s. v. פקד, Is. 26.16 etc. and Payne-Smith,
Dictionary, but the verbs can mean "muster, conscript" (cf.
פְּקוּדָא, פְּקוּדִים) which somehow the Chronicler missed. He translated according to the first sense "inquire, seek," hence his נדרשו;
but he should have translated נִפְקְדוּ even הִתְפָּקְדוּ Jud. 20.15, 17.
Our sentence should have conveyed the thought—"They were conscripted in the fortieth year of David's reign; and mighty men
were found among them in Yaʿazer Gilead."

22. We come now to a different category of phenomena which
are akin to mistranslations. The latter wind up with significations
in the translated text never intended by the author, as was predicated
above. The phenomena now to be discussed are not mistranslations. They are translations that have misfired; they yield a sense
it is true, but either exaggerated or underplayed, very much the
same way as one sees oneself in a distorting mirror. The figure is
there true enough, but parts may be undersized and other parts
exaggerated and grotesque.[17]

---

[17] To illustrate my meaning through reference to another contemporary
language, I shall give one example as a demonstration of the pitfalls of bilingualism.
Nevertheless, every word is technically correct, and I dare say that if a copy of
these rules were to be found a thousand years from now, they could be defended
as specimens of correct English, for each word could be "explained" through
an associative word or semantic development.

The following are some of the traffic regulations written to assist foreigners
arriving in Tokyo:

"When a passenger on foot heave in sight, tootle your horn, trumpet at him

a. For example:

II, 29.5 "And he said unto them, 'Hear ye me, O Levites, sanctify yourselves now, and sanctify the House of the Lord, God of your fathers, והוציאו את הַגִּדָּה מן הקדש.'"

נִדָּה is a strong word. "Take the menstruous things out of the sanctuary" is excessive hyperbolizing. With due regard to parallels that might be adduced, and as to how the word might be explained by association, I should still prefer to say that the Aramaic ריחוקא underlying the word (so the Targum here) should have been more mildly and appropriately translated תועבה. Very likely however the translation should have been טומאה. Comp. v. 16 where the priests carry out the order: ויוציאו את כל הטמאה . . . ויבואו הכהנים.

b. II, 11.23 וַיֶּבֶן ויפרץ מכל בניו לכל ארצות יהודה ובנימן לכל ערי המצרות וגו'. ויבן means "he understood." The Aramaic however ויסתכל (Payne-Smith סכל) means "he dealt wisely, shrewdly," much more than ויבן conveys. His shrewdness consisted, as the verse asserts, in scattering (so apparently ויפרץ; וַיִּפָּץ?) his sons throughout the contry, in giving them abundant food, and in marrying them off,—in short, keeping them satisfied. ויבן fails to convey his adroitness.

c. II, 20.9 אם תבא עלינו רָעָה, חֶרֶב שְׁפוֹט, וְדֶבֶר וְרָעָב   וגו'. Is not חרב שפוט a most unusual phrase? Like all these peculiarities of the Chronicler, we do not meet with the phrase before or since, except perhaps where the Chronicler himself is imitated in later Jewish writings. In Lev. 26.25 we have a striking phrase חֶרֶב נֹקֶמֶת which really should have been the translation here. The Aramaic had חַרְבָּא דִי פֻרְעָנוּתָא (comp. Onkelos in the Lev. passage). One of the lexical equivalents of שפט is פרע. Note especially Ex. 5.21 ירא

---

melodiously at first, but if he still obstacles your passage, tootle him with vigor, express by word of mouth the warning 'Hai-Hai."

"Go soothingly in the grease mud for there lurks the speed demon."

"Press the breaking of the feet as you reel around the corner to save collapse and tie-up."

The Japanese, of course, enjoy the mistakes made by Americans as when they hear an American, entering an elevator, ask for "mountains and sea," they know he only wants "the third floor."

—*The Daily Compass,* Friday, May 26th, 1950, p. 9.

עליכם וישפט 'יי and the translations of the Targums of Onkelos and Jerusalem. That the Chronicler had a special liking for this phrase in Ex. is seen from the fact that he has been influenced to a similar use elsewhere in his own book I, 12.17; II, 24.22. His liking for the phrase led him to translate with שפוט. But שפוט is vague compared with the savage חרב נקמת.

d. The next example may be considered either as a real mistranslation or else a nuance which the translator failed to perceive and hence his translation went wide of the mark. In II, 29.36 we have the statement that "Hezekiah rejoiced and all the people, because of that which God had prepared for the people כִּי בְפִתְאֹם הָיָה הַדָּבָר "for the thing was done suddenly." Now it was not done suddenly, unawares. On the contrary, as we read through c. 29, we see that elaborate preparations were made. Urged on by Hezekiah himself (v. 4 ff.), the priests purified themselves (v. 15); in sixteen days they finished the task of purifying the Temple. The answer to our problem is not that the whole thing was done suddenly, unawares, but *quickly*, i. e. in sixteen days. פתאם is an inadequate translation of תְּכֵיף; or rather בְּתֵכַף incidentally, for תכיף adverbially is always prefixed with *bet* which was carried over via translation into בפתאם, a form without parallel: elsewhere the form is universally פתאם (twenty-four instances in the Hebrew Bible as against this Chronicle occurrence). תכיף means "suddenly" but also "quickly" (Jastrow s. v. תכף).

e. In II, 19.2 ויצא אל פניו misses the mark for וּנְפַק לְקַדָּמוּתֵה "There went forth to meet him." קדמותה was translated too literally. II, 32.4 ‖ ויקבצו עם רב ויסתמו את כל המעינות ואת הנחל השוטף בְּתוֹךְ הָאָרֶץ "... and the brook that flowed through the midst of the land." בתוך הארץ as a phrase is unexampled in the Hebrew Bible. We have בתוך העיר, בתוך מצרים = בתוך ארץ מצרים etc. which are different matters. It is characteristic of the Hebrew to say *only* בקרב הארץ Gen. 45.6, 48.17; Ex. 8.18; Deut. 4.5. While on the one hand we may say בקרב המחנה (Deut. 23.15, 29.11) and בתוך המחנה, the phrase בתוך הארץ is never used. The Chronicler was unthinking when translating the Aramaic בְּגוֹא אַרְעָא ‖ II, 31.10 ויאמר אליו עזריהו הכהן הראש לבית צדוק ויאמר מהחל התרומה לבוא reads בית יי אכול ושבוע והותר עד לרב כי יי ברך את עמו וְהַנּוֹתָר אֶת הֶהָמוֹן הַזֶּה:

The meaning of the verse is that since the people had brought so abundantly to the House of the Lord, a great amount (of grain) had been left over. הָמוֹן is usually "wealth" or "people," but what is implied in the verse is the great store of grain left over. סְגִיאוּתָא in Aramaic means "plentitude" which indeed was the Aramaic before the Chronicler's eyes; but סגיאותא is of such variegated meaning that המון, which is equated often with the word in the Targums, flowed naturally from the Chronicler's pen when translating. Perhaps he should have translated simply רֹב ‖ In II, 28.23, Ahaz sacrificed to the gods of Damascus וְהֵם הָיוּ לוֹ לְהַכְשִׁילוֹ וּלְכָל יִשְׂרָאֵל. The Chronicler translated too literally again, and misconstrued his word grammatically in addition. For להכשילו, he had in his text a form probably like לְתַקְלוּתָה which he read as לְתַקְלוּתֵה making a redundant suffix to the לוֹ he has already in the sentence. But furthermore, while תקל = כשל is standard lexical equivalent in the Targums, תַּקְלְתָּא, תַּקוּלָא, תַּקְלָא in the various forms are used for מוֹקֵשׁ which is the regular word that would be required for such circumstance. His translation in short should have been in the Hebrew וְהֵם הָיוּ לוֹ לְמוֹקֵשׁ וּלְכָל יִשְׂרָאֵל ‖ II, 30.5 ויעמידו דבר =, וַהֲקִימוּ פִּתְגָמָא which means they enacted an edict, a law, not they established a thing—which is very wooden: *edict* is required,— note לעשות הפסח in the verse.

23. I should like to refer now to a stylistic phenomenon which appears in the Chronicler's function as translator. This phenomenon, astonishing and incredible as it may seem, has not been in evidence before in any of the documents that are regarded by the present writer as translated, *viz.*, Daniel c. 8–12 and Qohelet.[18] The evidence shows that the Chronicler was at times uncertain whether to take *miqtal* forms as infinitives or substantives.

In Syriac, the infinitive is always preceded by ל; in the biblical Aramaic likewise; only in the (later) Babylonian Aramaic does the infinitive with and without ל appear with the omission in the minority of cases; the same is true in the Mandaic; also in the

---

[18] For some of the stylistic evidence that baffled the translator, comp. Zimmermann, *JBL*, 57, 258–272, idem, 58, 349–54; and H. L. Ginsberg in his *Studies in Daniel*, p. 41 f. and the Notes, and in his *Studies in Koheleth*, p. 16 f.

Jerusalem Talmud and Midrash.[19] We should expect the Chronicler translator to be sharply aware of the difference between למקטל and מקטל; the latter could have hardly occurred infinitivally at so early a date *in Aramaic.* Yet it is evident that the Chronicler confused the two forms in his thinking, and translated one for the other. Again, if to belabor the point, only the translation hypothesis gives a plausible explanation of what takes place. Consider the following passages:

a. I, 10.13 וימת שאול במעלו אשר מעל בײ׳ על דבר יי אשר לא שמר וְגַם לִשְׁאוֹל בָּאוֹב לִדְרוֹשׁ:. The last word is certainly peculiar, and if we were to follow the critics (comp. BH[4]) we should delete the word and with one stroke end it all. But the Syriac to which textual critics appeal is notoriously truncated in Chronicles so that the omission may mean nothing at all. An Aramaic retroversion immediately shows up the source of the difficulty וּלְחַד לְמִבְעֵא בְּבְדִין לְמִדְרַשׁ. Very plainly, the Chronicler took למדרש as an infinitive, when as a matter of correct interpretation he should have taken it as מִדְרַשׁ (noun) plus ל. The original should have run: and to have recourse to necromancers for explanation.

b. In II, 13.4*b*, 5, Abiyyah, before the battle is joined, directs his address to the King, and the hosts of Israel, and says ויאמר שמעוני ירבעם וכל ישראל: הֲלֹא לָכֶם לָדַעַת כִּי יי אלהי ישראל נתן ממלכה הלא לכם לדויד על ישראל לעולם לו ולבניו ברית מלח. The expression לדעת is askew. Translated, it can only signify, "Is it not for you to know?" or "It is indeed for you to know." But that is not what the occasion calls for in the context. What we should expect is, "You have the knowledge" i. e. you know. This meaning, however, can only be obtained if we assume that the Aramaic had לא לכון מנדע = Don't you know? But מנדע was quite peculiarly taken as an infinitive (לדעת) by the Chronicler forming the awkward Hebrew of the text.

[19] Nöldeke, T., *Syriac Grammar*, trans. by J. A. Crichton, London, 1904, p. 224; E. Kautzsch, *Grammatik des biblisch-aramäischen,* Leipzig, 1884, p. 137; M. L. Margolis, *A Manual of the Aramaic Language of the Babylonian Talmud,* Munich, 1910, p. 83; Noldeke, T., *Mandäische Grammatik,* Halle, 1875, p. 386; the statement about the Jerusalem Talmud and Midrash may easily be seen in Dalman's *Dialektproben, passim.*

c. A similar instance we meet with in II, 5.11 ויהי בצאת הכהנים
מן הקדש כי כל הכהנים הנמצאים התקדשו אין לשמור למחלקות: Translation at once discloses the difficulty: "... for all the priests that
were present had sanctified themselves, and did not keep their
course" (JV) "... and did not then wait by course" (AV). אין לשמור.
למחלקות of course is difficult; the expression receives clarification
if we are guided from the Aramaic retroversion to אין מִשְׁמָר למחלקות.
Translate: "for there was no distinction (lit. watching) for class-
divisions." The passage is to be explained exegetically that the
Kohanim and Levites had equally sanctified themselves, a matter
which incidentally was of extreme importance to the Chronicler
psychologically, and in which he found great satisfaction. Comp.
on the exegesis "Rashi."

d. In line with this apparent confusion in the translator's mind
in re infinitives and substantives is the passage in II, 35.3 ויאמר
ללוים המבינים לכל ישראל הקדושים ליי תנו את ארון הקדש בבית אשר
בנה שלמה בן דויד מלך ישראל אין לָכֶם מַשָּׂא בַּכָּתֵף' עתה עבדו את יי אלהיכם
ואת עמו ישראל:. The point of the phrase is quite clear: it is not
for you to carry the Ark on your shoulders any more.[20] We
have to hark back to the Aramaic underlying document: לֵית
לְכוֹן מִטַּל בְּכַתְפָּא. The translator thought he ought to take מטל
as a noun, possibly מְטַל; hence his מַשָּׂא. However, he should have
rendered as follows אין להם לסור Comp. v. 15 . לֹא לָכֶם לְשָׂא בַּכָּתֵף
מעל עבודתם.

e. For a most convincing instance, I should like to refer to II, 26.5
וַיְהִי לִדְרֹשׁ אלהים בימי זכריהו המבין בראות אלהים ובימי דָרְשׁוֹ את יי
הצליחו האלהים. This verse deals with the beginning of Uzziah's
reign when he still "did what was good in the eyes of the Lord."
How is one, however, to explain the combination ויהי לדרש? The
Chronicler probably had in his text וַהֲוָא מְבַעֵא = והוא מבעא[21]

---

[20] Not "it shall not be a burden on your shoulders" (AV); "there shall no more
be a burden on your shoulders" (JV); Smith-Goodspeed; it shall ... The translations all miss the force of אין לכם.

[21] The lexical equivalent of דרש is either בעא or תבע in the Pe'al (as a rule).
Apparently, תבע never occurs in the Pa'el, but בעא does although rather on the
rare side. Still, the latter does occur in the Pa'el in the biblical Aramaic Dan.

"and he sought." As usual the compound Aramaic participle may serve for the perfect. The Chronicler, however, read וַהֲוָא מִבְעֵא; and notice that the latter he took as an infinitive again: לְדְרשׁ. For other examples of this genre which will not require now any further discussion see I, 16.5 and v. 42.

24. In this connection, with a misreading of הוּא הֲוָא / , we may now refer to a verse that had received discussion in another context: I, 22.14 וּלנחשת ולברזל אין משקל כי לרב הָיָה. After אין, היה is incongruous. The Chronicler misread הוּא for הֲוָא again as above. For another instance, self-explanatory, comp. II, 20.25.

25. There are some other phenomena, now, which should receive our attention. These examples of mistranslation occur elsewhere in translation into Hebrew viz., Daniel and Qohelet. I refer to the status of the Aramaic noun which the translators miscalculatingly, wrongly reproduce, or on the other hand fail to reproduce when necessary. This confusion was occasioned by the circumstance that the determinate state גברא in the course of centuries became blurred so that גברא came to be considered as איש and האיש in translation. Another reason for the confusion arose through the fact that the Aramaic will use the determinate state sui generis, whereas Hebrew will employ the undetermined state. One instance will serve. Dan. 5.4 has a series of determinate nouns in Aramaic which in Hebrew would be undetermined idiomatically, but,— which a translator might misconstrue. In the translation into Hebrew of Daniel and Qohelet, the instances of confusion were not rare. In Chronicles this does not seem to be a blind spot on the part of the translator. He seems to have been quite aware, to have the correct bearings, when he was supposed to render איש or האיש, following the example above. To me, this seemed surprising because the translated sections in Chronicles amount to a goodly number of sentences. Nevertheless in a number of instances the Chronicler translator markedly misconceived the status of the Aramaic noun and mistranslated.

4.33 (some correct to the Pe'al) and in the Targums punctuated as such. Comp. Levy, *Chaldäisches Wörterbuch* s. v. There are other equivalents to דרש which occur in the Pa'el which are not quite precise.

a. I, 22.5   וַיֹּאמֶר דָּוִיד שְׁלֹמֹה בְנִי נַעַר וָרָךְ וְהַבַּיִת לִבְנוֹת לַיי׳ לְהַגְדִּיל לְמַעְלָה

וְהַבָּיִת. לְשֵׁם וּלְתִפְאֶרֶת לְכָל הָאֲרָצוֹת אָכִינָה נָּא לוֹ. is misrendering
of בַּיְתָא; we should have וּבַיִת. The proof: in the next verse, we have
בַּיִת withouth the article(!), and correctly for the sense.[22]

II, 11.23   ויבן ויפרץ מכל בניו לכל ארצות יהודה ובנימן . . . . ויתן
מָזוֹן לָהֶם. הַמָּזוֹן לָרֹב וישׁאל המון נשים would have been the correct
rendition. It was not mentioned previously.

II, 26.19 which we have discussed before in connection with
a mistranslation וְהַצָּרַעַת זָרְחָה בְמִצְחוֹ likewise has been determinated
wrongly. It is clear we should have וְצָרַעַת. Comp. the correct
usage Lev. 13.9 ff.

26. We have now to dwell upon another linguistic phenomenon
that appears in Chronicles in a unique fashion. This is the little
particle דִּי (the later דְּ) which at times baffled, with its idiomatic
usage, the ingenuity of the translator, and he has therefore come
up with some astonishing Hebrew. Suppose we take a hypothetical
case to show how the translator, confronted by his difficulty,
attempted to solve it. As an instance, בַּיְתָא דִּי מַלְכָּא, let us say,
is in his text and means "the palace of the king." The translator,
eclectic as he was and as every translator has to be, nevertheless,
strove to reproduce every word of his text. ביתא with its determinate ending he would have translated הבית. Similarly מלכא =
המלך. How should he translate דִי? Well, sometimes, under the
circumstances described, where he had committed his pen to paper
with the two determinates, he did not know what to do with the
word די, for there is no equivalent of די in biblical Hebrew. So he
left it out in translation! With complete confidence in his readers'
understanding he felt sure they would understand הבית המלך
means "the palace of the king."[23]

[22] I have not dwelt incidentally on the extraordinary composition of the
sentences in Chronicles, and especially with regard to word-order. The Aramaic
is freer than the Hebrew: the verb frequently appears at the end; the object may
begin the sentence as well as not; the sentences are more winding, more lengthy,
less rhythmical than the Hebrew. Certainly this "strangely worded sentence"
(Driver) very definitely reflects the Aramaic *Vorlage*, and would never have been
composed in original Hebrew.

[23] The psychology of such translation comes about through these factors
mainly: that the translator has before his eyes the copy of the original, and it

a. Consequently we need not be surprised when we run into such strange instances as I, 15.8 והנבואה עדד הנביא, meaning "the prophecy of 'Oded, the prophet." A particularly interesting instance is where the translator left out two *di's*: I, 15.27 וכנניה השר המשא השוררים "And Kenaniah, the master of the song of the singers." Another instance: I, 28.18 ולתבנית המרכבה הכרובים "the pattern of the chariot of the kerubim."

b. The translator was not altogether happy, could not be happy, in this treatment and device, of leaving out the *di* in translation. In some fashion a mean had to be discovered to reproduce this Aramaic word in his Hebrew text. How could he have this particle reflected? His solution was to employ the ל in the Hebrew as a sign of the genitival relation. He probably knew empirically that the ל (e. g. מזמור לדוד of the Psalms) could be quite serviceable in that function. But,—this could work in some cases but not in all. A few examples will suffice to show how such employment of the ל is incongruous; it puts us indirectly on the track of translation again. For example, the Eastern Aramaic has a frequent idiomatic expression with דְלָא to express *without*: e. g. דלא לבא

---

is rarely possible for him, *all the time,* to disassociate himself from his newly translated text, off and alone, to see how it would look were his original not present, or how it would appear to the eyes of other persons. Secondly, if he knows that the original is extant and well known, and his translation is not to replace but to be co-equal with the original, since Jews did know Aramaic, he may allow himself a translator's license to do things ordinarily not permitted. I have not mentioned anything about the standards of the age for translation, the translator's own competence, his knowledge of Hebrew and Aramaic vocabulary, of syntax and the like. He knew too that his work was to a large measure a duplication of Samuel-Kings.

The processes of mistranslation anciently at work have been repeated in modern times. I cite the following instance: in E. Schürer's, *The Jewish People in the Time of Jesus Christ,* Eng. trans. II, vol. 2, 1885, p. 32 there is mentioned one "Antigonus von Socho." The translator working in the German, and no doubt in the midst of all the "vons," unconsciously thought that Antigonus von Socho must have been a name,—like von Hindenburg. It is not beyond the unconscious to commit a 2000 year old anachronism! "von Socho" can only be perpetrated by one who has the German text in front of her. She recovered herself, however, a few lines down (see note) with Antigonus of Socho without realizing of course the error she made a few lines before.

"without understanding," דלא חובא "without affection." Biblically
comp. דִי־לָא שָׁלוּ Ezr. 6.9 and the like., The ד here is so singularly
Aramaic that reproduction by ל will only create a puzzling Hebrew.
Yet our translator tried his hand at it, and therefore we get
for an example II, 15.3 וימים רבים לישראל ללא אלהי אמת וללא כהן
מורה וללא תורה as a star illustration of Hebrew not heard before
or since. For other examples of this sort, comp. II, 20.25 לאין משא;
I, 21.3 is a different kind of instance of how the translator handled
the ד.

27. In the light of the evidence presented, and the material
which the reader has now become familiar with, I should like
to offer a number of connected passages which will show, as I
believe, that the phenomena presented are not occasional, isolated
and casual, but form part of the very character of translation.
Thus I, 9.26: כִּי בֶאֱמוּנָה הֵמָּה אַרְבַּעַת גִּבֹּרֵי הַשֹּׁעֲרִים הֵם הַלְוִיִּם וְהָיוּ עַל
הַלְּשָׁכוֹת וְעַל הָאֹצְרוֹת בֵּית הָאֱלֹהִים. The Aramaic behind the Hebrew
in this verse ran as follows: דִּי בְהֵימָנוּתָא אִנּוּן אַרְבְּעַת גִּבָּרַיָּא דִּי תַרְעַיָּא
אִנּוּן לֵוָיֵא. A number of observations are to be made: 1. באמונה, as
was explained previously, has nothing to do with "faithfulness"
but is a *quid pro quo* for הימנותא "stewardship, office." Translate:
Because this was the function of the four "valiants." 2. The translator misunderstood the *di* in the Aramaic. He should have taken
it as a subordinate conjunction "as, because," not as a sign of the
construct to the following תרעיא. This part of the verse should
now be translated: because the gatekeepers were Levites. 3. It
follows that the translator prefixed the determinate ה wrongfully
in front of הלוים. The word should have been left undetermined
"Levites" not "the Levites." The two sources of confusion i. e.
the mixing up or misinterpretation of לוי as a determinate instead
of absolute for translation in the Hebrew, and misapprehension
of the particle *di*, led to the isolated, disjointed phrase הם הלוים
in the verse 4. Note also that the latter part of the verse contains
a number of constructs which the translator misconstrued de-
terminately: על הלשכות ועל האוצרות בית יי.

a. The passage in II, 14.10 may be elucidated through the sum
of interpretations secured previously. The text reads: ויקרא אסא
אֶל יְיָ אלֹהָיו וַיֹּאמַר יְיָ אֵין עִמְּךָ לַעְזוֹר בֵּין רַב לְאֵין כֹּחַ . . . אַל יַעְצֹר עִמְּךָ

אֱנוֹשׁ: The clause אין עמך לעזור is most peculiar to use with reference to God. Literally, it means "No one is with you to help." To get out of the difficulty, we must translate to make sense: O Lord, there is none besides thee to help (Smith-Goodspeed: Leroy Waterman) which however is reading into the Hebrew an esoteric syntax. The Aramaic hypothesis would propose as follows: לָא אִתַּי לְוָתָךְ מִסְתַּיַּע. לְוָת is employed equally as a rendering of אֶל and עִם in the Targums. It likewise should have been rendered here אֵלֶיךָ not עִמְּךָ. The Aramaic word behind לעזר is the lexical equivalent already mentioned מִסְתַּיַּע. But again the translator misrendered twice. In the first place, עזר means "help" and what we require here is "mobilize (army, troops)"; then again, the translator took מסתיע as if it were an infinitive! He took it as a *miqtal* form (= infinitive for him). To be brief, the Hebrew should have expressed something like this: no one can mobilize (array troops) against Thee. I strongly suspect that כֹּחַ in the sequence is also a misrendering of חַיְלָא "army." "With a large or no army" is simply hyperbole,—a rhetorical exaggeration that is extant retrospectly in the Hebrew text. The mistranslations that succeed one another here arise only as a result of the first misrendering that carries in its train the sequence.

יַעְצֹר is easily to be explained, as was intimated under the discussion of עצר = I מצי "be able" and II מצי = press, squeeze, as a wrong rendering of II for I.

28. In summing up the results of this study, the question that we should ask ourselves is: in what sections or chapters did the Chronicler make use of an Aramaic document? A conspectus of Chronicles and the chapters in which Aramaic idioms and mistranslations occur will indicate some conclusions: numbers beside chapters indicate the number of mistranslations:

Chronicles I		Chronicles II	
1	19	1	19 1
2	20	2 2	20 5
3	21 1	3	21
4 1	22 4	4	22 1
5 1	23	5 1	23 1

Chron. I		Chron. II	
6	24	6	24 2
7	25	7	25 1
8	26 3	8 2	26 3
9 2	27	9	27
10 1	28 1	10	28 5
11	29 2	11 3	29 4
12 4		12	30 5
13 3		13 4	31 4
14		14 2	32 2
15 4		15 1	33 1
16 4		16	34 1
17		17 3	35 1
18		18	36

29. The conspectus shows the distribution of the mistranslations, and how more deeply dyed, Aramaically speaking, some sections are over others. Apparently, the Chronicler made use of his Aramaic source more sparingly at first; we do not get four mistranslations (or translations) until I, 12. In II Chron. beginning with c. 28 through 31 he depended quite heavily upon his document. Perhaps his sources were fuller as he was approaching his own times.

30. In sum, there are some 90 instances of good evidence. The tell-tale clues in our sleuthing have been quite ample and pronounced, so that ingenuity was not strained to uncover what was in evidence all the time. There is no question that more and more students will add considerably to further our knowledge in this direction.

7

Complexion of the Document Underlying Ezra-Nehemiah

If Chronicles and Ezra-Nehemiah be one book, one composition, as tradition and the Masora transmit, and as it is agreed preponderantly by modern scholarship (EB, I, 763), then Ezra-Nehemiah like Chronicles should manifest marks of translation. Ezra-Nehemiah is written in the two languages of Hebrew and Aramaic. It is axiomatic again that an author would not write but in one language. An attempt will be made to indicate the evidence below for an underlying document in Aramaic, but one prefatory remark may be made. Probably the intent of the translator was to translate all of Ezra, just as he executed the translation of the material throughout Chronicles with an unflagging patriotic motive. One important consideration deterred him. The royal documents in Aramaic emanating from the authority of the Persian monarch should be kept, he thought, in the original language, and not be rendered into Hebrew. A translation would destroy the original character of the document and render it suspect. A further sense led him to keep in Aramaic the introductory statements transiting to the documents proper, the intrigue and crisis in the Temple construction, with the royal promise and fulfillment. Other matters as the annulment of foreign marriages, the new covenant, the "canonization" of the Pentateuch should be translated into Hebrew, as they touched and shaped the religious practice of the people.

The first indication that an Aramaic document underlies the Hebrew of Ezra-Nehemiah is the presence of Aramaic words in the Hebrew text. Thus Neh. 3.15 reads, "And the foundation gate repaired Shallun, the son of Col-hozeh, the ruler of the district of Mizpah; he built it, and covered it, and set up the doors thereof, and the bars thereof. . . ." For the word "covered" the text has the Aramaic וַיְטַלְלֶנּוּ. In the refrain-like pericope in the chapter, the phrase used previously is (v. 3) הֵמָּה קֵרוּהוּ וַיַּעֲמִידוּ דַלְתוֹתָיו.... and so v. 6. While capable of a number of interpretations, the word קרוהו must mean "they covered it with beams" (BDB, 900). וִיטַלְלֵנוּ, however, is pure Aramaic, never Hebraized. It means "cover", and is a regular equivalent of סכך in the Targums, cf. 1 Kings 6.9 וטלל ית ביתא; Jer. 22.14, employed for ספון, טללא/סכה Ps. 27.5, and likewise in the Peshitta as a noun employed for סכה, Jon. 4.5; Lev. 23.34. Because the translator made use of טלל in his daily Aramaic languages, he inserted in his translation what he saw in the Aramaic *Vorlage*.

He followed through with the same habit in Ezra 8.35. The text reads there צפירי חטאת where צְפִירֵי is simply Aramaic for שְׂעִירֵי. The same incorporation into the Hebrew text is found in the translation Hebrew of Dan. 8.5.8 (p. 9).

Unusual is the word הַנְּבִיאָה "the prophetess" in the text of Neh. 6.14 where the passage reads, "Remember, O my God, Tobiah and Sanballat according to these their works, and also the prophetess Noadiah, and the rest of the prophets that would have put me in fear". The mention of a prophetess in this connection is certainly surprising (Bertholet), and if we were to follow Ehrlich an impossibility altogether as Noadiah is a masculine name. Comp. Ezra 8.33. Ibn Ezra unhesitatingly identifies the prophetess with a prophet, the one of v. 10, who is named there as Shemayah b. Delayah with the following maladroit observation, "It is the consensus of commentators that this is Shemayah b. Delayah, and he is called so because of the statement 'Let us convene to the House of the Lord'. And the word 'prophetess' here [sc. takes the feminine form] because of the word Noadiah, which is feminine by attraction, and is not according to the substance of the matter . . . and to say that Noadiah is a woman who prophesied against him is false . . . and the word *we-gam* is epexegetical to Shemayah".[1] The word נביאה can be explained on other and much more simple grounds. Do not scholars recognize that the נביאה that confronts

---

[1] His observations are formulated in modern terms. The relevant passages read:
הסכמת המפרשים שהוא שמעיה בן דליה וקרא כן בעבור שאמר נועד אל בית אלהים שמלת הנביאה באה על דרך תיבת נועדיה שהוא כטעם נקבה בדבר ואיש על דרך הענין. . . . ולאמר כי נועדיה אשה התנבאה עליו שקר הוא . . . ומלת גם לנועדיה לרבות על שמעיה.

them is an Aramaic form? The determinate form נביאה in the under-lying Aramaic text looked like a feminine form to the Hebrew translator (for the precise form with *He*, comp. Ezr. 5.1; 6.14), and accordingly he reproduced mechanically this masculine determinate form with הנביאה, a feminine form externally in the Hebrew.

The plural פחוות is another sign of the fact that there is an Aramaic text substrate to our present Hebrew. In Hebrew the plural of פחה is פחות, 1 Kings 20.24; Jer. 51.23; Ez. 23.6.12.23; with suffixes. Jer. 51.28.57 (*paḥatu*, pl. *pa-ḥa-a-ti*), which the translator in Neh. when he does not forget himself writes according to the rule (Neh. 5.15). In Aramaic however the plural is פַּחֲוָתָא Dan. 3.2.3.27 and Targum to 2 Chron. 9.14, with the Hebraized plural פַּחֲוֹות. But notice that this plural is found only in translation Hebrew, Neh. 2.7.9; Ezr. 8.36. It is the suggestiveness of the Aramaic text that cued the formation of the Hebrew.

As another example of this genre, one expression because it was misunderstood was incorporated bodily into the Hebrew and then misvocalized. Neh. 2.16 runs: והסגנים לא ידעו אנה הלכתי ומה אני עשה וליהודים ולכהנים ולחרים ולסגנים וליתד עשה המלאכה עד כֵן לא הִגַּדְתִּי. Rashi, very acutely, emends the text tacitly (עַד עַתָּה) but indirectly provides the clue for the solution. The Aramaic text ran: עַד כֵּן "until now". The Aramaic word need not be written with Aleph, Dalman, *Aramäische Grammatik*[2], 258. Embodied in the text, the Masora had no choice but to vocalize כֵן since כָּן was or would be an Aramaic word. Translate the passage now, "And the rulers knew not where I went or what I did, and *until now* I had not told it to the Jews" etc.

The way some particles are employed also betray their Aramaic origin. In Ezr. 3.12 we find the combination זה הבית with the demonstrative preceding, whereas the norm is בית זה or הבית הזה. It is clear that this reflects the Aramaic דנה ביתא or דין ביתא, which the translator reflected following the order of his Aramaic text.

The Aramaic will also deploy the demonstrative particle with a proper name which the Hebrew does not have. Comp. Nöldeke, *Syriac Grammar*, par. 227. Palestinian Jewish Aramaic will say, "There is a story about a man from Jerusalem who went to Athens", להדא אתינס, or "Diocletian used to be a swineherd in Tiberias",

בהדא טיבריא lit. "in this Athens", "in this Tiberias", Dalman, *Dialektproben*, pp. 16, 22. Aramaic functionalizes the demonstrative הוא in a similar fashion. It is a demonstrative for ordinary nouns. Cf. הוא צלמא Dan. 2.32 "that image". In Ezr. 7.6 we find the phrase הוא עזרא which perforce has to be rendered "this Ezra" or more simply and idiomatically "Ezra". The phrase is found in translation Hebrew again in 2 Chron. 33.23 הוא אמון 1 Chron. 26.26 הוא שלמות ibid. 27.6 הוא כניהו See p. 85. There seems to be an analogous use in Greek with the development of the demonstrative pronoun *ho* in the usage with proper names. Quite obviously however if the Aramaic permits the demonstrative with names, and Hebrew does not countenance its usage, the conclusion about הוא עזרא must be that the phrase points to an Aramaic origin, and was simply copied in the Hebrew text.

The particle די, especially in its function as the particle of relation in the construct, is a difficult word for the translator. It quite baffles his ingenuity to render in an adequate fashion. Thus if we were to take a hypothetical example, say ביתא די מלכא he would translate ביתא with הבית, מלכא with המלך, but how would he express the particle די? He does a most surprising thing, but understandable in his helplessness. He leaves out די in the translation with the utmost confidence that his reader will understand that הבית המלך means "the house of the king". This explains certain phenomena in the book of Chronicles as 2, 15.8 והנבואה עדד הנביא meaning "the prophecy of Oded the prophet"; an extraordinary one at I, 15.27 וכנניה השר המשא המשוררים "And Kenaniah, the master of the song of the singers" wherein the translator left out the two *di*s. Comp. p. 137. The same phenomenon we find in the book of Ezra. Thus in 8.21 הנהר אחוא "the river Aḥawa", cf. the correct expression at v. 31; similarly in v. 29 הלשכות בית יי׳ "chambers of the house of the Lord", emended usually to לשכות (BH ad loc.); 9.1 העם ישראל "the people of Israel", and in Neh. 1.2 היהודים הפליטה "the remnant of the Jews".

In another direction, the prepositional Lamed furnishes a substantial amount of confusion to the translator. The particle, among its usages, may serve as a mark of the direct object in Aramaic like the Hebrew את, as well as a sign of the dative case (dative of reference, dative of ownership, the ethical dative) as well as the indirect object. The syntactical usage of the Lamed fluctuates widely in Ezra-Nehemiah, as well as in Chronicles, via the translation medium. A clear cut instance of misapprehension of the Lamed particle is found in Neh. 8.7 where the passage runs: וישוע ובני . . . . והלוים מבינים את העם לתורה . . . Perforce we must translate: Also Jeshua, and Bani . . . and the Levites caused the people to understand the Law . . . (JV). It must be clear, however, that the passage must run in the Hebrew: והלוים מבינים לעם את התורה. The translator misapprehended his Aramaic which in all likelihood read ולויא מסברין לעמא לאוריתא. Clearly the translator did not comprehend the syntax of the two Lameds wherein the first should have been taken indirectly, and the second one as a direct object. Comp. the instructive ex. in Margolis, p. 78 "Teach your sons the Torah".

There are a number of examples where the translator's hand betrays itself in the incompetent handling of tense. The Aramaic as mentioned elsewhere (p. 20) has its own idiosyncracy in the deployment of the participle. Without any regard to the temporal mode antecedently, the Aramaic may stop abruptly in a narrative and without further ado employ the participle for the present or future. It may employ the participle in a long connected passage where the tense would obviously be aorist. The participle will also combine with the auxiliary verb *hawa* to express the simple preterite, or a continuous passage of time. For a misuse of syntactical rule, we may look at a passage in Neh. 3.26: . . . והנתינים היו ישבים בעפל According to the text we must translate, "And the Nethinim were dwelling" or "used to dwell", although we perceive that the preterite "they dwelt" would be the most proper interpretation, and so indeed the Jewish Version; the RSV emends, and translates by the present participle "living", while the American translation sticks to the text "were living". But as indicated, the Aramaic participle combines with *hawa* in many instances to form but a simple preterite = ישבו. Manifestly, the translator copied word for word which in Aramaic would be correct, but altogether awry in the Hebrew. In Neh. 11.21, we have the parallel והנתינים ישבים בעפל where we must translate again "And the Nethinim *dwelt* in Ophel", and so the Jewish Version correctly. The translator again failed to seize upon the correct temporal nuance of the oscillating Aramaic participle. He saw יתבין and should have rendered ישבו.

The non-sequitur in tenses is further exemplified in the Hebrew of Ezr. 10.6 where in the series of four imperfects with the Waw Conversive the verse ends with a participle: כי מתאבל על מעל הגולה where התאבל would be the norm. מתאבל again simply represents the fluctuating usage of the Aramaic participle.

As another example of this genre which carries within itself both an awkward construction of tense, and a mistranslation as well, we may glance at Ezr. 10.19: וַיִּתְּנוּ יָדָם לְהוֹצִיא נְשֵׁיהֶם וַאֲשֵׁמִים אֵיל צֹאן עַל אַשְׁמָתָם "And they gave their hand that they would put away their wives, and being guilty (they offered) a ram of the flock for their guilt". Batten, *Ezra and Nehemiah*, 349 thinks that the verse requires editing, and emends "I appointed", presumably ואשימם though he does not spell out the Hebrew which anyway is inapposite and unHebraic (appoint an offering?). Kuenen conjectures ואשמם "and their guilt-offering" and apparently this emendation is followed by the American and RSV translations: "And their guilt-offering was a ram of the flock for their guilt". The JV, following apparently the older Revised Version, has added the words (they offered) in parentheses; Torrey, acutely, "they fined". Patently, ואשמים as a sequel to ויתנו at the beginning of the verse, is completely askew by all the rules. With the observations about the participle as set forth above, it is clear that ואשמים represents the Aramaic וְחָבִין.[2] As a participle with its shifting temporal function, it should have been translated as an aorist.

In addition, it was mistranslated. חב, while having the meaning of "sin" in Aramaic, bears as well the signification of "be liable, responsible" in the sense of being required to fulfill a duty or obligation. The passage therefore should be translated, "And they pledged themselves to divorce their wives, and they held themselves liable for a ram of the flock for their transgression." חב incidentally may take a direct object, which would be quite the syntactical rule in Aramaic, but hardly so for אשם in the Hebrew.[3]

---

[2] אשם/חב Targum Lev. 4.13.22.27; אשם *ashem*/חיב Gen. 42.21.
[3] אשם actually is a stative verb as its form evidences.

The translator, as remarked, was not completely at home in some idiomatic usages of particles. Mention was made of his trouble with *di / de* (supra p. 136 f. and see p. 154 for *hen*). In Onqelos and the Jerusalem Targum, a compound such as בדיל meaning both "because" and "on account of", as well as other compounds, Dalman, *Grammatik*[2] 237 might prove to be a source of confusion. Thus, if two *bedil*s should follow one another, the translator might insensibly render both the same way. He did this in Neh. 6.12.13:

וָאַכִּירָה וְהִנֵּה לֹא אֱלֹהִים שְׁלָחוֹ כִּי הַנְּבוּאָה דִּבֶּר עָלַי וְטוֹבִיָּה וְסַנְבַלַּט שְׂכָרוֹ לְמַעַן
שָׂכוּר הוּא לְמַעַן אִירָא וְאֶעֱשֶׂה כֵּן וְחָטָאתִי וְהָיָה לָהֶם לְשֵׁם רָע לְמַעַן יְחָרְפוּנִי.

The translation would run as follows, "And I discerned and behold, God did not send him; for the prophecy he spoke concerning me, Tobiah and Sanballat had hired him. In order (?) that he be hired, so that I be afraid; and were I to do thus, then would I fail;[4] then it would be for them (!) an evil reputation so that they might calumniate me".

It is clear that the translator rendered one particle wrongly, and put the whole verse out of kilter.

1. In Aramaic בדיל אדחל was translated correctly as למען אירא.[5]

2. Because the translator had in his mind's eye to translate למען אירא/בדיל אדחל i.e. *bedil* with the Imperfect (Dalman, 237), he translated the first *bedil* likewise, but wrongly. He should have rendered with *ki* "because he was hired", not "so that he be hired" as is extant in the Hebrew with its poor and awkward sense. For *lahem / li* (!), as a circumlocution, and so in effect the Greek here, cf. Driver, *Notes . . . on Samuel*[2], 199. [6]

---

[4] "Miss" Job 5.24; Prov. 19.2. Comp. BDB s.v.

[5] למען/בדיל ד(י) Gen. 18.19 passim.

[6] In 1 Sam. 3.13, the change takes the form of a Tikkun Soferim, comp. *Mekilta* c. 12 where they are enumerated although there are variations; comp. F. Buhl, *Canon and Text of the Old Testament*, English translation, p. 103–04. It is well known however that the Hebrew or Aramaic speaker will alter the idiom if he has occasion to refer to something unfavorable about himself. In the Bible 1 Sam. 25.22 "May God do to the enemies of David . . ." where David refers to himself. In the rabbinic literature these ideas are likewise met with, Dalman, *Grammatik*[2], 109. Similarly *Midrash Ekah* on 1.4, "She said to him, 'The father of that man (yourself) could not procreate. Did not that woman (I, myself) do right that she went and fornicated and brought you into the world so that you inherit this property?'", Dalman, *Dialektproben*[2] p. 18.

There are quite a number of mistranslations in Ezra-Nehemiah. The translator knew more Aramaic than Hebrew, otherwise he would not have permitted himself that kind of Hebrew defiant of meaning, etymology, and syntax. But matter-of-factly, he is no more abnormal than any of the Greek translators. Just as a Greek translator will confuse roots, misconstrue the syntax, assign meanings to words they never have, or gloss over difficulties that he does not know how to handle, or skip a strange word in the Hebrew because he does not know it, or paraphrase, or fail to provide the proper vocalization, so does the Hebrew translator from the Aramaic all too often suffer from the same frailties. Some of these mistranslations are slight but quite evident; others show how much the translator betrays himself; still others are of the greatest significance, for the retroversion to the substrate Aramaic casts a completely new light on the meaning and structure of the verse.

Thus it is quite evident that a mistranslation occurs in Neh. 12.43 where the passage reads: וַיִּזְבְּחוּ בַיּוֹם הַהוּא זְבָחִים גְּדוֹלִים. If we translate literally as the Jewish Version has it, "And they offered great sacrifices that day", it will be undisputed that the size of the sacrifices is the last intent of the verse's description, to say nothing of the fact that the locution and the idea are found nowhere else. גדולים is simply a mistranslation of שגיאין which means both big in size and *many*. The phrase should have been translated as זבחים רבים.

There are two instances where the translator misrendered the Aramaic קם. This Aramaic word doubles in meaning for "stand up" and "stand", whereas the Hebrew uses two separate words for those significations: עמד means "stand" while קם means only "rise". Comp. p. 112 f. Because the latter in the Aramaic and Hebrew forms are identical in appearance but not in meaning, the translator will confuse at times the one with the other. Thus 7 times in the Bible, incidentally in translation Hebrew only, the locution "stand in one's place" is extant as ויעמדו על עמדם, עמד על עמדם, עמד על עמדך etc.[7] However in one instance our translator forgot himself and rendered וַיָּקוּמוּ עַל עָמְדָם Neh. 9.3. That this is a mistranslation is shown by the antecedent ויעמדו in the previous v. 2; that is, they had already been standing;

---

[7] Dan. 8.18; 10.11; Neh. 9.3; 13.11; 2 Chron. 30.16; 34.31; 35.10.

they did not rise again. The Aramaic read most likely וקמו על מקמהון.
He misconstrued the sense of the same קם again in Neh. 9.4 (perhaps under the influence of his previous (mis) translation of
v. 3):וַיָּקָם עַל מַעֲלֵה הַלְוִיִּם not "There arose (!) on the stairs Jeshua.
. . . etc." With the sense of what this text demands, the American
translation and the RSV translate "stood", but the Jewish Version
following the masoretic text renders "stood up" despite the in-
congruity.

A number of passages offer the strange unHebraic phrase הֹשִׁיבוּ
נָשִׁים נָכְרִיּוֹת "They married foreign women", Ezr. 10.2.10.14.17.18,
Neh. 13.23.27, the dissolution of which marriages both Ezra and
Nehemiah took measures to carry through. The expression has
not been employed before or since in the Hebrew, the ordinary
locution being לקח אשה, נשא אשה. If recourse be had to the Aramaic
however, the phrase becomes understandable. יתב אנתתא in the
Haf'el "marry a wife" is instanced in Mandaic literature[8] (Nöldeke,
Mandäische Grammatik, 361), as well as in Syriac (Payne Smith,
199; Brockelmann, *Lexicon* 312). The translator reproduced
hebraice the Aramaic expression in the document before him.

Neh. 2.1 contains the phrase לא הייתי רע לפניו, literally, "I was
not bad before him", although it is supposed to mean "I was not
sad". Actually the whole intent of the passage is so to portray
Nehemiah that in his capacity as cupbearer to the king, he maintained a cheerful countenance and disposition, and that he was
never *ill-favored*. The Aramaic expressed this by לא הוית באיש
קדמוהי. The vocalization should have been *be'ish / ba'esh* "ill-
favored" which the Hebrew translator read or interpreted as *be'ish*
meaning "bad".[9] In addition, when we retrovert to the Aramaic,
there appear a number of wordplays in v. 2. The passage runs: ויאמר
לי המלך מדוע פניך רעים ואתה אינך חולה אין זה כי אם רע לב ואירא
הרבה מאד. It would now appear that 1), פניך רעים = אפיך בישין;

---

[8] Comp. T. Nöldeke. *Mandäische Grammatik*, 361; C. Brockelmann, *Lexicon
Syriacum*, 312 has another reference for a Syriac usage. His other exx. seem to be
based upon the Peshitta translation of הושיב אשה where these passages occur in
Ezra and Nehemiah.

[9] Both the active and passive forms may be elastic enough to comprehend
both meanings of "ill favored" and "bad".

2. חולה = ביש;[10] 3. רע לב = ביש לבא cf. ביש גדא "unlucky".
Accordingly in the verse, רע appears each time in a different connotation, with a different significance. Thus, the first phrase means:
you do not look physically sick; the third phrase: you must have a
malignity, a desire to do evil, in your heart. For these variegated
meanings of באש, and hence in the underlying Aramaic a characteristic wordplay, comp. Brockelmann, *Lexicon*, 57. In this connection,
note the syntax of אשר in v. 3 where it introduces a participial clause
very much like the usage of the Syriac *kad* (kedi) and where we
should translate: Why should not my countenance be sad and the
city, the place of my fathers' sepulchers being waste, and the gates
thereof consumed with fire?

This misunderstanding of *b̄ish* again occurs in Neh. 2.10 and
we should translate; "And when Sanballat the Horonite, and
Tobiah, the Ammonite military man (Aramaic plḥ') heard of it,
they were very displeased that a man should come and seek the
welfare of the children of Israel. The phrase is וירע להם רעה גדולה
and it should not be rendered "They were deeply hurt" (Moffatt)
or "It grieved them exceedingly" (Jewish version) but as RSV "They
were displeased", *aramaice* וּבָאֵיש לְהוֹן בִּישׁוּתָא שַׂגִּיאָה. Comp. p. 56.

Seemingly a problematic word with the translator is the Aramaic
word קוריא. It is philologically associated with the Hebrew קריה
"city" but the Aramaic goes its own way in evolving the meaning
of the environs of a city, the surrounding country of the city.
Thus the Peshitta to Mt. 13.24; 19.20 renders *agros* by קוריא.[11]
For other exx. comp. the lexica of Payne Smith and Brockelmann,
and see Luke 8.27 and 9.10 for confusions between "city" and
"open country". Now it is quite apparent that the translator in
Ezr.-Neh. confused these meanings on a number of occasions. The
settlement at Jerusalem was quite small at first (Neh. 7.4) and much
time passed before the Temple was built, and the wall repaired and

---

[10] ביש means "ill". Comp. on Gen. 35.8, *Targ. Yerushalmi* II למבקרא ית בישיא
"to visit the sick"; *Qoh. Rabba* to 4.6 ומפלגא לבישיא "And she distributes (the
apples) among the sick".

[11] Other passages are: קריתא/*agros* Mark 5.14; 10.29; 15.21; Luke 17.7. Comp.
O. Klein, *Syrisch-griechischen Wörterbuch zu der vier kanonischen Evangelien*,
Giessen, 1916.

fortified. Yet we are persistently told that the people would go back to their cities, *'arim*, certainly an incongruous description of affairs. AV, JV, following the Greek *polesin* translate (Ezr. 2.70) cities . . . cities, and (3.1) cities; RSV: towns . . . towns . . . towns, idem, Moffatt. The Cambridge New English Bible renders *suburbs* . . . towns . . . towns. The related apocryphal Esdras 5.46 has *country* . . . villages . . . *place* (*chora* . . . *komais* . . . *en tois idiois*); Hartom in *Ketubim Aḥronim*, 107 *'erez* . . . *kefar* . . . *'ir*. Some commentators therefore assume that "cities" should not be taken literally.[12] The proper and satisfying explanation is that the translator misapprehended the word קוריא which as indicated has two distinct meanings of "city" and "farm/field". Accordingly, Ezra 3.1 should be translated as follows, "And when the seventh month was come, the children of Israel being on their "farms" (*not* "in their cities"), then the people gathered together as one man to Jerusalem". And similarly Ezr. 2.70, "So the priests and the Levites, and some of the people (Aramaic locution), and the singers and the porters and the Nethinim dwelt in their fields-and-farms and all Israel on their fields-and-farms".

In Neh. 10.38, we have again this misunderstanding of קוריא. The passage reads, "And that we should bring the first of our dough, and our heave-offerings, and the fruit of all manner of trees, the wine and oil to the priests, and to the chambers of the house of our God; and the tithes of our lands to the Levites; for they, the Levites, take the tithes in all the *cities* of our work" (ערי עבדתינו). The latter phrase "cities of our work" certainly strikes one as strange. The Levites picked up the tithes that were due them on the spot, and indeed this is made manifest by the verse itself "bring . . . tithes of our land to the Levites". The reader will now surmise that the last part of our verse should read, "For they the Levites take the tithes in all the fields of our work", i.e. שדי עבדתינו. The translator should not have rendered by "cities".

Quite interesting for the proof of translation is the verse in Ezra 3.10 where the text reads: ויסדו הבנים את היכל יי' ויעמידו הכהנים מלֻבָּשִׁים בַּחֲצֹצְרוֹת והלוים בני אסף כמצלתים וג'.The translation would

---

[12] "איש לעירו ist nicht wörtlich zu nehmen" (Bertholet).

run, "And when the builders laid the foundation of the Temple of the Lord, they set the priests in their apparel with trumpets, and the Levites, the sons of Asaph with cymbals, to praise the Lord according to the direction of David, king of Israel" (Jewish Version). The translators of JV did the best they could, but it will be conceded that the phrase מלבשים בחצצרות lit. "clothed in trumpets" (!) is most extraordinary. The Peshitta gives us, at any rate, the required meaning "clothed and *holding* the trumpets". Now E. Nestle in his *Marginalien und Materialien*, 24 had made the observation that the text in 2 Chron. 35.2 where the Hebrew reads ויעמד הכהנים על משמרותם ויחזקם לעבודת בית יי׳, the Greek reads . . . kai katischusen autous   that is ויחזקם is correctly taken in the sense of "encourage". The counterpart of this verse in Greek Ezra, he goes on to remark, reads (1.2) estolismenous taking ויחזקם in the Aramaic (Syriac) sense of "arrayed, appareled". (*stole* is employed for לבוש in Gen. 49.11; Es. 6.8.11; Is. 63.1; similarly *stolizo* Es. 8.15; 4.4; 6.9.) It is a reasonable hypothesis therefore that in the back of our Hebrew מלבשים of our Ezra text there was this Aramaic word מחזקים. However, our Hebrew translator, instead of rendering by מלבשים "appareled", should have taken the verb in the other sense. He should have vocalized (Aramaic) *maḥzeqin* "holding", cognate Hebrew *maḥziqim*. We have immediately an unforced natural portrayal of the circumstances: the priests were *holding* the trumpets in their hands while the Levites were holding the cymbals to praise the Lord. The Aramaic is again the key.

Equally cogent as an example of mistranslation is the text in Neh. 3.34. The Hebrew passage runs: וַיֹּאמֶר לִפְנֵי אֶחָיו וְחֵיל שֹׁמְרוֹן וַיֹּאמֶר מָה הַיְּהוּדִים הָאֲמֵלָלִים עֹשִׂים הֲיַעַזְבוּ לָהֶם הֲיִזְבָּחוּ הַיְכַלּוּ בַיּוֹם הַיְחַיּוּ אֶת הָאֲבָנִים מֵעֲרֵמוֹת הֶעָפָר וְהֵמָּה שְׂרוּפוֹת. The conventional translation reads, "And he spoke before his brethren and the army of Samaria, and said, 'What do these feeble Jews? Will they restore at will? Will they sacrifice? Will they make an end this day? Will they revive the stones out of the heaps of rubbish, seeing they are burned?'" This translation avoids the pitfalls, and glosses over most smoothly the difficulties of the Hebrew.[13] The whole verse bristles with problems

---

[13] The two preceding translations follow closely the Jewish Version, 1917.

but in this connection I shall deal only with three. היעזבו להם is problematical. RSV translates "Will they restore things?" while on the other hand the American translation renders "Will they fortify themselves?" BDB regards the text as corrupt (p. 737). The Aramaic equivalent of עזב is שבק[14] and the translator in Chronicles for example had quite a number of difficulties with this Aramaic word (p. 110 f.). It has a much more wide and ranging connotation than its Hebrew counterpart עזב. The Aramaic שבק signifies "leave behind, bequeath, pardon, permit, forgive, send away, divorce", some meanings that עזב does not have. A good quid pro quo rendering here would be היניחו להם (cf. Rashi) "Will they *permit* them?" שבק is employed for הניח in the Targums as in Gen. 42.33; Jud. 16.26; Ez. 41.9.11 and elsewhere. Our translator used one of the most frequent meanings of שבק and rendered almost mechanically with עזב. For the continuity see the discussion presently.

Likewise bizarre is the phrase היחיו את האבנים. One cannot make stones live again. In Aramaic the almost universal lexical equivalent of חיה in the Pa'el is *qayyem*[15] and the form in the underlying Aramaic text was undoubtedly יקימו. However it is evident that the Hebrew translator mispointed the word. He should have read *yeqimu* imperfect Haf'el, and the meaning should have been "Will they raise up these stones?", the only comportable sense, not יְקַיְמוּ "make live".

The third difficulty is the staccato unnatural rhythm and abrupt sequence throughout the verse; the questions do not hold together with any logic: will it be allowed them, will they sacrifice, will they finish in the day, will they raise up the stones. It appears that the Hebrew translator misunderstood the Aramaic construction of the verse. He failed to apprehend both the meaning and syntax of the Aramaic particle הֵן (targumic, talmudic, אִין) corresponding to Hebrew אם. Like the Hebrew counterpart, it may introduce a question, cf. Job 6.12 and Targum, and it may serve in a different direction with the signification of "if". If the translator should see

[14] שבק = עזב Targum Onqelos Gen. 2.24; 28.15; 39.6 and elsewhere. In the Peshitta, Ex. 2.20; Ps. 27.9.

[15] Pi'el of the Hebrew is reproduced as the Pa'el in Aramaic as in Onqelos Gen. 7.3; 12.12; 19.32.34; Ex. 1.17.18.22 and elsewhere.

before him a series of four *hen* s, or even two, for an Aramaic sentence need not have an interrogatory introductory particle at all, the translator might be confused. He was. He comprehended the two *hen* s (or perhaps even four) as signs of interrogations throughout whereas he should have understood the two *hen*s as *if*. There are really only *two* questions: 1) will it be permitted them if they sacrifice? 2) will they finish in a day if they raise up the stones from the dust heaps? With regard to the first question, permission seems to have been required by royal edict (Ezr. 6.9 and the Elephantine Papyri # 21 (Cowley's ed.)). The Aramaic restoration provides a meaningful and logical interpretation of the verse.

A striking reproduction of an Aramaic word via a Hebrew cognate is found in Neh. 7.3. The sense of the passage seems to be this: Nehemiah orders that the gates of Jerusalem be not opened until sunrise; and until the gatekeepers stand at their posts (see below) "they shall close the gates, and take hold (?); then shall they station the dwellers of Jerusalem on guard, each man at his post, each man opposite his house". The term "take hold" does not seem to be congruous in the sequence. A frequent locution in Aramaic is אחד תרעא "close the door, close the gate".[16] This verb, it is obvious, was in the underlying Aramaic text, but the translator in a primitive sort of way established a philological cognate with ואחזו. Actually therefore we have a mistranslation. He should have rendered with וְיַבְרִיחוּ and the English translation should be, "And they shall close the gates, and make them fast" lit. "bolt them", (cf. the noun אחדא "bolt").

In dealing with other anomalies in this verse, it should be noted that the translator failed to do justice to the Aramaic participle, and construed peculiarly an enigmatic segment in the verse that juts out in a very puzzling fashion. How does עד הם עומדים, beginning a new thought in the verse, relate to what follows? "While they are standing" is to be construed with what? Batten p. 263 regards the phrase as "meaningless", emends to "while it is still standing" *it* referring to the sun (!) and reconstructs the Hebrew ועוד היא עומדה

---

[16] Comp. Targum Jos. 2.7; Ez. 46.2. The Hebrew word is שַׁעַר.

and concludes that the time indicated is shortly "before sunset".
BH proposes עוד הֹהם עומד. We can hardly say that we have hit
upon the right solution. It would appear to me that the translator
failed to grasp and fix the tempus of the Aramaic participle at this
point. As discussed above, the Aramaic participle is capable of the
most elastic free-swinging function, of representing the past,
present, and future, completely independent of any other moods or
verbal modes in the verse. עד אנן קימין, as the Aramaic construction
was, should have been translated more precisely for the exigencies
of the verse as עד [אשר] יעמדו. Now all the members of the verse fall
into place, "Until they should stand at their post, the doors should
be closed and made fast".

The third chapter of Neh. needs much in the way of clarification
and reconstruction. In the large, the chapter describes the rebuilding
of Jerusalem by the various families and settlers, starting with the
High Priest and his kinsmen in the first row and place. They built
(or rebuilt, בנה the verb) the various "gates" with the required
roofing, portals, bolts and bars (vv. 3.6.13.14.15). A recurring refrain in the construction process is ועל ידו החזיק . . . some fifteen
times, with a secondary modifying counterpoint מדה שנית . . .
ועל ידו החזיק (Neh. 3.11 + 4 times). In the first place, a remark
should be made on the Hebrew term החזיק. The usual interpretation
is "they repaired" (comp. the translations) which superficially
might be quite plausible, except that new constructions and new
edifices seem to amount to nothing at all, and hardly anything but
repair work was carried through. From the context, the term
החזיק really means *take possession* in a legal fashion, the extended
meaning of the biblical החזיק, found in the rabbinic חזקה. Apparently
the Pi'el as well as the Hif'il may be deployed in this sense, comp.
Neh. 3.19. Certainly the term "repair" cannot be suitable in 3.28–29.
Summarizing, then, the meaning should be "they took possession",
not "repaired". Actually however the term in the original Aramaic
text was החסנו which in its varied meanings has the signification
"take possession", comp. Dan. 7.22, and this cued the translator
to render with its *lexical* equivalent החזיק in the Hif'il.

3.11 has the puzzling term that Malkiah "took possession" מדה
שנית. What should the "second measure" mean? As Rashi remarks,

the term "measure" here does not apply.[17] The Aramaic would supply us with the key, מושחא תנינא which means "second rank, second station",[18] and in our present passage "second *row*". The whole chapter now recounts a recognizable procedure. Allotments were made to the returning immigrants plot by plot, the more distinguished ones favored with the well-placed acreage, and others behind them in the second row. The whole intent of this chapter is to provide, in substance, a record of deed and property, and for the general community a statement of holdings. So that a typical statement about this parcelling would now read as follows:

"After him there took possession the Levites, Rehum son of Bani; next to him there took possession Hashabiah, the ruler of half the district of Keilah, for his district. After him, their brothers took possession, Bavvai, son of Henadad, the ruler of half of the district of Keilah. And next to him there took possession Ezer son of Jeshua the ruler of Mizpah in *the second row* (JV 'another portion' (!)) over against the ascent to the armory at the Turning." (Neh. 3.17–19).

Incidentally in Neh. 3.30 we have the strange combination of a masculine and feminine מדה שני although the translator remembered to follow the rule of agreement in Neh. 3.19.20.21.24.27; but in v. 30, in the final instance, and when his mind wandered, he forgot himself and wrote the masculine שני because of the masculine תנינא in the expression מושחא תנינא. The suggestiveness of the underlying text makes for the unconscious error. Comp. for example Gen. 20.9 חטאה גדולה, Onqelos חובא רבתא (but not so in Sperber's edition), Targ. Yerushalmi correctly חובא רבא. Even when the translator has done the correct thing over and over again, he will lapse. Comp. Gen. 24.28 הנערה, Targum Yer. הריבא (!) instead of רביתא. For other exx., cf. Zimmermann, *Book of Tobit*, 134.

The verse in Ezr. 7.9 presents some extraordinary difficulties especially in the phrase הוא יסד המעלה מבבל. The previous verse essays to fingerpoint a date when the great ascent took place: the

---

[17] מדה שנית: בנין החומה אינו נופל לומר לשון מדה בבנין השערים . . . שלא מצינו בכל הפרשה בבנין השערים לשון מדה.
[18] Brockelmann, *Lexicon*, 406.

people of Israel came to Jerusalem in the seventh year of Artaxerxes (v.7) which is the fifth month (v. 8). Then v. 9 continues, "For upon the first day of the first month, began he to go up from Babylon, and on the first day of the fifth month came he to Jerusalem, according to the good hand of his God upon him". The Hebrew expression is most anomalous: יסד means "found, establish" and it is unnatural to say "establish an ascent'''; המעלה doubtlessly means "ascent", employed however for a description of inanimate objects, e.g. מעלה העיר 1 Sam. 9.11, but not for people, at any rate nowhere in the Bible. The phrase *ad hoc* must signify that on the first day of the first month there was an organizing of an emigration or expedition from Babylon.

The problem in the verse revolves mainly around יְסָד. It was misvocalized (comp. BH ad loc.) and the word itself mistranslated. The vocalization *yesud* is unexampled; read *yasad* on the basis of the Greek *ethemeleose*. The Aramaic word supplying the solution was תקן misconstrued in the substrate text. *Taqqen* is a standard equivalent in the Targums for *yasad*[19] but it carries with it a variety of significations, its focal meaning "found, establish", but also concomitant meanings of "arrange, order", modernly speaking "initiate, organize". The meaning of "arrange" would make the phrase illumined with new clarity. In addition מעלה is a *quid pro quo* rendering with the Mem preformative, the feminine ending, and the normal lexical equivalent of מסקתא (סלק). In rabbinic literature, one who comes from Babylon to Israel is always described with the verbal סלק.[20] We may render now, "For he arranged for the ascent from Babylon". Observe that מסקתא may be employed for human beings, comp. Targum to II Chron. 9.4 while מעלה does not countenance this usage.

One Aramaic idiom, unrecognized in the Hebrew, but coming through via translation is recoverable at Ezr. 3.8. The passage reads, "Now in their second year of their coming to the house of

---

[19] תקן/יסד Targ. Hab. 1.12; 1 Chron. 9.22.
[20] Comp. *Beẓa* 38a כי סליק ר׳ אבא "When R. Abba went up from Babylon to Palestine"; *Yer. R. Ha-shanah* II, 38b כד סליקת להכא "When I came up here (to Palestine)".

God, to Jerusalem, in the second month, *began* Zerubabel the son of Shealtiel, and Jeshua the son of Jozadak, and the rest of their brethren the priests and the Levites, and all they that were come out of the captivity unto Jerusalem, appointed the Levites, from twenty years old and upward to have the oversight of the work of the house of the Lord". The word italicized is הֵחֵלּוּ in the Hebrew. The difficulty is that החלו patently has no complement as to what was begun (Bewer, *Der Text des Buches Ezra*, 15) and of course the text is regarded as suspect (Ehrlich נקהלו). In Aramaic the word שרי denotes "begin". In the course of its development, however, its primary meaning was weakened a good deal so that it became otiose in the Aramaic sentence.[21] Thus שרי אמר simply connotes "he said". This type of expression we frequently meet with in the Gospels, a striking one (*pace* all critics) in Luke 3.23 "And Jesus himself began to about thirty years of age . . ." See C.C. Torrey, *Four Gospels*, 305. An identical locution is present in the Ezra passage here and should be rendered the same way. . . . החלו ויעמדו reflects the Aramaic שריו . . . . וקמו and should be translated simply "they stationed". The translator, as his wont, rendered word for word.

It is now possible to deploy our information for the solution of a number of problems in a connected passage. Again the Aramaic supplies us with a resolution of the difficulties. Chapter 1 of Ezra offers the usual unHebraic puzzling constructions, but with recoverable Aramaic as the guide, solutions will present themselves easily.

The very first verse reads: וּבִשְׁנַת אַחַת לְכוֹרֶשׁ מֶלֶךְ פָּרַס לִכְלוֹת כלה. דְּבַר יי' מִפִּי יִרְמְיָה הֵעִיר יי' אֶת רוּחַ כֹּרֶשׁ מֶלֶךְ פָּרַס וגו' signifies "put an end to, complete, finish, waste, consume", and the Hebrew word does not suit the context here. It does not mean "At the conclusion of the word of the Lord from (?) the mouth of Jeremiah". The underlying Aramaic was משלם (and so the Peshitta at this point) and is the usual lexical equivalent of כלה. Comp. Targum Onqelos Gen. 21.15; 41.53; Ex. 39.32. The Aramaic word שלם provides the correct clue because it means not only "put an end to" but also *fulfill*, a meaning which כלה never has. The Hebrew translation, it may be presumed, should have taken the cast of למלאות דבר יי׳ precisely as in 2 Chron. 36.21. The translator in Dan. 9.2, too, understood his Aramaic and rendered correctly there.

V. 3 contains either a nuance that was not correctly perceived, of a mistranslation,—the line may waver between the two—, and the difference between the Hebrew and the Aramaic may involve a nice but important distinction. The text: ויבן את בית יי׳ אלהי ישראל הוא האלהים אשר בירושלם. The king in his proclamation had implicitly acknowledged that YHWH was the God of the heavens and earth (v. 2). So the chronicler *pro rege*. The implication is that while YHWH is the God of the heavens, at the same time he is the God of Jerusalem. It would be much more in consonance with the monarch's character and psychology to declare that YHWH is the God of Israel, the god (sic!) whose abode is in Jerusalem. The Hebrew translator very understandably made an off-the-road erroneous translation for to him there was only one God in Jerusalem. The analysis shows this: his Aramaic was אלהא which he should not have rendered by Elohim. The difference for us would be God and *god*, and it is the latter that the king intended, and the distinction is real. Observe again the idiomatic use of הוא אלהא (p. 107) "*the* god in Jerusalem".

Proceeding along in the chapter, v. 4 contains a number of misrenderings. The text reads: וְכָל הַנִּשְׁאָר מִכָּל הַמְּקֹמוֹת אֲשֶׁר הוּא גָר שָׁם יְנַשְּׂאוּהוּ אַנְשֵׁי מְקֹמוֹ בְּכֶסֶף וּבְזָהָב וּבִרְכוּשׁ וּבִבְהֵמָה עִם הַנְּדָבָה לְבֵית הָאֱלֹהִים אֲשֶׁר בִּירוּשָׁלָיִם. All the modern translations have their difficulties. The Jewish version, probably the most literal of all, departs markedly from the ordinary sense of the words to give a rational translation, "And whosoever is left, in any place where he sojourneth, let the men of his place help him with silver, and with gold, and with goods, and with beasts, beside the free-will offering for the house of God which is in Jerusalem". The RSV, "And let each survivor . . . . be assisted . . . with silver and gold . . . besides freewill offerings". The American translation (Leroy

Waterman), "Whoever is left in any place where he resides as an alien, let the men aid him with silver and gold . . . . as well as with voluntary offerings . . ." (!) Moffat, "Whenever any such survivor resides, let the men furnish him with silver and gold . . . as well as freewill offerings . . ."

The expression וכל הנשאר "all that remain" is obviously unsuitable to the context. Why should the "men of his place" furnish one who is "left" in the place where he sojourns? and what is the relationship between the one who "remains", and actually is departing for Palestine, to those in the majority who really are remaining behind? In retroversion the word שאר in its naked form, without conjugational accretions, is a close synonym to the Aramaic יתר (and so the Peshitta here in the verse). The Haf'el passive מיתר could easily be misunderstood and mistranslated as נשאר. The Hebrew translator should have taken the word as *honored* (and thus in one of its significations, Brockelmann, 313). A good rendering would have been נכבד. The Jewish community was to appoint a man who was trustworthy and honorable to carry out this commission.

The next word to be considered is וינשאהו lit. "raise him up" which in the context of gold and silver is inapposite in the verse. "Aid" and "furnish" of the translations, more to the point, are free. Undoubtedly the Aramaic word in the underlying document was וינטלונה which the translator failed grammatically to comprehend. He took it as a Pa'el form and in this sense the word bears the meaning of "raise up", Deut. 32.11; Is. 57.15 et passim. He made an understandable error. He should have read the word as a Haf'el which in this conjugation means "put upon one, lade one with, 'load' one up" and cf. 2 Sam. 24.12 in Hebrew. This makes good sense with the sequel of gold, silver, goods.

Likewise, the conjunction in the locution עם הנדבה is peculiar, and the definite article is strange. Perforce we must render with the different translations "besides the farewell offerings" (RSV), "as well as the voluntary offerings" (American translation) which are free renderings and do not account properly for the strange syntax. Moreover the gold, goods etc. were in themselves voluntary offerings. The Aramaic document would supply the solution again. That text read לות נדבתא (Ezra 4.12; 7.16 partial parallel). לות means "with" and so the Hebrew translator but wrongly. The word also means "to" (ל) as found in the Targums passim. נדבתא should have been rendered indefinitely (p. 10); in short the phrase should have been rendered in the Hebrew לנדבה "for a free offering". The whole verse now makes for the following appropriate harmonious thought, "And anyone who is honorable, in the place where he sojourns, let the men of his place supply (lit. load) him with silver, gold, goods, beasts for a freewill offering for the house of God which is in Jerusalem".

At the end of Neh. c.2, in reply to Sanballat and Tobiyyah who try to shake Nehemiah by scorn and provocation, Nehemiah responds, "The God of Heaven, He will prosper us; therefore we his servants, will rise up and build; but as for you there is no portion, nor righteousness, nor memorial in Jerusalem". The Hebrew at the end of verse 20 reads וְלָכֶם אֵין חֵלֶק וּצְדָקָה וְזִכָּרוֹן בִּירוּשָׁלָ͏ם. There is a question of nuance here which in the translation process was missed. In the context, "portion" is understandable, although another possibility will be offered presently. צדקה of course means a right act, an act of righteousness, and the current translations, JV, RSV, Moffat, American of necessity truncate righteousness to right, in the sense of "just claim" although צדקה apparently would have that meaning peculiarly here. 2 Sam. 19.29 quoted by BDB as "right" is in a different set of circumstances (Qimḥi: "kindness") and is not parallel to our verse. זכרון likewise has its puzzle. How has the meaning "memorial" relevancy in this context?

Again, in the complex of these anomalies, Aramaic retroversion from the presumed underlying document, supplies the pertinent and satisfying clarification. Through easy reconstruction, the Aramaic undoubtedly read ולא אתי לכם חלק וזכו ודוכרן בירושלם. The whole phrase implies more than what meets the eye. While חלק means "portion", and so may be taken here, it is quite believable that it represents the Aramaic ḥālāq (Ezr. 4.16) meaning "territory, a region over which one has jurisdiction"; BDB, 1093

translates "possession". Either rendering is preferable to "portion".
As will be seen in the sequel, this interpretation adds pungency
to our passage under discussion.

The second word צדקה has a standard equivalent זכותא in the
Targums, passim. The Aramaic word however acquired its own
semantic development. Like the Hebrew זכות, it signifies "merit,
meritorius claim"; and the latter meaning is the one to be assigned
here, not "righteousness".

The third word is the Aramaic דכרונה wherein again, philologically cognate to זכרון, it evolved its own nuance. The Aramaic
word denotes "memorandum", specifically the royal memorandum
as in Ezr. 6.2, that King Darius was sought to look for in the archives
(Ezr. 4.15), which, when brought to light, enabled the Judeans
to resume the construction of the walls and the Temple precincts.

Now the direct counter to Sanballat's taunt becomes clear.
Nehemiah declares that Sanballat and his confederates not only do
not have any property or possession in Jerusalem, but no claim of
merit whatsoever, not even a memorandum as a warrant from the
king. The argument accumulates with pulverizing force. Sanballat
does not have a leg to stand on; he actually possesses nothing; nor
does he have a claim for possession; nor does he have a royal
memorandum for a claim. The old translation: portion, right/
righteousness, memorial should be abandoned.

In Neh. 11.17 there is likewise a phrase which is most bizarre
in the Hebrew from the point of view of syntax, and which hardly
makes for any rational exegesis at all, but which, with the key we
possess, becomes logical and comprehensible. The passage reads:
"And Mathaniah, the son of Mica, the son of Zabdi, the son of
Asaph, chief of the beginning (?) gave thanks in prayer . . ."

The text to be discussed runs in Hebrew רֹאשׁ הַתְּחִלָּה יְהוֹדֶה לַתְּפִלָּה.
With the Greek, we should most likely read הַתְּהִלָּה "praise", which
relieves the problematic phrase to a degree, although *ex parte* the
Aramaic it is more probable that the Hebrew translator did not
recognize שירתא "song", and confused it with שירותא "beginning",
Dalman, *Wörterbuch*, 402. יהודה לתפלה cannot be translated "gave
thanks *in* prayer", so JV, RSV, for it is evident that "prayer" is in
the accusative. יהודה actually reflects ישבח (comp. Targum Ps.

136.1 and passim) which however is the usual word for "sing, chant" e.g., תושבחתא לדויד/מזמור לדויד Targums, passim. The Aramaic probably read רישא די שירתא ישבח לצלותא "The chief musician chanted the prayer". Note the word-play. ישבח however was mistranslated as יהודה "give praise" instead of "chant". Cf. Neh. 12.46.

Neh. 6.8–9: "Then I sent to him (Sanballat) saying, 'There are no such things done as you say, but you imagine them out of your own mind'. For they would all have us fear, thinking, 'Their hands shall slacken from the work not done'. But now strengthen my hands". The Hebrew to the latter part runs וְעַתָּה חַזֵּק אֶת יָדָי. It is conceded by commentators that the last part of the verse is completely at cross-purpose with the first part. Batten assumes that the phrase is a fragment of a prayer (p. 255) which however Ehrlich (p. 197) denies. It would seem clear that Nehemiah would hardly turn to God in prayer at this juncture, for this would be a disruption of his discourse and most decidedly abrupt. The Aramaic comes to the rescue. The passage ran וּכְעַן חַיִל לִידִי. The meaning and translation would be, "Now I have the power!" The central part of the verse is in reality parenthetical, while "I have the power" is to be connected with "but you imagine them out of your own mind". The translator erred in two places: he took the original ḥayil "strength, power" as a verb in the imperative i.e. ḥayyel "strengthen!", and the Lamed as the nota accusativi, whereas he should have construed it as the datival Lamed indicating possession. "My hands" was likewise misvocalized as a plural for the singular, the consonants again being identical. The significance of the verse is that Nehemiah is putting Sanballat on notice that he cannot frighten him because Nehemiah has power now. Nehemiah implies more possession of power than he has, just as Sanballat threatens more than what he can carry through. The translation brings out the inherent connection between the prior and latter division of the verse with the parenthesis in between: Then I sent to him saying, There are no such things done as you say, but you are fabricating them out of your mind (for they would frighten us, intending the hands shall slacken from the work that it be not done) and I have power now! Nehemiah's position may have been strengthened at this point, and he may have had the confidence that he could withstand Sanballat.

Another Aramaic locution is discoverable in Neh. 6.18. We are told that Nehemiah ousted members of the High Priest's family who were intriguing against him. They were בעלי שבועה "men of oath" to the High Priest, as the verse designates them, and were intermarried with him as brothers-in-law and in other close familial relationships. On the surface of things, there seems to be nothing at fault with the phrase בעלי שבועה although it is unusual that for so common an idea, the phrase is not found anywhere else, neither in the Bible, nor in the Mishna, nor the Talmud. In the circumstances portrayed that they were banded together by close ties, the expression most commonly used would have been בעלי ברית[22] "men of the (same) covenant", or more freely "men of the same party". This immediately suggests the possibility to the alert reader that the phrase מ(א)רי קימא was misconstrued, because in the Targums for instance קימא is a standing equation both with שבועה and ברית[23]. In short, the Hebrew translation should have been בעלי ברית.

In Ezr. 8.17, a place called כספיא המקום, mentioned twice in the verse has hitherto not been identified. Catching one's attention is the postpositive *ha-maqom* "the place", a strange designation. In Aramaic of course the retroversion would be אתרא which has not only the meaning of "place" but more pertinently "country, region". Cf. Brockelmann, *Lexicon*, 55b as well as instances where the Peshitta reproduces *chora* in Mt. 2.12; 8.28. In talmudic usage, it is also apparent that אתרא has the meaning of "country, town, region". E.g., "Foolish Babylonians, because they dwell in a country (*'atra*) of darkness, say or make statements that darken us" *Menaḥot* 52a; "I saw a region (*'atra*) and it was three parasangs by three parasangs" *Er.*55b; "Nehardea, the town (*'atra*) of Samuel..." *Shabb.* 116b. Ezr. 5.8 יהוד מדינתא would offer an analogy to the postposition of כספיא אתרא "the *region* of K.".

[22] Comp. Gen. 14.13 in the Peshitta בעלי קימה, Onqelos אנשי קימה but the Targum of Jerusalem מאריה קימיה; and again the same linguistic phenomena but with a different connotation Jud. 8.33; 9.4.

[23] ברית/קים Gen. 6.18; 9.9.11; שבועה/קים Gen. 26.3; Lev. 5.4; Num. 30.3; Deut. 7.8.

A most convincing and final example of the evidence for an antecedent Aramaic document, to the present writer at least, is found at Ezr. 10.44 where the verse ends the book כָּל אֵלֶּה נָשְׂאוּ נָשִׁים נָכְרִיּוֹת וְיֵשׁ מֵהֶם נָשִׁים וַיָּשִׂימוּ בָּנִים. The usual translation renders ad hoc, "And some of them had wives by whom they had children" (JV); "And they put them away with their children" (RSV, with the footnote that the Hebrew is obscure); 1 Esdras 9.36 "And they put them away (Gk. apelusan = וישיבו apparently; cf. Ex. 33.11 Hebrew and Greek; Batten proposes this reading with reservation (p. 351); he suggests "returned them to their mothers"). The American translation: . . . and they cast them off with their children.

The varying translations certainly indicate the difficulties of the text. As Ehrlich (Miqra ki-peshuto, ad loc.) further observed, it is ridiculous to repeat statements that men married foreign wives, and, following the text literally, then had children with the wives after the plethora of marriages that had taken place. The key to the problems here lies with the Aramaic. In Aramaic סם בנין signifies "to adopt children", cf. Brockelmann, Lexicon, 470b, 471b. At once the verse receives the proper illumination. All the above mentioned men (in the chapter) had married foreign women. Some of them had married women and had adopted their children. This is the novum in the verse. The Judean men had married foreign women with their children, and had adopted these children as their own. The point is that while a divorce may be carried through with regard to the wife, it is not easy to disown officially adopted children. While in those days the wife might be sent away, the children would remain on the father's hands as his responsibility. Despite Ezra's reform, the legal complication might have been a tangle, to say nothing of the bond and the affection a father may have had for his children.

Appendix I

It should be evident that the examples cited in the preceding pages should satisfy one that the books examined: Daniel, Esther, Jonah, Ezra-Nehemiah-Chronicles have been translated from Aramaic originals. The proof stems from every variety of faulty rendering: misunderstanding of Aramaic constructions, mistranslations, misapprehension of syntax, mechanical renditions, misvocalizations, misinterpretations of nouns for verbs and vice versa, word-for-word translations and hence distorting the sense of the verse, stock translations, failure to comprehend elusive particles, the relative pronouns, the conjunctions and the prepositions. The Hebrew renderings differed from one another in the various books. The translators of Jonah and Esther were quite skillful; only occasionally did particles elude them or the meanings of certain words. Both employed the Waw Conversive, for example, quite effectively. The translator of Daniel was the worst offender of all. He inadequately comprehended the determinate and indeterminate state of the noun. He knew less Aramaic, or fumbled more than the others, including the Chronicler. His apocalyptic theology interfered much with his translation; his syntax is far gone; his chapter 11 is astonishing on every count (and so Montgomery). The Chronicler, on the other hand, was quite taken in by stock translations, and of these there are an appreciable number. It may be noted that the translators of Nehemiah and Ezra are not to be identified with that of Chronicles. We do not find in Ezr. Neh. the awkwardness and absurdities that are found in the Chronicler's translator. Comp. his translator at I Chron. 2.18.30; 3.1; 5.2.23 and elsewhere.

It may be possible to point in some degree to the locale where the translators operated. In a separate publication, I was able to narrow the composition, as well as the translation of Qohelet (*Inner World of Qohelet*, 123f.) to Babylon. Not only does the language of the book betray translation, but the book's milieu, the climate described, the use of silver as the monetary medium instead of gold, the familiarity of the writer with Akkadian and Sumerian locutions, the quotation from the Gilgamesh Epic,—all show that the book's origin is Babylonian. Similarly, the retroverted Aramaic shows itself to be of a particular kind, that of a proto-Syriac i.e. Eastern Aramaic. Of the books studied in the present volume, the book of Esther manifests itself most clearly where it was composed. The Persian and Aramaic words, the Persian names, the knowledge of the etiquette of the court, the postal service and its nomenclature, the use of Babylonian motifs, the post-exilic and Babylonian milieu (p. 98) evidence the Mesopotamian origin, specifically Seleucia on the Tigris. In Esther, the recovered Aramaic from the Greek versions and from the canonical Hebrew רישא, תנינא, שני, איקרא "children", "transfer", "again", "a second time" show the Eastern Aramaic provenance. Jonah presents something of a problem; the material is too scanty. On the one hand, the author knows of Joppa as a sea-port, and of Jonah taking a ship to sail to the end of the world, the storm at sea, the nautical vocabulary, hence he would be Palestinian. The presence of the big fish is indecisive, equivocal, folkloristic. On the other hand, the words קורבנין, אלימא meaning "strong", "gifts" and misinterpreted as "dumb", "sacrifices" are indicative of Babylonian Aramaic.

Ezra-Nehemiah-Chronicles represent a complex. It is quite possible that Chronicles may have had its locale in Palestine. Not so Ezra-Nehemiah. These leaders came from Babylon, and the language shows its origin. Cf. such expressions as הותב אנתא סם בנין, מיתר, מושחא "marry a wife", "row", "honored", "adopt children", again Eastern Aramaic.

With regard to Daniel, the assumption of many scholars that older material was collected, perhaps composed, by a Jew in the Eastern Diaspora (O. Eissenfeldt, *The Old Testament*, 524) would be confirmed by the presence of Eastern Aramaic words as they come through in the retroversions: לא אתי לה, עד זבן, מן שליא, חסן סרח, פלח i.e. "suddenly", "for a while", "he shall die", "be ill", "fight", "desolate". Later, a Jew in Jerusalem secondarily (ibid. p. 527) did the editing and translating.

Appendix II

I Chron. 12.16

A retroversion from the Aramaic provides the correct restoration to a puzzling text at I Chron. 12.16. The preceding verses tell how the Gadites, "mighty men . . whose faces were like the faces of lions, and swift as the roes" came in their enthusiasm and loyalty to join up with David in his fight against Saul. Then v. 12 continues: These are they that went over the Jordan, in the first month when it had overflown all its banks; and they put to flight all the valleys (?), both toward the east and toward the west, Hebrew text וַיַּבְרִיחוּ אֶת כל העמקים למזרח ולמערב. Commentators and translators (JV, The American Translation, L. Waterman) presume that the text means that the Gadites put to flight all the inhabitants of the valleys, following the Targum reading "the dwellers of the valleys". Perhaps בישבי was omitted. Nevertheless some difficulties remain. Their exploit in crossing the Jordan at the flood is noteworthy, but to put to flight the inhabitants, and to the east and the west is puzzling. The Gadites came from the east. The Aramaic gives an interesting alternative enhancing the heroics of the Gadites: ואפכו ית עומקיא (cf. the Targum). They *reversed* the flood depth of the Jordan, going north to south, to the east and west. They probably dammed up the river so that they could cross. This interpretation tangibly connects with the first part of the verse describing the Jordan's expanse and onrush. The translator misunderstood rt. (ה)אפך 1) reverse 2) put to flight. Comp. its usage for ברח/Ps. 139.7 and frequently for the good synonym נוס 1 Sam. 4.16 as well as its lexical employment for שוב in the Peshitta Gen. 43.12 (Hofʻal Ps. 18.37; Jos. 5.2; Jer. 36.38. עמקים = depths as in its usage for מצלות Ps. 68.23; Ex. 15.5.

Bibliography

This list contains the works more frequently cited.

Texts and Versions

Biblia Hebraica, ed. R. Kittel. Textum masoreticum curavit, P. Kahle, 3–4 ed. A. Alt et O. Eissfeldt, 1949.

Peshitta, ed. S. Lee, 1923.

Targums, as found in the standard Rabbinic Bibles; ed. A. Sperber, The Bible in Aramaic, 4 vols. so far, 1959–

Talmud Yerushalmi, Krotoschin, 1866, repr. 1948.

Talmud Babli, Vilna ed. 1928.

Midrash to Esther and Song of Songs, vol. IX, ed. Soncino.

Biblia Vulgata, Madrid, 1953.

Josephus; Works, ed. B. Niese; latest ed. in the Loeb Classics by Thackeray, Marcus, Feldman.

Grammars

Dalman: G. Dalman, Grammatik des jüdisch—palästinischen Aramäisch,[2] (1905) und Aramaische Dialektproben[2] (1927), repr. 1960.

Margolis: Margolis, M. L. A, Manual of the Aramaic Language of the Babylonian Talmud, 1910.

Epstein: Y. N. Epstein, Babylonian Aramaic Grammar (in Hebrew: Dikduk Aramit Bablit), 1930.

Rosenthal: F. Rosenthal, A Grammar of Biblical Aramaic, 1961.

Nöldeke: Nöldeke, T., Mandäische Grammatik, 1875

Nöldeke: Nöldeke, T., Compendious Syriac Grammar, trans. J. A. Crichton, 1907.

Dictionaries

Levy: Jacob Levy, Neuhebräisches und chaldäisches Wörterbuch über die Talmudim und Midraschim, 4 vols., 1876.

Chaldäisches Wörterbuch über die Targumim, 1881.

Kohut: A. Kohut, Aruch Completum, 1878–92.

Jastrow: M. Jastrow, Dictionary of the Targumim., the Talmud Babli, and Yerushalmi, and the Midrashic Literature, 1886–1903.

Dalman: G. Dalman, Aramäisch–neuhebräisches Handwörterbuch zu Targum, Talmud, und Midrasch, 1901.

Brown, Driver, and Briggs: F. Brown, S. R. Driver, C. A. Briggs, Hebrew and English Lexicon of the Old Testament, 1907.

Gesenius-Buhl: William Gesenius' Hebräisches und Aramäisches Handwörterbuch über das A. T., 17ed., repr. 1949.

Payne Smith: J. Payne Smith, Compendious Syriac Dictionary, founded on the Thesaurus Syriacus of R. Payne Smith, 1902.

Brockelmann: C. Brockelmann, Lexicon Syriacum, 1928.

Openheim: A. L. Oppenheim et alii, The Assyrian Dictionary, Chicago.

Lane: E. E. Lane, Arabic-English Lexicon, 8 vols.

Commentaries and Special Studies

Bevan: A. A. Bevan, Book of Daniel, 1893.

Montgomery: J. A. Montgomery, Book of Daniel.

Torrey: C. C. Torrey, Notes on the Aramaic Part of Daniel, Trans. of the Connecticut Academy, 1909, p. 241–82.

Ginsberg: H. L. Ginsberg, Studies in Daniel, 1948.

Bewer: J. Bewer, Commentary on Jonah, 1912.

Hoschander: J. Hoschander, the Book of Esther in the Light of History.

Torrey: Torrey, C. C. "The Older Book of Esther", Har. Theo. Rev., 1944.

Moore: C. A. Moore, Esther.

Batten: L. W. Batten Ezra–Nehemiah.

Curtis: E. L. Curtis and A. A. Madsen, Chronicles.

Modern Bible Translations

King James Bible (Authorized Version), current text, AV.

Revised Standard Version, 1953, RSV.

The Holy Scriptures, Jewish Publication Society, 1917. JV.

The Holy Bible, a new Translation, by James Moffatt, 1922.

The Complete Bible . . . an American Translation, eds. J. M. P. Smith and E. Goodspeed, 1939.

The New English Bible, Oxford and Cambridge U. Press, 1970.

The New American Bible (Catholic) 1970.

General Index

I. Hebrew and Aramaic Passages and their Relation to the Underlying Aramaic

Neh.		Neh.		Neh.	
7.3	154	10.38	151	12.43	148
8.7	145	11.17	162	13.23	149
9.3	148	11.21	145	13.27	149
9.4	149				

II. *Aramaic Words and Forms*

III. Hebrew Words and Forms

IV. Words and Forms

References

This list contains the works more frequently cited.

Texts and Versions

Biblia Hebraica, ed. R. Kittel. Textum masoreticum curavit,
P. Kahle, 3-4 ed. A. Alt et O. Eissfeldt, 1949.
Peshitta, ed. S. Lee, 1823.
Targums, as found in the standard Rabbinic Bibles; ed. A. Sperber,
The Bible in Aramaic, 4 vols. so far, 1959-
Talmud Yerushalmi, Krotoschin, 1866, repr. 1948.
Talmud Babli, Vilna ed. 1928
Midrash to Esther and Song of Songs, vol. IX, ed. Soncino.
Biblia Vulgata, Madrid, 1953.
Josephus; Works, ed. B. Niese; latest ed. in the Loeb Classics by
Thackeray, Marcus, Feldman

Grammars

Dalman: G. Dalman, Grammatik des jüdisch-palästinischen Aramäisch,[2]
(1905) und Aramäische Dialektproben[2] (1927), repr. 1960.
Margolis: Margolis, M. L. A Manual of the Aramaic Language of the
Babylonian Talmud, 1910.
Epstein: Y. N. Epstein, Babylonian Aramaic Grammar (in Hebrew:
Dikduk Aramit Bablit), 1930.
Rosenthal: F. Rosenthal, A Grammar of Biblical Aramaic, 1961.
Nöldeke: Nöldeke, T., Mandäische Grammatik, 1875.
Nöldeke: Nöldeke, T., Compendious Syriac Grammar, trans. J. A.
Crichton, 1907.

Dictionaries

Levy: Jacob Levy, Neuhebräisches und chaldäisches Wörterbuch über
die Talmudim und Midraschim, 4 vols., 1876. Chaldäisches Wörter-
buch über die Targumim, 1881.
Kohut: A. Kohut, Aruch Completum, 1878-92.
Jastrow: M. Jastrow, Dictionary of the Targumim., the Talmud Babli,
and Yerushalmi, and the Midrashic Literature, 1886-1903.
Dalman: G. Dalman, Aramäisch-neuhebräisches Handwörterbuch zu
Targum, Talmud, und Midrasch, 1901.
Brown, Driver, and Briggs: F. Brown, S. R. Driver, C. A. Briggs, He-
brew and English Lexicon of the Old Testament, 1907.
Gesenius-Buhl: William Gesenius' Hebräisches und Aramäisches Hand-
wörterbuch über das A. T., 17 ed., repr. 1949.
Payne Smith: J. Payne Smith, Compendious Syriac Dictionary, founded
on the Thesaurus Syriacus of R. Payne Smith, 1902.

Brockelmann: C. Brockelmann, Lexicon Syriacum, 1928.

Oppenheim: A. L. Oppenheim et alii, The Assyrian Dictionary, Chicago.

Lane; E. E. Lane, Arabic-English Lexicon, 8 vols.

Commentaries and Special Studies

Bevan: A. A. Bevan, Book of Daniel, 1893.

Montgomery: J. A. Montgomery, Book of Daniel.

Torrey: C. C. Torrey, Notes on the Aramaic Part of Daniel, Trans. of the Connecticut Academy, 1909, p. 241-82.

Ginsberg: H. L. Ginsberg, Studies in Daniel, 1948.

Bewer: J. Bewer, Commentary on Jonah, 1912.

Hoschander: J. Hoschander, the Book of Esther in the Light of History.

Torrey: Torrey, C. C. "The Older Book of Esther", Har. Theo. Rev., 1944.

Moore: C. A. Moore, Esther.

Batten: L. W. Batten Ezra-Nehemiah.

Curtis: E. L. Curtis and A. A. Madsen, Chronicles.

Modern Bible Translations

King James Bible (Authorized Version), current text, AV.

Revised Standard Version, 1953. RSV.

The Holy Scriptures, Jewish Publication Society, 1917. JV.

The Holy Bible, a new Translation, by James Moffatt, 1922.

The Complete Bible . . . an American Translation eds. J. M. P. Smith and E. Goodspeed, 1938.

The New English Bible, Oxford and Cambridge U. Press, 1970.

The New American Bible (Catholic) 1970.

ERRATA

Page 76—line 11: should read **איקרתא**

line 17: add for **איקרתא** cf. Brockelmann, 307; Payne Smith, 196

Page 85—last line should read see p. 144

Page 98—note 20 read **איקרתא**

Page 104—line 21 read or

Page 118—line 10 read Pharaoh

Page 129—line 10 read demonstrating

Page 167—line 14 read **איקרתא** , line 32 read Eissfeldt

Page 173—index R line 1 read ben, line 2 read Reckendorf

Page 178—column 1 line 10 read **אנתתא** , column line 11 read **איקרתא**